AND THE MORROW IS THEIRS

and the morrow is theirs

The autobiography of
Miss Sue Ryder O.B.E.

THE BURLEIGH PRESS
BRISTOL

First published 1975

© Miss Sue Ryder

ISBN 0903173018

Printed in England by
BURLEIGH LTD., AT THE BURLEIGH PRESS, BRISTOL
and Published by them for the Sue Ryder Foundation

CONTENTS

PREFACE

Throughout the writing of this book I have been conscious not only of the persons and places named in it but also of many more whom I have not been able to mention. I think of all those specialist and other doctors faithfully tending physically and mentally handicapped children, of radiologists and neurologists, of others caring for the dying, and of T.B. patients who made it a pleasure and privilege to nurse and work with them. And I think also of the thousands who on my path through life have inspired me by their courage and cheerfulness in extreme adversity, by their power to draw out the best in men and women of goodwill.

All these seem to me to have proclaimed by their necessities, and to have proved by their example, how mankind may seek and find unity in a common bond of service. Named or unnamed here, they have my heartfelt gratitude.

ACKNOWLEDGMENTS

I want to thank all the people who have given me most invaluable assistance in research and in checking historical data, and all those who have encouraged and supported me, who together have made the writing of this book possible.

The Right Honourable Baroness Ward, for permission to quote from her book *F.A.N.Y. Invicta.*

Lady Hermione Cobbold, for permission to quote from *Antony Viscount Knebworth.*

The following for permission to reproduce the photographs.

W.T.S. (F.A.N.Y.) Annabelle; British Broadcasting Corporation; *The Times;* Grimsby *Evening Telegraph;* S. Jardine; Doncaster *Evening Post;* D. M. McKenzie; Interpress, Poland.

I have tried to acknowledge all the sources I have used but to anyone I have unintentionally omitted I ask their indulgence.

Macmillan & Co. Ltd. for permission to print "Thanksgiving" from Fruit-Gathering by Rabindranath Tagore.

Tribute by Dame Anna Neagle C.B.E.

It is some years since I met Sue Ryder and learnt of her war experiences and her endeavours on behalf of those who suffer so indescribably.

Now, in reading her book I am overwhelmed by the extent of her achievement in founding a Living Memorial in Britain and many parts of the world, to succour the disabled and sick of all age groups.

Of course Sue Ryder is one of those very rare people who is herself inspired and an inspiration to all who know her. Her compassion carries her far beyond the point of mental and physical exhaustion—with her it would seem the spirit takes over from, and gives strength to mind and body. The impossible becomes possible in her concern for those who suffer.

May this book make it clear to us all that, no matter how small our contribution, we can be of service by expressing our own deepfelt sympathy and by our prayers.

THANKSGIVING

Those who walk on the path of pride crushing the lowly life under their tread, covering the tender green of the earth with their footprints in blood;

Let them rejoice, and thank thee, Lord, for the day is theirs.

But I am thankful that my lot lies with the humble who suffer and bear the burden of power, and hide their faces and stifle their sobs in the dark.

For every throb of their pain has pulsed in the secret depths of thy night, and every insult has been gathered into thy great silence.

And the morrow is theirs.

O Sun, rise upon the bleeding hearts blossoming in flowers of the morning, and the torchlight revelry of pride shrunken to ashes.

Rabindranath Tagore
from FRUIT-GATHERING.

CHAPTER 1

Home is Where You Start From

I was born on July 3rd, 1923, in Leeds, Yorkshire. My Mother had had four previous children delivered at home, but as she had lost a baby and I was the youngest by six years, she was advised to have the facilities of a hospital. She loved children and liked large families, though she told me she dreaded the pain of giving birth. My father's first wife died leaving him with five children and he married my mother, Mabel Elizabeth Sims, in Oxford on 11th July, 1911.

We lived in Scarcroft near Leeds, and (until the early thirties) for four months of the year at Thurlow in Suffolk. In Yorkshire, though Scarcroft was a village on the main Leeds-Wetherby road, our pleasant home was almost within walking distance of terrible slums. As a child I visited the people in them, and the children came over to us for outings and to play in our fields and garden. I remember preparing food and bags of sweets for them, and enjoyed joining them in the excitement of their outings away from the back-to-back houses and narrow cobbled streets—the only place they had to play.

The poverty I saw shocked me, and the fact that there were people who ate off newspapers instead of table cloths, and slept without sheets because they owned none, although they had—understandably—great pride and cheerfully scrubbed their houses, including their front door steps, on their knees in a perpetual struggle against the industrial grime of their environment. Mama and her friends worked very hard, and voluntarily, on slum clearance and hospital and school boards. Those were the days when the State left a great deal of responsibility to members of the community, and family units were still strong. We also visited those in the villages and on the

1

farms where the Yorkshire spirit of hospitality and frankness was very evident, and we were invited into the cottages and offered delicious tea cakes and fresh bread, which in those days were baked at home.

My first memories are of the Leeds General Infirmary where I had been operated on for tuberculosis of a gland in my neck. There were prayers in the wards every morning. I loved the surgeons and the nurses, and though the discipline was strict, the standard of care for the individual was high and very personal. They always appeared to have time for us, were ready to answer my many questions, and gave us all the feeling that they really cared for us. Later, at home, I transformed the drawing room into an operating theatre. I persuaded friends staying in the house to join in, we gowned, scrubbed down and masked, and one of us was carried on to the operating table. The local doctor said to Mama: "Your daughter will certainly become a physician or surgeon, or perhaps a builder."

We were extremely fortunate in having a lovely garden with lawns, a rose and a Dutch garden, a rose pergola and a long walk between wide herbaceous borders to the kitchen garden beyond. The conservatory led off the drawing room, with wrought iron grilles through which could be glimpsed the rain water which was channelled off the roof and stored in an underground tank, for the head gardener Preston allowed nothing but this rain water to moisten the precious plants which grew there—the two kentias in copper-bound oak tubs, the great trails of crimson-pink bougainvillea, the hanging baskets of lobelia of the most intense blue, long trailing fuchsias, and masses of different ferns and moon-flowers. I remember the beauty of a white-flowered variety of ivy-leaf geranium called l'Elegante, hydrangea, Stephanotis, and the arum lilies at Easter. The conservatory had a warm, earthy smell that was clean and pleasant.

Being so much the youngest, with my brothers and sisters away at boarding school, I naturally spent a great deal of my time during the term with my parents. My father, who was already middle-aged when I was born,

2

was quiet and reserved, spending more time in working on the family farms and reading and writing, than in talking. When he spoke, however, he proved to have an unusually wide vocabulary and the ability to express his thoughts with great clarity. Papa had won at least one prize for history at school but his father made him read maths at Trinity College, Cambridge instead of history which was his natural bent. At Cambridge he rowed and was awarded a cup for sculling at Trinity. His day started with a cold bath and physical exercises. Conservative in dress, he always wore a high, stiff white collar. He was a great believer in outdoor life, liked walking and was a skilful and intrepid horseman. He liked simple food: baked apple, tomatoes, baked potatoes. As children we were allowed downstairs for Sunday lunch and a cold supper—which we helped ourselves to as the staff had the evening off. After the age of eight we joined our parents for all meals and in the presence of people from very varying walks of life we learned much. It was customary always to rise when an adult entered the room, to open the door for an adult, and to shake hands when meeting. Once two members of the Royal Academy stayed, F. W. Elwell and A. J. Munnings, to paint the barn, and I used to enjoy watching and listening to these two famous artists. Papa enjoyed entertaining in the sense of inviting people for meals and discussions. Cocktail parties were not in vogue or considered right in our family. Although so different in age, I loved Papa deeply and while we went riding together to visit the farms we would discuss different subjects. At mealtimes, unless there were guests, he would often read while Mama did crosswords. If we children made too much noise he would say: "Stop this damned nonsense or I will send you out of the dining room."

It was my mother, however, who had the greatest influence on my childhood and indeed on my entire life, playing an important part in my later work and giving me her unfailing interest, encouragement and active help. She had been brought up in somewhat straitened circumstances by her widowed mother, who managed, neverthe-

3

less, with the help of friends, to give her a wide education, later taking her abroad to Florence and Paris to study the history of art and languages. My Mother was a woman of many talents and interests, which she loved sharing while learning from others. She was a good writer, conversationalist and mimic, with a deep understanding of architecture, music and painting. The most striking of her gifts was perhaps her very warm and real interest in people, their wants and needs, and even in old age she remained a vital and outgoing person. She had a great sense of fun, and a friend once remarked about her that she should either have been a Bishop's wife—or an actress. Mama was ingenious at inventing games, and amongst her inventions was one in which everybody was invited to wear something they had bought for 3d. or 6d. at Woolworths. It was a great leveller as this included imitation jewellery and caused great amusement. Also, a book called *I have got your Number* was much enjoyed. Mama was in every way an unworldly person. I remember, for example, one evening in their room Mama remarking when she had just come in from a long and heavy day of visits and meetings plus an official luncheon, "Well I wish to goodness people would save time and money on food and use this in feeding others in need."

Mama's father, Herbert Sims, had been an Anglican priest who had won a cricket Blue at Jesus College, Cambridge, and also on occasion played for Yorkshire. He died young at St. Cuthbert's Church, Hunslet, a poor parish in Leeds. My Grandmother, Elizabeth Sims (*Simmie*), was strict, alert and tidy. She had few clothes but wore these with dignity and always changed for Dinner. She kept meticulous lists of presents for those in need, and information about them. She was an authority on Bradshaw's famous time-table covering all railway services in Britain, and used to tell me stories of how the poor lived and put up with awful conditions. We talked too of the contrasts in town and country houses. When maids were employed they felt, in some households at least, a sense of belonging and of security, if their employers had a social responsibility.

4

Religion influenced both my parents' lives—and my own—from the beginning. We attended church at Shadwell and Bardsey: for the beautiful Norman church of Bardsey I bought with my own pocket money a Crucifix which still hangs above the pulpit today.

The house at Scarcroft was a busy one and there was always something happening: callers arriving, people coming in for help or advice, visitors to be looked after and businessmen dropping in to the estate office. Tramps and the homeless were not simply turned away at the door with money: they were asked in to have a hot meal and occasionally a bed, and each was looked upon as an individual, a person with dignity. We children were always interested to know why they had chosen the life they had.

It was the era when very few people possessed cars, and walking and bicycling (even on tandems) were popular, especially on Sundays and Bank Holidays. Crowds of people streamed past, and the sound of their voices carried into the house, which was separated from the road only by a yard and, further down, a long wood. In the neighbourhood, and no doubt too in other parts of the country, camping was very popular, for comparatively few could afford holidays. They therefore either camped free or paid 3d. for part of a field to a local farmer. We too loved sleeping out, but Mama always tried to cover us with a mackintosh sheet, as the dew was heavy. I remember her coming down in the middle of the night to see if we were all right. One morning on waking we saw that three horses had got loose and were coming towards us at full gallop but luckily they veered off at the last moment.

It was also a period of mounting distress. The men who had survived the First World War had been promised a better country in which to live, but instead they were faced with unemployment, a dole that barely held body and soul together, and a period of economic collapse which culminated in the Great Depression. When farming was at its hardest and taxation at its height, my father gave financial aid which he could ill afford to people suffering hardship or out of work.

5

Every year we undertook the journey from Yorkshire to the other family estate at Thurlow in Suffolk, where we spent four months of the year. A special railway coach was reserved for us and our luggage, which was marked with red tape. These memorable journeys ended, however, in the Thirties when the Depression also hit my father. I remember him coming into the library one Sunday morning and expressing deep concern at the huge number of the unemployed and the financial crisis and then explaining to us the necessity of having to give up the house at Scarcroft. From then on we lived permanently at Great Thurlow.

The village of Thurlow is spread out between the churches of Great and Little Thurlow, with its trees and hedges and cottages in gardens full of flowers—almost as it remains today. There is still the old Jacobean brick house in the village where the fire glowed as we opened the door, the Cock Inn, and the house with the pump outside. There were the Forge, the baker's, the cobbler's and the game-keeper's cottages, the Rose and Crown Inn where the Women's Institute gave concerts. A feature of the village was the Elizabethan almshouses with their tiled roofs, mellow red bricks and well-kept gardens, which I visited regularly with my mother. To those unable to cook or cope for themselves, we took meals, which I often brought to them in the basket of my bicycle. I liked doing this, as I enjoyed talking to people. They were very friendly and open, and I started in this way to have an insight into their disabilities, problems and joys. Each person, adult or child, was an individual to whom one listened and from whom we learnt. There was Mrs. Wright, who lived on her own to a great age (over ninety): she was bedridden and liked companionship and to recall the past. Gertrude, in a neighbouring village had a kidney disease and was often in bed—her room lay up a very steep, narrow staircase. Dr. Wilkin, who was everybody's family doctor, and Mrs. Tweed as well as other District Nurses and friends talked with Mama about their rounds of the sick, and so the people, the children and the visits remain in my mind very vividly. There was a great variety and diversity in the different people's stories and circumstances.

Mama often took me to the local psychiatric hospital, called then by the terrible name of the Workhouse. Here, too, we got to know the individuals by name, and we liked asking them over for tea parties and games.

Like other villages, Thurlow too had its characters, the most notable of whom was a woman with the habit of communicating through telegrams delivered by the patient postman. The only hall in the village large enough for plays and meetings was owned by her. Sadly, she was an alcoholic and in consequence unpredictable. She was extremely kind-hearted and was forever giving things. She would give wedding presents like a piano or a pony, and then ask Mama to go and get them back, and finally the postman decided that he would ask for wallpaper, which she would be unable to ask for back. She once threw the village into confusion by tossing apples from a basket into the audience at a public meeting, and on another occasion dispatched boxes full of kippers and peaches to my mother via the postman for distribution. They were then followed by a telegram: "Advise immediately if kippers have arrived." Alec Sadler, the only postman in the village, was kept extra busy delivering both the kippers and the telegram. In spite of the individual idiosyncrasies, however, there was a very deep sense of community at Thurlow, which makes me feel that I belong there even now, more than thirty years after the death of my father and the sale of the family home.

On one side of the church at Great Thurlow with its square, solid tower, a pair of white gates and an avenue of chestnut trees led to the Hall. In springtime the grass beneath the trees was golden yellow with aconites. The Hall was a large Georgian house, its simple lines softened by the creeper which covered it. A high brick wall hid from view the kitchen garden and the greenhouses, and behind were the rose garden, the lawns descending to the stream, and the old trees—copper beech and oak and yew. I had my own very small patch in the kitchen garden where I spent much time, for I liked to see things grow and bear fruit, and I loved the smell of sun, damp earth, mint and tomatoes. I enjoyed the fun of pinching grapes and leaving only the stalks, much to the gardener's annoyance; punting under the curved bridge, listening to the call of pheasant and partridge, and the smell of lilac and acacia coming in through the windows.

Up to the age of nine I had lessons at home with my mother, although a French teacher came some years during the summer holidays. My mother taught me all the elementary subjects, and I would sit with her on the sofa listening to her talk about different countries and peoples, their cultures, folklore and history. I became interested in music. Each spring there was a local musical festival at Clare in which many villages took part. The standard they aimed for was high and the adjudicators came from well-known schools of music. My mother was a hard-working co-founder and president. The choir master at Thurlow, who lived at Haverhill, was a perfectionist. He rehearsed relentlessly one evening each week in our drawing room, and the ringing tones of the large-bosomed soprano (who performed with joy and enthusiasm) would echo through the house. He was my first piano-teacher, and although I never became proficient, he must have given me a liking for it, for I see in my mother's diary: "I went to the churchyard and returned to the church to find Sue perched on the organ stool, pulling out stops and playing five finger exercises with great assurance and effect, Gavin blowing for her. We raced back over the fields." Alas, I can no longer play, but the love of music has remained and increased, and it means much to me.

Christmas was for us all, perhaps, the highlight of the year. For weeks beforehand we prepared and made presents, especially for those we knew would not be receiving any. Whatever the weather, my mother drove herself to Yorkshire (considered a considerable distance in those days) to present her gifts, occasionally taking me or one of my brothers with her. She was sometimes criticised for this, but her warm-hearted nature made her see how important the *personal* side of giving was, and each present was made or chosen with special attention to what the recipient would like. Carol singers and bellringers called and were entertained, but above all it was the mystery and beauty of the Christmas story that dominated everything else, and all through Advent we were being prepared for the joy of the birth of Christ. Usually the whole family came for Christmas, and I had the companionship of my two half-nieces, Anne and Peggy, who were nearer my age and who later became an architect and a nurse respectively.

But I was closest to my three brothers; John, who later became an historian, Michael, a physician, and Stephen, who read history too, but eventually took up farming. Stephen was a good mimic, while Mama was in the habit of constantly playing practical jokes, and I suppose I have inherited her sense of humour. One evening I offered to help out at dinner and dressed up as a parlourmaid in a black dress with a white apron. Apparently the only person who recognised me was the Vicar, who said to Mama, "How unusual to see someone enjoying a meringue behind the screen near the sideboard." Also we remember Papa becoming slightly indignant when I took the port round twice.

On Saturday afternoons we usually were allowed to accompany Papa to the Museum and bookshops in Cambridge, and he would show me the way in which the books were arranged and explain their contents. We spent hours there, but John, my eldest brother, lost count of time as he became so absorbed in reading. Occasionally I would be sent back to fetch him, and one evening he was locked in, not having noticed that the shop was closing.

From the age of eight I helped to look after the dairy; my half-sister gave me two cows and I began my own small herd of Jerseys. I took this work seriously, studying farm books and magazines so as to be sure that I was doing everything correctly and thoroughly. After milking we separated the milk, and then I would clean the dairy and scrub the flagstones. People from the village came with their enamel mugs and jars to the door of the top dairy to buy the milk which I would ladle out to them, marking it off on the register. One large family always asked for

9

skimmed milk, which was cheaper, but I did not think that was right, and let them have the ordinary full cream milk. Buttermaking was done in the other dairy near the laundry, at first in the old wooden tubs, which were quite heavy for me to turn, and later in the three-minute churn. I would roll the butter, salt it and make it up into pound and half-pound packs, and then clean up the churns and equipment. It was hard work, but I enjoyed it, and at twelve, because my father encouraged me and possibly because he thought I was proficient enough, I entered for a butter-making competition at a local show. Together with Argent, the head dairyman, who instructed me so thoroughly, and his colleague, I helped deliver the calves.

In the carpenter's shop I learnt about the use of tools and the different kinds of woods, making a table, a trolley and a bookcase. The repair and maintenance programme taught me, in the course of time, the different materials needed to renovate the buildings on the home farm and the various cottages and farmhouses. My father encouraged me to go round and listen to and ask questions of the men who were responsible for the regular maintenance, so I was aware of their trades and the time the work took, but above all, of the quality, and of the service they gave. I was allowed to choose the colour schemes too. When tractors became redundant or farm machinery out of date, my father also permitted me to bargain with scrap merchants to secure a good price for them. In the house Nelly Martin, the kitchen maid, taught me how to scrub; and I enjoyed observing and learning from the cooks who showed me how to cater for numbers.

There were more conventional pastimes too: blackberrying in our favourite woods, riding over the countryside I loved so much, all the activities of the house—the music and charades, the play-reading and games, the practical jokes and the dances I was allowed to attend, for I was very fond of dancing. My mother loved reading aloud and making up stories. She also wrote a pageant about the History of Thurlow in which the entire village joined in helping and taking part, the proceeds being divided between the Chinese Red Cross and the building

10

fund of the village hall. Miss Annie Bainbridge the head housemaid, affectionately called Bay, and friends spent hours in the workroom making the costumes. From her we also learnt how to do housework and all that this entailed without the many mechanical gadgets we have these days. She had served in several well known households such as Temple Newsam and the house of the explorer Gertrude Bell. Bay stayed on for 43 years and became Mama's devoted companion.

We all had a full and busy life, with no time to get bored, there was never a dull moment, and the participation in community activities brought us together in a way that is almost impossible to describe. There was a Mr. Bulkley who could not pay his rent—nobody apparently knew where he came from and he took over (presumably under false pretences) one of the farms. Our agent told Papa he was armed, and felt he could not go back to ask for the rent again. Shortly afterwards Mr. Bulkley was living with us. Weeks later Mama and Papa said to each other: "Well, what are we going to do with him?" Neither felt it kind to ask him to leave, as he was alone and odd. He talked to many of us and asked me, amongst many other things, to mend the puncture on his bicycle with a needle and black cotton. Weeks later he rode off, sup osedly to open a sweet shop in Cambridge, but he came back frequently and without warning, and knew that he would always find a bed and food.

For Papa, who after all was a very busy man, the constant activity in the house must have sometimes been trying. We remember him wistfully walking about the house, finding the library, drawing room and dining room full of people. He had a complete routine for each day, which began with early morning exercises and continued until late in the evening, and apart from all his other activities he was also a great champion of countries which were trying to gain their independence.

Mama went to Holy Communion every day when she could. On Sundays the family invariably attended church, either going to the service at Great Thurlow adjoining the grounds, or, more often, walking across the fields to Little

11

Thurlow, sometimes as the five-minute bell was ringing and the Rector, with flapping cassock, could be seen hurrying across his garden to the church. In summer the side door of the church near the altar was left open so that we could see the sun glinting on the grass among the headstones, and in winter hot air would blow through the gratings in the floor and the candles were lit in the brass candelabra. The Litany of the Saints was said regularly. There was a smell of beeswax, and an organ which had to be pumped by hand, and on either side of the altar there were brass tablets inscribed with the Ten Commandments —"Thou shalt not kill", "Thou shalt not covet", etc.

The box pew of the family is still there behind the choir stalls on the left of the altar, high, dark and polished, and today there is a plaque on the wall which reads: "In loving memory of Charles Foster Ryder, a constant worshipper in this House of God, Lord of the Manor of Little Thurlow. *'What doth the Lord require of thee but to do justly and to love mercy and to walk humbly with thy God'* "

Underneath to my mother, is inscribed:- *"He that dwelleth in love dwelleth in God,* and *the souls of the righteous are in the hand of God "*

On the other wall a wooden plaque made from his aircraft propeller commemorates William Harold Ryder, my youngest half-brother, who was killed near Arras while flying during the First World War. Papa wore a black tie for the rest of his life.

CHAPTER 2

The Years of Transition

Although our own home life was happy, the tragedies, the sorrows and the unsolved problems remaining as the aftermath of the First World War weighed on many people's minds, for there was hardly a family that had not been affected; millions had lost their lives and thousands were left mutilated. Written and verbal descriptions of the battles and the terrible drawings and photographs of disfigured men and buildings haunted me as a child.

Many individuals living and working around us had been involved in the fighting and the nursing, and as few seemed reluctant to talk, I learnt much by listening to them. Several had been affected by the gas attacks on the Western Front from April 1915 onwards. A figure I remember used to bicycle regularly along the local roads, swearing at anybody who passed—he had been shell-shocked and was disturbed, with no other occupation than bicycling on through the four seasons of the year.

In general there was at that time far more respect for and attention to those who had died. On Armistice Day the whole nation united to remember them by observing a two minutes' silence, when *every* person and vehicle stood still, regardless of where they were or what they were doing, while often the names of those from the village who had died in action were read out in church or at the local War Memorial, and we sang:

I vow to Thee, my country, all earthly things above,
Entire and whole and perfect, the service of my love;
The love that asks no question, the love that stands the test,
That lays upon the altar the dearest and the best;
The love that never falters, the love that pays the price,
The love that makes undaunted the final sacrifice.

And there's another country, I've heard of long ago,

13

Most dear to them that love her, most great to them that
know;
We may not count her armies, we may not see her King;
Her fortress is a faithful heart, her pride is suffering;
And soul by soul and silently her shining bounds increase;
And her ways are ways of gentleness and all her paths are
peace.

By Cecil Spring Rice.

The sacrifices others had made in defence of liberty
seemed worse and the price they had paid even higher,
however, when one considered how all this was subsequently taken for granted by many people.

Quite apart from the actual fighting, fifty-one Zeppelin
attacks made on the civilian population had killed 500
people, and Mama used to tell me that in the night a
member of the household would come to her door and
say "The Germans are over the stable yard". It was, however, the terrible number of thirty-seven million lives (or
more) lost in monstrous circumstances which kept recur-
ring to my mind while we drifted on to the next abyss. We
were waiting for another statesman to confirm again what
Gray had said on 3rd August 1914: "The lamps are going
out all over Europe; we shall not see them lit again in our
lifetime."

Reading the prose and poetry produced during and after
the War—Siegfried Sassoon, Rupert Brooke, Julian
Grenfell, Wilfred Owen and others—I felt we were being
unfaithful to the writers and those for whom they had
written. It seemed we had devalued the quality of their
lives.

Somebody who to me seems to have personified the
same qualities in a different and later time was Antony
Knebworth. His biography, by his father the Earl of
Lytton, is a book that still moves me. Antony's judgement
sometimes went sadly astray and there is painful poignancy in the misplaced optimism of his forecast of 1933,
but I admire the sensitivity with which he wrote it:

"I have a feeling that 1933 is going to be a year memorable
in the life of our country, and of the world and of our
family. It is the high tide—the high tide and turn of all

14

Sue Ryder with her husband, Group Captain G. L. Cheshire, in the grounds of the Sue Ryder Home and Headquarters at Cavendish, Suffolk.

A view of the general office, Cavendish.

Mama (Mrs. Mabel
Elizabeth Ryder).

SUE RYDER—
CHILDHOOD AT
THURLOW.

that is depressing. And the year is going to mark the beginning of a new world, a new light, a great hope, and a great happiness. But it is only a feeling, and had better be left there, with heart in mouth, and a great prayer."

Antony himself died in an aeroplane accident in 1933, and his father wrote:

"On the afternoon of Sunday, April 30th, he came unexpectedly to Knebworth in his Moth with Roger Bushell, a brother officer. It was a perfect spring day and everthing was at its loveliest. Antony and his friend played tennis, and after tea sat talking with his mother while she was gardening until nearly eight o'clock. Then the two flew back to London together. The last I saw of him was disappearing into the glow of the sunset above the trees. . . .

"Thus in an instant, without warning, without anticipation, he who had always been so full of life passed into the Great Beyond, and took with him all his high hopes, aspirations and great endeavour.

"Of that flower of youth which perished in the Great War he had written, 'When they were dead they were great'. His own death was as much in the service of his country as theirs had been, although no enemy hand had struck him down. In this, if in little else, he was rich. At the moment of his death he was almost without any material possessions. He was singularly free from any possessive ties. Perhaps this was because he had an unconscious knowledge that he was destined to sojourn here for so short a time. But in that short time he had tasted life to the full. He had always lived dangerously and had taken the test that life could give. In return he had also given himself heartily and generously to the service of others whenever opportunity offered.

" 'Mummy, do you think I shall ever be famous?' he had once asked. It was not given to him to achieve what brings fame. But if he is remembered, it will be for what he was, and not for what he did. What he was is best set forth in his own letters.

"That is why we who received and treasure them have wished to share some of them with others, in the hope that many may come to realise, as we do, that at the thought of him this old world seems to recapture the vigour of

15

youth, hopes soar high, despair vanishes, hearts grow bold and limbs are strong again."

This boy was a person I admired, not only for his writing, but also for his outlook on life; and to quote from another of his letters:

> "It seems to me immensely unimportant whether we live or die, are gay or sad, but very essential never to give up trying one's utmost. Let us be thankful for what was good, hope for the future, love, laugh and praise, and one day perhaps we shall know."

1933 brought the rise of Nazism and the passing of racial laws in Germany—and once again dark shadows lengthened over Europe. We had Jewish friends staying near Thurlow who had managed to get out of Germany, and they told us—and others too—that pogroms had begun and would get worse, and that more and more people, including Socialists and Christians, were being arrested. The concentration camps of Dachau, Esterwegen and Oranienburg Sachsenhausen had started, and the system of terror began. Having become so aware of all the implications of the First World War through all that I had heard and read, I began to feel that every day we lived brought us closer to the Second.

In the meantime I had been sent to my first school as a weekly boarder. I was extremely homesick, not because of the place itself or the lessons, but because I missed my parents and the activities at home so greatly. It was the only thing about which I can clearly remember not agreeing with Mama. At one point I ran away, but after a mile or so decided that it would not have the desired effect, nor would I necessarily be accepted back by Papa, who was a strict disciplinarian and considered that a woman should learn a trade or profession and be independent regardless of her status in life. I wept and wept every night and felt the more desperate when nobody appeared to understand, for they probably thought the mood would pass. When I left, the Headmistress who bore me no grudge wrote:

> "Sue has worked well throughout the term and really knew her work for the examinations. She is cheerful and gay by nature and most helpful and reliable in both form and in the house."

After looking round, Mama went to see Miss Sheldon, Miss Hindle and Miss Bird, co-founders of a comparatively new school at Benenden in Kent, and at the age of twelve I went there as a new girl. The school had started in 1923, very much on a shoestring, as the Founders could only contribute £300 between them towards the initial expense until six months later when a Company was formed to ensure the continuity of the school. I think we were all conscious in those early days of improvisation that it was a courageous venture and we felt it was up to us to help to make it a success. This, and the fact that there was "freedom within the law" made us feel responsible and trusted. Although the school was surrounded by fields and woods with lovely azaleas and rhododendrons, we did not have any sense of isolation and felt we belonged to a vital community of nearly 300 people and we shared fully in the life of the village and the Church. We had many contacts with the world outside through visitors, concerts, lectures and with children from the London Settlements who came to stay, and with other children. One of the Founders wrote to me:

> "You ask about the beginning of the school. We wanted it to be a friendly normal happy place where learning to live life as a whole went side by side with a sound academic training. We hoped that you would all find a philosophy which would help you in meeting difficulty, trouble and opportunity, and that in planning your lives you would always be aware of the needs of others and serve them with compassion and understanding. The atmosphere of friendliness, gaiety and the forward-looking spirit of the early days is still part of the school's character and tradition. It seems summed up in the school lesson: *Think on these things* (Philippians 4, 4-9).*

17

AND THE MORROW IS THEIRS

Philippians 4 (verses 4-9)*

Rejoice in the Lord alway: and again I say Rejoice.
Let your moderation be known unto all men. The Lord is at hand.
Be careful for nothing; but in every thing by prayer and supplication
  with thanksgiving let your requests be made known unto God.
And the peace of God, which passeth all understanding, shall keep
  your hearts and minds through Christ Jesus.
Finally, brethren, whatsoever things are true, whatsoever things are
  honest, whatsoever things are just, whatsoever things are pure,
  whatsoever things are lovely; whatsoever things are of good report;
  if there be any virtue, and if there be any praise, think on these
  things.
Those things, which ye have both learned, and received, and heard,
  and seen in me, do: and the God of peace shall be with you.

"My memory of you as a schoolgirl is very clear, as if caugth by a snapshot. You were standing quite alone in the courtyard, a small, still figure, fair-haired. I watched you for a few minutes and wondered what you were thinking about. In a school community it is rather rare for people to wish to be alone, and I always hoped that I should know something of their future; these people who were friendly and enjoyed life but yet felt the need sometimes for the pleasure of solitude. I still wonder what you were thinking about—perhaps you were planning one of your practical jokes!"

History, Geography, Domestic Science, English and Economics were my favourite subjects, while Mathematics and Science remained forever beyond my grasp. Our Carpentry teacher we found strict at the time—though later I had every reason to be profoundly grateful for what I had learnt under her guidance.

A part of the weekly school routine which I remember especially is the School Service on Sunday evening, to which I always looked forward, the more so when Miss Bird gave us one of her Benenden Angel sermons. Prayers have always meant a great deal to me, and the following two school prayers are especially memorable.

The Prayer for Seniors (Old Girls, Past Members)
We commend, O God, unto Thy Fatherly care the Seniors of this school, beseeching Thee that Thy loving kindness and mercy may follow them all the days of their life. Succour them in temptation, preserve them in danger, assist them in every good word, and keep them ever in the way that leadeth to eternal life: through Jesus Christ our Lord. Amen.

18

The Prayer for the School
Grant, O God, that as the years pass by there may go forth
from this place a great company, who, strengthened by Thy
Grace, and inspired by Thy Spirit, shall serve Thee faith-
fully, for the welfare of their fellow-men, and for the honour
of Thy great Name: through Jesus Christ our Lord. Amen.

I remember the choir singing Walford Davies' *God be in my Head* and Stainer's *Sevenfold Amen* and walking afterwards down the drive called Lime Avenue in our navy blue cloaks, the lights twinkling in the leaded windows of the main house behind us.

The grounds were 380 feet above sea level. Memories of the cold remain—chilblains were common. I remember too the games' field exposed to the winds over the Weald and particularly Dinky Dick Read's laughter and her fast running. "We would wind up illicit gramophones, stuffed with silencing serge bloomers, to listen to Jack Buchanan and Fred Astaire. The older girls held highbrow discussions on T. S. Elliot." I learnt later that sometimes in the eighth week of term, always a difficult time, when we were unusually tiresome in school, a whole day's outing would be announced, during which we walked miles, with nosebags, frying pans and sausages—regardless of the weather—and returned in a more tractable frame of mind. I believe the staff also welcomed these occasions.

Letters were very important to me, and each day some member of the family or a friend would write. I can still see them laid out and waiting for me on the quarry-tiled windowsill of the house. There was great intimacy between the members of our family, and I wrote to Mama at length, keeping notes of what to tell her each day and usually starting the letter with a quotation. "With every rising of the sun, think of one's life."—"All yesterdays, just let them sleep."—"Not to seek to summon back one ghost of that innumerable host." I would then go on and tell her what I had been doing:

"I made a *complete* fool of myself in French this morning. 10 out of 10 for English made up for it a wee bit, and, of *all* things, I somehow managed to shoot 3 goals in lacrosse this afternoon. We had talks from a variety of speakers.

19

Yesterday a woman who is a missionary in East Africa came and talked for one hour about the school there, which is supported by this school and how, when she first went, she had to take over from another who was ill. Forty mission schools dotted over a vast area and one girls' school where she had to teach. She also told us all about the nursing in the villages around and how she helped with the locals to build a church."

We enjoyed the treat of hearing musicians, amongst them Solomon and Cortot and Myra Hess and the Casals Trio, who came and played to us in the School Hall.

Every Saturday morning one of the School's Founders held a session on Current Affairs. We sat on the main staircase and on the floor in the Entrance Hall. A synopsis was given of what had appeared in the Press, including *The Spectator* and *The New Statesman*, also on the B.B.C. about the principal events of the week. Time was allowed for many questions were asked which covered a very wide range. Discussions at Benenden, as at home and elsewhere, were concerned with the calamitous and deepening crisis. I loved economics and at the age of about thirteen ended an essay on taxation, "the state may use taxation for revenue purposes, moral purposes, social and medical purposes, political and, most important today, war purposes . . . in actual fact, large portions of our taxes go towards paying for past and future wars." This essay was written in 1938, and it was returned with the words "and future" crossed through in red.

Many of us became increasingly concerned about current problems and injustices, both at home and abroad. I wrote to my mother: "There is a Jewish girl here from Northern Italy. She's in my dorm. and tells me in graphic detail about the arrests, suspicions and the Fascists. Her family only just got out in time, thousands were left. Many won't realise or believe the fate which awaits them. Equally the majority of people don't understand the full horror of what is happening and being planned. Afterwards they'll say it's exaggerated or could have been averted. If one didn't believe in God and justice in the next world, one might despair."

20

I had always thought that I would like to go in for nursing or study medicine, although I was most doubtful of being able to cope. One of my brothers was a doctor, and as a small girl I had enjoyed looking at and reading his books. However, as was the case with thousands of others, Hitler had other plans for my future.

After Hitler's rise to power in 1933 and the passing of the Racial Laws in 1934, the following years had seen the German Army marching unopposed into the Rhineland, Austria and Czechoslovakia.

We were shocked and dismayed by the attitude of Chamberlain and indeed many members of the Government—even a few Members of Parliament had attended the Nuremberg Rallies—the complacency and the reasons they gave shocked me for we had heard and indeed been taught that the Versailles Treaty would inevitably bring serious consequences in addition to the world monetary crisis.

Those who welcomed and believed in Chamberlain's statement after his return from Munich seemed both unrealistic and unfair to the rest of the world and in particular to the countries on the Continent each of which in turn would be over-run.

According to the League of Nations' Armaments Year Book 1938 the Army in Czechoslovakia consisted of—

12 Infantry Divisions (2 Brigades each).
2 Brigades of Mountain Infantry.
12 Light Field Artillery Brigades.
4 Cavalry Brigades.

In addition they had a complex system of Reservists. If they had been allowed to choose their own course and had been supported fully by their Allies, there might have been a different outcome.

Our old portable blue radio at home was much used and a visitor from Germany insisted upon hearing Hitler's screeching voice at the Nuremberg Rallies. She also read out parts of *Mein Kampf* and we were revolted by this too. It gave a dreadful insight into what the Nazis planned.

21

The summer of 1939 was a particularly lovely one, and the still, sunny days continued on during the last week of August, the week before war was declared on Germany. Everywhere there was a feeling of tension, and the cloudless golden days seemed to pass unbearably slowly while we waited for news. There were prayers every evening in the village church at Great Thurlow; specially fervent prayers for some miracle to avert the war that appeared to be inevitable. In Cardinal Newman's favourite prayer I found a measure of tranquillity, or at any rate a hope of tranquillity, that helped to ease the strain of those days:

> *O Lord, support us all day long of this troublous life, until the shades lengthen and the evening comes, and the busy world is hushed, the fever of life is over, and our work is done. Then Lord, in Thy Mercy, grant us a safe lodging, a holy rest, and peace at last: through Jesus Christ our Lord. Amen.*

On September 3rd war was declared. The old life had ended for good.

CHAPTER 3

Go Out into the Darkness

The congregation at Great Thurlow was in church as usual at 11 o'clock on Sunday, 3rd September 1939, and there we heard Neville Chamberlain's announcement from 10 Downing Street that Britain was at war with Germany. The War had started two days earlier with Hitler's invasion of Poland, a crime the direct and particular effects of which were destined to have a special and lasting influence on my whole life. We felt a sense of very deep shame when the Prime Minister in his broadcast mentioned the failure of the ultimatums his Government had sent to Berlin after the expected invasion and the bombing and killing in Poland had begun, an ultimatum vainly demanding a German withdrawal. In March 1939, and indeed at Munich already, the Czechs had been sold down the river, and now, owing to unbelievable political blindness, history had moved on to a point where it had become too late to be of any assistance to the Poles whose territorial integrity we had guaranteed and with whom we had signed a mutual defence treaty. When I see the pre-War British Embassy in Warsaw and remember the crowds who assembled there calling for the Ambassador and cheering him because they vainly believed that we would send arms, I marvel at the Poles' lack of bitterness today.

Immediately after the broadcast, sirens sounded, but people reacted calmly. It was in fact a false alarm. Thereafter followed a series of alarms which typified the start of the eight month period of the phoney war.

The nearest bomb to us was subsequently dropped near the sheep pen on the Home Farm. My brother Stephen's friend, John McAnally, aged 21 (who was to be killed on 7th July 1941 as a Pilot in 214 Squadron), watched with us from the door of the cellar, and we talked about the courage of the Poles and their resistance and how remarkable the cavalry were to fight on horseback against the

23

German tanks. We expressed indignation at our inability to help them and the knowledge that we had let down their country and our common cause.

Evacuees from London were given rooms in our home, and for a few months I worked in a local hospital, to which quite a number of evacuees from the East End were admitted. Many of them were children who had left their parents behind and were frightened, especially as they might never see their homes or parents again. The majority were women and children who had never had the opportunity of seeing the country before. They came from slum areas and were used to sharing a bed. Some we had to persuade to bath and change their clothes and a few were infected, so that we introduced them to DDT. It meant coping with all the difficulties arising from different social attitudes and from personal handicaps—lice, incontinence and smells—and besides the discipline that had to be exerted, which involved teamwork, diagnosis and treatment of illness were required, and we enjoyed attending to all the little needs of the individuals. There was constant tiredness to contend with; our feet swollen from walking through long covered ways between the different departments of the hospital (including the theatre), and it was a constant temptation to snatch forbidden moments of rest sitting on the bread bins in the small ward kitchen.

Rightly, the discipline and routine were strict, and if we failed and got slightly behind, the Ward Sisters were quick to reprimand us. Pride in our uniforms was important, starched aprons had to match the hem of the dress—to the calf of the leg—and we wore black stockings. There were different colours for the frocks and caps according to the status of the nurses and the organisations who worked there, besides the Pros (Probationers—later Student Nurses) as we called them, who were on duty. If we were sent for we removed the cotton or organdie cuffs and rolled down our sleeves before reporting to Matron's office. We did not have curtain cubicles, and whenever a patient wanted a bed pan, wash or blanket bath, one had to carry a heavy wooden screen the length of the long ward. I remember there was a young girl of nine (a blue baby) with a heart condition, who had convulsions and as we had no oxygen tent, she was resuscitated with an oxygen cylinder and was kept under very strict observation before she died. I enjoyed making and keeping temperature charts for different fevers and the simple training and the examinations I subsequently passed proved extremely useful in the wards, but even more so later on in life.

There were great restrictions on lighting because of the blackout regulations and we would go round with a torch. Four reports had to be written up by the Night Sister and it was usual to receive three visits by the General Night Sister. It was exacting to prepare the trolleys, especially for the Surgical Ward. Drums and sterilisers were prepared daily and each needle and syringe sterilised before use. Bandages had to be washed, boiled and re-rolled and the gauze we had to cut and fold. There were no disposable sputum mugs. Mouth trays appeared on each individual locker and there was a special day for lockers which entailed washing them out completely. As we did not have proper trolleys, the wet and foul laundry had to be specially folded. Each ward had its own linen and when an inventory was taken, we occasionally had to borrow from another ward. In those days there was fasting from 10 p.m. prior to an operation. The day started before 6 a.m. in order to get all the bed patients washed, their beds made (three minutes were allowed to make a bed and this one always did with another nurse), drugs distributed and dressings changed. Visiting hours were strict and if a patient deteriorated, he was moved up towards the door. Backs were rubbed down after every bed round with methylated spirits and boracic powder. Each Ward Sister naturally insisted upon us carrying out her own particular principles and, if necessary, a nurse who had gone off duty who had failed to put away a medicine glass would be sent for to put it back in the medicine cupboard. Each morning there would be a retinue consisting of the Ward Sister, a Consultant and Physician on the regular ward rounds, when we had to maintain silence.

In June 1940 a few of the wounded were evacuated from France. They were the first battle casualties that we

25

had seen. Some of them, full of fun, teased us even to the extent of getting me into trouble with the Sister because I had given a blanket bath to the wrong patient.

After Dunkirk preparations were made in earnest in the village of Thurlow and a very serious-minded man gave lectures, which the majority of villagers attended, on what action we were to take in the event of an invasion. Pamphlets were distributed called *If the Invader Comes*, and we fully expected the landings and invasion. The duties of the L.D.V. (Local Defence Volunteers—later the Home Guard) and A.R.P. (Air Raid Precautions) Wardens increased.

The troops who had been brought back exhausted from the miracle of Dunkirk continued their training and marching, but it was evident that few carried weapons. Some people were assigned to making Molotov Cocktails, while others were told what their duties would be in the event of an invasion and these included looking after the wounded and cooking food in the woods.

We were told that the church bells were to be rung everywhere once the parachutists had landed, and at night the glow of the fires from the oil tanks at Tilbury which had been bombed, was visible 60 miles away. Several Dorniers were shot down in the vicinity and one crew surrendered to a farmer who only had a pitchfork; another crew were so arrogant that they were taken to an R.A.F. Station and watched some of the ground crew playing cricket to give them an idea that the British were far from panicking.

Churchill's speeches and the general spirit of the country gave a sense of purpose and united everyone. His memorable speech on 4th June 1940 made us feel determined that, regardless of all odds, we would resist to the last:

"Even though large tracts of Europe and many old and famous States have fallen or may fall into the grip of the Gestapo and all the odious apparatus of Nazi rule, we shall not flag or fail. We shall go on to the end. We shall fight in France, we shall fight in the seas and oceans, we shall fight with growing confidence and growing strength in the air. We shall defend our island, whatever the cost may be. We shall fight on the beaches, we shall fight on the landing-grounds, we shall fight in the fields and in the streets, we shall fight in the hills. We shall never surrender.

"And even if, which I do not for a moment believe, this Island or a large part of it were subjugated and starving, then our Empire beyond the seas, armed and guarded by the British Fleet, would carry on the struggle until, in God's good time, the New World, with all its power and might, steps forth to the rescue and liberation of the Old."

The response by R.A.F. Fighter Command was one of the decisive battles of world history. Perhaps it was fortunate, perhaps not, that so very few of us knew at the time how savagely the margin between possible salvation and defeat was shrinking. But we did "hang breathless" on its fate, and if we thought at all we could but realise and marvel that those pilots were enduring and triumphing over the appalling strain of constant duelling against enormous odds. During the battle a number of the dog fights took place above us, and in the early mornings we saw German planes in formation flying inland, a sight never to be forgotten. There were also very special days that remain vivid in one's mind. It's true that the heat and passion and fog of battle inflated the claims made immediately on either side, but honest exaggeration certainly gave a needful and worthwhile boost to morale, and victory mattered far more than statistics. Two of the crucial days were August 15th, when we now *know* the Luftwaffe's losses were 75 aircraft and the R.A.F.'s were 34, and September 15th, the last, when *they* lost 60 aircraft and we lost 26. This was also the day when Churchill, on a visit to 11 Group Fighter Command, asked where the reserves were and was told there were none. But by then Hitler had made his fatal mistake. On September 7th the Luftwaffe's main onslaught was switched from the R.A.F. stations to civilian London—and the invasion of England was called off.

So London and other big British cities had to "take it",

and did. Many of those enduring the nightly blitz were remarkable people. So few, relatively, had adequate shelter: the cupboard-under-the-stairs became something far more vital to survival than anyone had ever dreamed it could be. Anderson Shelters were popular and useful. Thousands made a weird communal life for themselves for months on end on the platforms of the London Underground—it was strange that they could sleep except for sheer weariness, some sang and hot drinks were distributed to them whenever possible. They emerged at dawn or after the "all clear" to discover whether their homes still stood. Other thousands adapted themselves with astonishing facility to utterly unfamiliar duties in instant, dire and often macabre peril. I do truly think that that was Britain's "finest hour". No one would like to have such an experience again, but it did give us a togetherness that we have not recovered since the war.

Mobilisation meanwhile was acquiring a new meaning. The National Service Act had been rushed through Parliament at the outset of the War. It was to be supplemented later by a law making everybody, men and women alike, aged 18 to 60, liable to some type of war work.

I decided to join the FANY as a volunteer.

The FANY (First Aid Nursing Yeomanry) was the first women's voluntary corps to be registered in this country. It was founded in 1907 by a Captain Baker who, while lying wounded on a battlefield during the Sudan campaign, had visualised nurses galloping from field hospitals to the wounded on the battlefield. rendering first aid and remaining until the horse ambulance arrived, which explains why the Corps started as a band of mounted nurses.

At the outbreak of the First World War the FANY's worked with the Belgian and French Armies near the line and in dangerous and difficult places, but in January 1916, as a result of the famous Calais Convoy and other distinctions, recognition was at last given by the British Army and they were allowed to work with the British as well. Training continued between the Wars, and during the Second World War a very valuable contribution was made by the FANY's who worked with Special Operations Executive (S.O.E.), an organisation specially formed on 19th July 1940 in accordance with a War Cabinet memorandum for the purpose of "co-ordinating all action by way of subversion and sabotage against the enemy overseas". (Other sections served in over 30 countries). The functions indicated initially by the Corps had changed since its conception. The head of S.O.E. was a firm believer in our capacity to do difficult and secret work and he was also convinced that security was impeccable. He gave encouragement to all, but especially to those of us in our teens.

The FANY still exists today and may be called upon in national emergencies. Their main peacetime commitment is a mobile R.T. Team on call to the Metropolitan and City of London Major Incident Units (i.e. Plane and rail crashes and Thames flooding).

Training for the first course took place at a large country house at Ketteringham in Norfolk. We received 11/2d per week. It was a tradition in the FANY to be addressed by one's surname only, which included the Commandants: there was little hierarchy, and only a small number of internal ranks.

Each morning began with drill, at that time taken by a sergeant from the Devonshire Regiment, whose accent made his commands even more difficult to follow. The FANY Commanding Officer inspected us, paying particular attention to our appearance: hair had to be well above the collar, and our shoes were polished vigorously every day—the insteps were expected to be as clean and shiny as the uppers. It was luck as to who got the right leather for the Sam Browne belts, and these too had to be polished to resemble a mirror. We even resorted to trying to find ox blood stain to polish them with. Route marches were included in the training, as well as corps history, map reading, night vision, mechanics and driving, etc., and in addition to the practical work we had to pass written and oral examinations in all these subjects.

It was during this period that I met Anna, who trained as a wireless telegrapher, and also Diana (nicknamed Dipsy) Portman. Dipsy and I became the closest friends, remaining so up until the time of Dipsy's death in 1945: she was about my age and similar in height—about five feet. Although she had a very serious side to her nature, she enjoyed life enormously, and we shared an interest in nursing, ballet and music. We also appeared to have the same sense of humour.

The course lasted for about three weeks, and then lists were put up with our names indicating to which sections we had been posted. We reported to S.O.E. headquarters in Baker Street (only known afterwards to the public), a rabbit-warren of offices and a prosaic threshold to a new world. When we signed the Official Secrets Act we were, without realising it, signing our names to a new way of life. The familiar, ordinary world was left behind, and I never returned to it.

I was always reminded of King George VI's Christmas broadcast in 1939 and the quotation he used from Minnie Louise Haskins:

> "I said to the man who stood at the gate of the year, 'Give me a light that I may tread safely into the unknown', and he replied, 'Go out into the darkness and put your hand into the hand of God. That shall be to thee better than a light and safer than a known way'."

CHAPTER 4

These Hearts were Woven

These hearts were woven of human joys and cares,
Washed marvellously with sorrow, swift to mirth.
The years had given them kindness. Dawn was theirs,
And sunset, and the colours of the earth.

Rupert Brooke.

In Churchill's words—"You are to set Europe ablaze."

During the War many men and women escaped to Britain from different occupied countries. While the majority joined the Services, many also volunteered or were picked for S.O.E. Many of these volunteers had already fought with great bravery in their own countries— they had also witnessed defeat, withdrawal, bitterness, collapse. They were Dutch, Norwegian, French, Belgian, Danish, Polish and Czech. The Norwegians were left bewildered by the Allied withdrawal and they made their escape by an incredible variety of routes, a few even via the Trans-Siberian railway and Canada. The Danes, Dutch and Belgians were equally worried about their families and the fate of friends. The Poles had witnessed two or even three disintegrations.

Special Operations Executive was established in July 1940, its task being to organise and co-ordinate resistance to the common foe—Hitler. Discipline and esprit de corps were essential qualities.

In S.O.E. there were different stations, referred to by numbers and serving different purposes. Amongst others there were training stations where agents were prepared for their future activities, and Ops. and holding stations where they waited prior to being dropped.

Station 17 in Hertfordshire was one of the small arms and saboteur schools where agents were trained to carry out resistance work in occupied countries, and here a number of FANY's worked with the "Bods", as the individual agents were affectionately called. One of our tasks was driving them, escorting them to Ringway (the Parachute Training School) and to special courses, as well as maintaining their vehicles and working as cypherers. We looked after them, acting as their confidantes, and tried also to bring some kind of stability to a life which, for many, held only a precarious promise for the future. In return, however, for whatever we did to help them they gave far more back to us. It was a time my companions and I were never to forget.

At an Ops. Station, when the signal came through, we took it in turns to go to the Group Leaders to tell them: "Ops. are on." Preparation and briefing had been completed by the quiet, very well-mannered Briefing Officers from London. Not infrequently the Bods had to be driven down to the airfield along the familiar roads of Hertfordshire, Cambridgeshire or Suffolk. The aircraft took off during the moon periods, originally from a runway converted from the race course at Newmarket, but later on they flew from Stradishall and Tempsford airfields. Each nationality had its own changing hut and, for security reasons, was kept apart from the others. A number of Bods had already flown on futile missions, some as many as eight times, when either the Reception Committee could not be located or visibility in the region of the landing area was too bad.

At the Ops. Station and during the journey (more often too, if necessary) complete checks were made to ensure that none of the agents carried any clues that would give him away—such as labels on clothing—and also to ensure that each had his or her compass, forged identification card and money, poison tablet (sometimes hidden in the top inside part of the jacket) and revolver. All messages, pass-words and other information had to be carried by word of mouth only.

The FANY's prepared sandwiches and flasks for the flight—sometimes an agent's last meal was from a "hay-box". Though the pre-mission hours were naturally very tense, there was also a wonderful mixture of humour and

32

cheerfulness among the Bods, and I can't remember any false bravado; on the contrary, it was real wit that came through. Whenever the atmosphere was especially tense or a feeling of dread pervaded, someone in the small group would rally the spirits of the others. No written word can recapture the warmth of the atmosphere throughout the Station.

The agents delighted in talking about their own countries: it seemed to help them, perhaps because it eased their homesickness and enabled them to express the pride they felt. They had, too, an extraordinary humility and a religious faith which was exemplified in the way they prepared themselves for their missions and made their confessions to a priest who would come to the Ops. Station especially for this purpose. Later in North Africa and Italy Mass would be said in the open (even in winter), or in some very simple shelter.

The Poles at the Ops. Station often sang and danced, for they were gay and musical, and they taught us some of their folk songs as well as songs composed in the War.

Christmas at Ops. Station was unforgettable. The Bods according to their nationalities took over the Station, including the kitchen and managed despite rationing to prepare part of their old traditional Christmas Eve supper. The Poles observed *wigilia* (vigil). Hay was laid on the table to represent the manger and, after the first star appeared, we handed each other a blessed wafer (øplatek). This was broken and a greeting expressed. Barszcz (beetroot soup) and fish (in peace time, carp) were prepared. On one occasion, our Polish Christmas Eve meal included *golabki* (cabbage rolls with rice and meat). This was clearly a mistake for meat is not to be eaten by Polish Catholics on what to them is a day of abstinence. But on this occasion, we all ate *golabki* amidst laughter and the mistake was discovered when the dish was almost empty. To many of those present this was their last Christmas on earth. We learnt and sang their carols and taught them ours. At midnight, Mass was celebrated. We could not exchange presents for obvious reasons, but I remember one Bod who handed me his parachute badge.

33

He wrote *"until we meet at the Central Station in Warsaw"*. We were naturally unable to invite them because of security to our own homes and this made us feel all the more united. I recall too there was an escape practice which included swimming across a cold stream. In all I spent 21 years away from home at Christmas.

The Norwegians would describe the light Northern nights, the way they had been brought up to use skis, and the distances they covered on them while working in the Resistance, the pine forests, the fjords. Peter, a young Norwegian, felt that after the war it would be impossible for him to remain in his own country, for he couldn't imagine settling down to an ordinary life after his life as an Agent and talked of emigrating, but did not know where he wanted to go. The other Bods were shocked by his attitude. Some said they would study medicine or social work, and they spoke about rebuilding their countries, for both their cities and their lives were in ruins. Less than a year was to pass before Peter was captured and shot.

Walking back across the deserted fields after an un-official evening out playing shove ha'penny at the local pub the Dutch would talk of Amsterdam, the canals and the flowers, and of the pre-War breakfast tables laden with different varieties of cheese and sausages.

They were fighting for Britain and for freedom for their own countries, and they knew what lay ahead for them if they were caught. They were going into situations from which they might never escape, and even if they were not killed, they would be deprived of their liberty. Yet the choice they made would in the end give them a far greater freedom.

At Station 17 a small group of French Canadians did part of their training for the Dieppe raid, which took place on the 19th August 1942, at a cost of 3,642 Allied servicemen killed, wounded or taken prisoner.

Little or nothing was ever to be known of the seven Czech parachutists who were dropped into Czechoslovakia on a mission to assassinate SS General Reinhard Heydrich, the ruthless Reich "Protector" (Governor) of their country. The decision to assassinate Heydrich was taken because of the appalling brutality to which the Czechs were subjected under his régime. Though it was known that the seven agents had little or no chance of escape and that the civilian population would suffer severe reprisals if the purpose of the mission were discovered, it was felt that Heydrich must be stopped even at this cost.

From the moment they landed in Czechoslovakia the seven boys endured a constant nightmare as they tried to find a safe hiding place. After the assassination, which took place on the outskirts of Prague, the nightmare intensified as the Germans searched for them, and as one hiding place after another was discovered, the boys found themselves on the run yet again. Eventually they were denounced to the Germans, who cornered them in the crypt of a church in Prague, but they put up an heroic fight before they were killed.

The reaction of the SS and the Gestapo to the assassination was indescribably savage: there were waves of arrests; hundreds of innocent civilians were rounded up; every man in the village of Lidice was shot, all women taken to a concentration camp, the children handed over to SS families for germanisation and the locality burned to the ground. Ležáky, the other village marked out for reprisal, was also destroyed.

The following top priority cable was sent by Himmler to SS Gruppenfuhrer Frank:—

Top Priority Cable
Special Train 'Heinrich'
No. 5745—27 May 1942

> To SS Gruppenfuhrer Frank
> Prague
> For Immediate Delivery
> SECRET

1. I agree to the proclamation.
2. The 10,000 hostages to be arrested must above all contain the intellectuals of the Czech opposition.
3. One hundred leaders of this Czech intellectual opposition are to be shot the same night.

I shall telephone you again tonight.
Signed
H. Himmler.

The Czechs were stunned for while they had expected reprisals, they had anticipated nothing on this scale. One of the Czechs echoed his country's grief when he said, "It will be difficult ever to be the same again"; and I was reminded of the shame I had felt in 1938 when huge crowds in Britain had celebrated Chamberlain's return to London while Prague was in sorrow.

The men and women who trained as agents had to be in top mental and physical condition and to possess initiative; they were self-reliant and discreet, and capable of standing up to tough and arduous training and work. From many volunteers comparatively few were accepted.

Certain of the Bods returned to Britain to risk their lives all over again for S.O.E., some of them having experienced capture and imprisonment at the hands of the Gestapo. Their anger at the occupation of their countries and the atrocities committed there made them prepared to face any risk in an attempt to do battle with the devil; but on the other hand there were also those who questioned their ability to cope with the boredom of living and working in the Resistance, the frustrations, and the perpetual strain of maintaining their disguise.

The men and women who were trained as wireless/telegraph operators included the bravest, for if they were caught with a set in the suitcase which they carried, they knew they faced death. To escape detection they frequently had to change the place from which they transmitted messages, and to avoid capture they often had to disguise themselves—sometimes at barely a moment's notice. Later in the War, in Southern Italy, a British Naval Commander seconded to our section said, "Well, if you want to risk your bloody neck, don't expect anybody to be there to fall back on."

Many Polish air-crews operated in the different sections of special duties operations. They incurred heavy losses, for they had to fly without fighter protection and were harassed by night fighters and by very heavy flak, in addition to which they often had to contend with appalling weather conditions which caused icing on the wings of their aircraft. The crews referred to the slow heavy

Whitley aircrafts as coffins, but gradually they were replaced by Halifax bombers, adapted to carry an extra fuel tank which increased their range to 2,100 miles, although their speed was only 150 miles per hour.

The courage and endurance of the aircrews and of the Bods they carried was superb: as well as the special dangers they faced from fighters and flak because they were operating singly and in small groups, they also had to endure the bitter cold, the noise of the aircraft, the absence of heating and seats, and uncertainty as to whether the Reception Committee would be waiting for them at the dropping zone. The curfew forbade people in Occupied Europe to leave their homes between dusk and dawn, so the risks the Reception Committee took were incalculable. *Containers of supplies to be dropped with the agents were loaded into the bomb bay of the aircraft, while lighter packages were kept in the hull and thrown out by the despatcher when the dropping zone was in sight. It was not unheard of for these air-crews to fly five nights in succession if that would help the Resistance and ensure the success of an operation. But, tragically, in such circumstances exhaustion and heavy casualties were inevitable.

We got to know some of the crews in Special Squadrons well. I remember John, aged nineteen, the navigator of a Whitley bomber, saying that his home had been bombed and his mother killed in the London Blitz of 1940. His younger brother was serving in the Merchant Navy and his father in the Fire Brigade, and he showed great concern for them. Some weeks later he told me: "Now I can understand far more about the Bods and the work we are involved in, for since I last saw Dad his team was sent to another town and he was killed in a raid, and Peter's boat has been torpedoed and blown up in the Atlantic by a

---

* Containers with Sten guns, Bren guns, Piats (anti-tank guns), revolvers, ammunition, gammon grenades, hand grenades, plastic explosive, instantaneous det. fuses, safety fuses, and detonators were loaded into the bomb bay of the aircraft, while lighter packages of tins of meat, biscuits, margarine, American rations and medical equipment were kept in the hull and thrown out by the despatcher.

U-boat." I was struck, however, by the lack of rancour in his tone. Not long afterwards as I was standing with some Bods by an aircraft that was about to take off, John left the cockpit and leaning over the fuselage said, "We must keep smiling as you all do." He, his crew, and the Bods were lost on their long flight back from Poland, shot down over Denmark. They were returning to Tempsford because they did not find the Reception Committee.

It would be impossible to give details of the hundreds of missions to Occupied Europe which were flown by these crews or of the courage shown on each. 138 Squadron alone flew on 2,562 such missions, dropped 995 parachutists, 29,000 containers and 10,000 packages—and lost 70 aircraft and their crews. Very few received any official recognition or decoration, for they belonged to a world where anonymous heroism both during and after the War was the norm. They seemed to be linked in a chronological way with those who had suffered in the First World War, and with those who have been afflicted ever since—the persecuted, the sick, the hungry, the millions everywhere, up to the present day, whose names and whose heroism are known only to God.

Deep friendships were made, transient but precious, for we were all 'ships passing', and there was the unspoken knowledge between us that we would most probably not see each other again, which made important the short time spent in each other's company. In some ways it was an unreal world: in others it enforced an inescapable reality.

Farewells have followed me through my life. I have always felt a sense of sadness and poignancy on leaving both people and places, even though I may have known the individual concerned for only a short time or been to a place on no more than a brief visit. It was especially hard for people who had lived so close to each other to leave each other's company and we admired greatly the way the Bods did this.

Sometimes we remained on at the airfield when the aircraft had taken off, or else returned to our Ops. base to be with the other groups. Occasionally the place was deserted because everyone was on a mission, and then it was filled with memories. During the night or the early hours of the morning a telephone call would come through that we were to return immediately to the airfield, and sometimes we found that an aircraft had already landed with its Bods and packages, having had a fruitless flight. At other times we would wait near the runway for the aircraft to return, and then the despatchers in each aircraft would give us news of what had happened, sometimes bringing back messages or notes scribbled on a cigarette packet. One read: "What was your life? A ray of light that rushed astonished through the night."

The writer of the note—man or woman, boy or girl— would be far away in his occupied country facing a situation which in spite of thorough briefing and training called for every ounce of courage and resourcefulness. As we read the message, we could not help wondering what dangers the writer was facing at that moment. Perhaps he had already been killed or betrayed; he might be in a railway carriage travelling to the next destination on his mission; or perhaps he was in a remote mountain village, making contacts, deciding whom he could trust, gambling his life and the mission entrusted to him on the honesty he recognised in another man's eyes. Or perhaps luck had deserted him and he had already been captured and stood with his hands above his head and a Gestapo gun in his back.

Which was the reality? The music, the briefing, the discussions and the laughter, or the danger and fear that lay ahead? Perhaps all of them had equal importance according to the occasion.

S.O.E. necessarily had to operate behind a heavy veil of secrecy: the only address that we used and could give to friends and relations was "Room 98, The Horseguards, London SW1" and mail was collected from there and brought to the Stations by despatch riders. There was much coming and going of people from Headquarters in Baker Street, but their names were not, strictly speaking, allowed to be mentioned.

No contact with local people in the area of the Station

was permitted and cover stories were given, though at times these must have struck the locals as somewhat less than convincing. A group of puzzled locals gathered one day on the road outside Audley End House, near Saffron Walden, Essex (then used as one of the training stations) and gazed across the wide lawns as a number of Bods, taking part in a training exercise and disguised as Germans, held off an attack. And at one railway station in Hertford I was embarrassed to hear someone mention to me, "strange noises and low parachute drops made up your way."

Security at more secluded stations presented less of a problem, but even here the risk of discovery could not be eliminated. One remembers the day at Ops. Station 20 when everyone was engaged in small arms firing practice and an astonished woman advanced through the woods saying: "I have always understood this place to be a transit centre for the wounded."

With all the care to maintain security that was exerted by those who served at the stations, it was deeply disturbing to learn that the Gestapo were able to show a captured Bod a photograph of one of the training stations in Britain.

At Station 20, small and enclosed, holding Polish agents and occasionally a Czech too, I shared a room with Elizabeth, who had made the fastest time of any courier between Poland and England. She was both gay and frightened, and we admired her the more because she was courageous rather than fearless. On the wall of her room she hung a picture of two young people standing on a river bank holding hands, with the inscription: "A Moment Out of Time." Elizabeth seemed to lead a charmed existence, and when it was her turn to be dropped she would joke with the others in the aircraft saying: "Ladies first!" The last time she was dropped a message was received from the despatcher saying that her drop from the aircraft had been successful; but her luck had run out, for she never returned.

Within a week or two Dipsy arrived at the Station from Thame and shared this same small room with me. She was a wireless operator and she hung a poster on the wall, which showed a wireless/telegrapher operating a wireless set, overshadowed by the figure of a German listening as she transmitted and about to pounce on her.

Though our days passed quickly and were full, we at the training stations occasionally had an overwhelming urge to get out for a while. This was not permitted, but all the same we would go out from Station 17 for a swift ride in the surrounding country on the light collapsible bicycles which were practised on and then packed into containers and dropped into enemy-occupied countries. Such escapades earned us a ticking-off from the C.O. if we were caught. Sometimes there were bets about climbing the water tower, and the more high-spirited were known to have put minute, partly defused time bombs in pockets or under pillows. We had to have relief, for we were all young.

Though books or films about S.O.E. often catch the excitement involved in the work, they rarely recapture the dreadful fear and anguish that most of the Bods, if not all, experienced. The romance which is invariably introduced into such works seems overdone. We had those platonic friendships which people say are impossible: they do not seem to realise what such friendships really mean nor the necessity for them.

About three hundred Bods went through the Stations while we were with them, which meant three hundred "Goodbyes", and a questioning of all accepted values. In the heightened awareness of life and death, it was quality and not quantity that counted: in the final analysis, faith, loyalty, courage and truth were all that mattered.

It has been said that I was born with some instinct, a sort of sixth sense, which made me especially sensitive to atmosphere. I therefore noticed with particular vividness how extremely responsive the Bods were, and as a general rule how cheerful. During the War, when discipline had to be maintained, I found that they were able to keep up also a wonderful relationship both with each other and with the FANY's, to many of whom they used to give some complimentary nick-name. All of us undoubtedly were the better for having been together and exchanging thoughts, whether about the fundamentals of life or about personal or confidential matters.

The Resistance, of which the Bods formed so essential a part, was a situation unlike any other. Yet in the years to come, when in the presence of those who had suffered some misfortune or illness, I was to have the same kind of feeling, as if there were a common identity between the two. With them too, the moment of saying farewell has always moved me deeply.

We used to sit and talk—the Bods remarked how strange it felt to be in an English country garden one day and in Oslo, The Hague, Warsaw or Prague the next. I remember particularly the Ops. Station near Watton-at-Stone, where a wall of the main room was covered with a massive contour map of Poland, while on the other walls hung emblems from some of the groups—a collar, a jacket, a shirt; each bearing its owner's code name. From whatever country they came, these men and women usually had great optimism, although some said they didn't want to be alive to see the aftermath—to them the present moment was everything. If they lived, they might marry unhappily or get cancer or become alcoholic. "Better to die now than that," they thought. The Bods were referred to as the 'silent parachutists' and later their maxim was *We were unknown then, we shall remain unknown now.*

I remember often listening at night to groups of parachutists as they talked deeply about life: the mistakes that had been made, and what they believed could be done with peace when it came. I began then to think of ways in which the qualities they possessed and showed—tolerance, faith, courage, humour and gaiety—might be perpetuated. I thought that instead of trying to remember all those who had died fighting or in camps by means of a plaque or monument, one should go out and provide assistance and comfort to those who are sick, and in need, wherever they might be, regardless of nationality or religion, creating in this a "living memorial" to the dead.

42

CHAPTER 5

Service Overseas

In 1943, when aircraft losses became heavier, especially on the route across Denmark and the Baltic Sea to Poland and Czechoslovakia, it was decided to tranfer one of the special squadrons to North Africa and later to Italy.

We were then operating from an ops. and holding station in Buckinghamshire, and the aircraft were taking off from Tempsford in Bedfordshire. When we were told who had been chosen to go overseas, there was great excitement. We were instructed to check over our uniforms, including the greatcoats (which were designed with a double line of buttons fanning out from the waist to the shoulders, scarlet lining and deep cuffs), and we believed these greatcoats, or the other type known as "British warm", and battledress would ultimately be needed for the victory parade if we reached Warsaw and Prague.

We were allowed to telephone our mothers to say we would be going away, but we were not permitted to give any clue as to where we were going or how we were travelling, and we also had a week's leave, which went by very quickly. At that time I was able to endure great physical tiredness, but on occasion, both during and after the War, I was able to compensate for this by sleeping up to twenty hours at a time when on leave. I could imagine no better feeling than going to bed realising I could sleep on, and my mother used to spoil me by bringing breakfast up to me. My family rarely asked questions, but Mama was perturbed and had consulted the mothers of Dipsy and another friend, Pammy, who suggested that we should have our last tea at the Berkeley or some such place in London. We were highly embarrassed by the idea that questions might be asked.

The nature of our work meant that we had to have cover stories, and these were all the more necessary because the authorities knew we would be in close contact

43

with other servicemen and women. We were told that we were to wear the Polish eagle on our FANY uniforms, even though we were also partly attached to the Czech section. The Poles were delighted to provide the eagles (their national emblem) for us, and we sewed them on to our uniforms. I remember Dipsy saying: "Just think if we had been allowed to wear the crests of the other Bods— Dutch, Belgian, French, Danish, Norwegian! Well, in any case, we shall always remember them, and we shall certainly miss them!" Neither of us had ever served with the French section.

Both Dipsy and I decided at the holding station to preserve our notes and the other small souvenirs which the Bods of the different nationalities had given us at the training or ops. stations. Dipsy left hers in a cake tin with a sealed letter to her mother which was opened in the presence of Mrs. Portman when I came back briefly in 1945; it was very touching. Mine I put in a box marked "S.R." inside a container specially made by a Bod. I remember that we talked to one another very late at night in the bathroom with the taps running, which we considered to be the safest place. We recalled the different people and the ops. they had left on, remembering especially those who had been dropped more than once. Dipsy had received part of her WT training at Thame and later we met at Grendon Underwood, a Signals Station near Oxford, a dreary place which I believe has now been converted into a prison.

I suppose because we realised we were never likely to meet them again, the different Bods and their various missions were very vividly present in our minds during those last nights in Britain. For example we thought of the nine Norwegian Bods and Operation Swallow, a raid they'd carried out successfully against the heavy water plant at Telemark, which had required superb planning, great courage and tremendous luck. These Norwegians destroyed both the hydro factory and the ferry on which the Germans were attempting to evacuate the remains of their heavy water supply. That the Germans failed in the race to produce the atom bomb was due largely to the success of this raid and of an earlier raid by a group of British Commandos.

In London we saw one or two FANY's who had been serving with the Polish Brigade in Scotland and had worn the word *Poland* on their uniforms since 1940. Naturally they considered themselves part of the Polish Brigade, and they expressed surprise on seeing our eagle, not knowing that we belonged to S.O.E. nor what that entailed.

On enlisting, the FANY's bought their uniforms, new or second-hand; a kitbag, a sleeping ("flea") bag and a canvas gas mask were part of their equipment. The mask had to be carried at all times. One issue of khaki drill, consisting of lightweight battledress, was free. Regulations were strict, and after a certain date in spring KD (as it was known) had to be worn with the sleeves rolled up above the elbow. The FANY's who were being posted abroad stocked up with boot polish and soap, and they were given an extra allowance of coupons for stockings.

We were billeted in London opposite the FANY Headquarters, which were in the vicarage of St. Paul's Knightsbridge. Our billet was high up in a draughty room in the Alexandra Hotel, which had already been damaged in the Blitz. Later, after the War, a memorial plaque to the FANY's who had died was unveiled by H.R.H. Princess Alice of Athlone on the wall of St. Paul's Church, in the presence of Field Marshal Earl Wavell.

My mother came to London especially the day before we were due to embark. We prayed together in St. Paul's Church, and then I saw Mama into a taxi at Hyde Park at the start of her journey back to Thurlow. As the taxi pulled away she leaned out of the window and said: "Please come back to see us before you leave to work in Prague and Poland for years." Undoubtedly my mother already had an intuition of the course my life was to take, and I hoped the taxi driver would not repeat her words if he had heard them. Much water was to pass under the bridge before we saw each other again very briefly in 1945.

Dipsy and I enjoyed going to Floris in Jermyn Street and having a free spray of scent; then we listened in a

45

Bond Street record shop to Tchaikovsky's Rhapsody on a
theme of Paganini, to Brahms' Violin Concerto and to
"Softly awakes my heart" from *Samson and Delilah*.
These were treats to be packed in on almost our last
day.

After embarking at Addison Road Station we travelled
overnight in a heavily blacked-out train which seemed to
stop at every station before finally reaching Liverpool,
making the journey seem endless. In the docks we waited
in a damp warehouse while embarkation on to the troopship proceeded, and it was afternoon before we trudged
up the gangplank carrying our kitbags. We were allocated
two berths with four other girls in a cabin which, before
the War, had accommodated only one or two passengers.
The sight of the Clyde in Scotland where the troopship
joined the assembling convey in the misty and mellow
atmosphere remained in my memory for a long time.

A company of the Rifle Brigade who were also on
board caught sight of us in our FANY uniforms and
wondered who we were. There could be no disclosure
about our assignment, and this proved much more
difficult on a crowded troopship than it had been at the
training station, where we had been isolated from outsiders. Strict security had to be maintained at all times,
but our cover stories must have been weak, for members
of the crew and fellow passengers often expressed surprise
at what they were told, and asked us awkward questions
about our past service and where we had been.

For some of the hundreds on board the troopship the
feeling of optimism and cheerful good humour remained
throughout the voyage to North Africa; but overcrowding,
particularly for the unfortunate troops below deck and for
others, who were sleeping on the stairs, eventually led in
most cases to a tremendous feeling of boredom, broken
only by regular boat drills and occasional attacks on the
convoy. Three ships were lost. The crew often talked
about the thousands of servicemen who, from 1940, had
spent weeks on troopships sailing round the Cape to join
the Eighth Army, and of others who had had equally
boring and monotonous or dangerous weeks at sea

above:
Sue Ryder with Krishna
and Prem.

right:
In India.

below:
A leprosy patient who can
still dance and sing,
though she has lost her
hands and part of her feet.

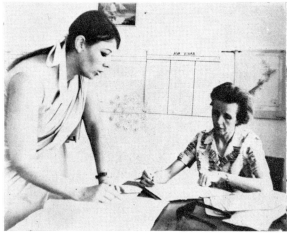

Young tradesmen erecting a new Home.

Sue Ryder Home, Oxenhope, Yorkshire.

Sue Ryder Home, Hickleton, Yorkshire.

Sue Ryder Home, Stagenhoe, Hertfordshire —with the proposed extension.

before fighting in the campaigns against the Japanese in the Far East.

During the voyage we had time for deep thought and for entertaining great hopes of linking up with the Yugoslav Partisans into Hungary and beyond or possibly of breaking through the Alps. There was speculation too about the formation of a Second Front—how? when? where?

After disembarking in Algiers we walked, carrying our kitbags and sleeping bags on our shoulders, to a billet— a pension of doubtful repute. During our first night there some Americans of the First Army had an orgy of drinking and were sick on the stairs, and we helped to clear up the mess. We were made very uncomfortable by the intensely cold nights which succeeded the brilliant sunshine of the day. Amongst the local population there was a general distrust of the French, a shortage of food, and great poverty.

Some of my friends joined FANY's posted to the East of Algiers—ISSU 6 as the unit was called—which was concerned with building up and organising the Resistance in Southern France and Corsica, and "the jargon of sabotage was on our lips". Muffet Panting (who had lost her parents in the Far East in Japanese camps, her husband and brother in other theatres of the War), was subsequently dropped in Corsica. I myself also moved on, and, leaving Dipsy and the others behind, including Joannie our mutual friend, two or three of us flew to Tunis in a Liberator with the crew of a special flight of which Wing Commander S. Król was the captain. Amongst all the squalor the beauty of the sunrise and sunset was breath-taking, and I was reminded of the descriptions given in letters written to me by friends who had fought in the campaigns across all of the two thousand miles stretching into the desert.

During my stay in Tunis the Town Major offered me a bath, and two prisoners of war from the Afrika Korps, who had to heat and carry the water, told me they were convinced that Germany would win the War. In Tunis too we met men from the Eighth Army, some of whom wore scarves instead of ties round their necks and suede boots instead of the usual Army footwear. It was confirmed by these men that their commanders were not sticklers for the conventional appearance of their troops.

We were billeted on the outskirts of Tunis, where the Arabs were so short of food that they used to come to the billet and barter eggs for tea leaves. On one occasion I was surprised when friends burst into our room carrying loaded revolvers. They rushed over to the window and saw a local Arab, whom they had noticed on their way into the billets, climbing the wall with a knife between his teeth; but he ran off, and we presumed he had been looking for food to steal. We also suffered severely from mosquito bites, and once when the Unit was to be inspected by the Commander-in-Chief, I was unable to be present as the swelling from the bites was so acute.

Our handpicked group of FANY's now travelled on to Italy, for there had been only two or three long flights from Tunisia to Poland and Czechoslovakia. Conditions here were rough. In one place, at a farm we called Tara (from *Gone with the Wind*), where there was no heating and the only electricity was generated by a windvane, we were billeted upstairs while sheep and goats occupied the ground floor. My kitbag and camp bed had been lost, but the Poles made beds from blankets nailed on to orange boxes, and put up pieces of canvas sheeting to give partial privacy for a loo.

The Germans had told the local people in Italy various tales of what would happen to them when the Allies landed, and the Italians expressed astonishment and even fear at seeing a girl in trousers and battledress and a man in a kilt (which they called a "skirt"). They said: "When we saw you we did not know how to react; we'd been told that you would kill the lot of us when you arrived." Some villages seemed deserted, for the inhabitants, if they were not under fire and in the immediate battle areas, shut themselves up in their small and often poverty-stricken dwellings and waited anxiously to see what was going to happen.

One of our Commanding Officers, Colonel Trevor Roper-Caldbeck, wrote of that time: "At first I was not altogether happy at the thought of having women in that situation, but the four who came as an advance guard were superb. Their courage, cheerfulness and guts in the face of every obstacle amazed me, and I cannot speak too highly of the way they tackled any task."

The intense cold, especially during the winter of 1943, was unforgettable. The only heating was from a round charcoal brazier, and if it burned all night the fumes became lethal. We thought we would never be warm again, and at night we lay awake thinking about a hot bath and clean sheets. But we came to terms with it, as did others. One of the air crew gave me his spare flying suit, and I remember wearing it at night, inside a sleeping bag. Rum bottles filled with hot water served as improvised hot water bottles, but if the bottles broke during the night the cold and ice in the morning were terrible.

There were long tedious drives through blizzards in the mountains, with Italians begging for rations (bully beef, hard biscuits, margarine) or left-over food, and troops sitting on the back of the 15 cwt. truck discouraging children from stealing the kit. Improvised stoves were erected outside which functioned on two drops of oil and one drop of water. The FANY's gave up wearing ties and caps, and replaced them with Balaclava helmets and scarves.

In an extract from a note I found the following: "You must have had an appalling journey. Mike said you had left before dawn and my fears were all confirmed. We were under three feet of snow and it snowed hard all Tuesday. We are ghostly white figures moving about in snowsuits and snow shoes."

A friend, Johnny, wrote to me at this time of the 'great pale platitude'. "Have you read Max Beerbohm's lecture on Lytton Strachey? After speaking of Strachey's purely unsentimental genius as a writer of English prose, he finishes up with a denunciation of the century's incredible new religion, the worship of the common man. 'I am an old man,' he says,— 'and I don't like new religions. But in the year 2000 man will be unchained and will rise to his feet and find something a bit better to worship. But in the meantime, in the great pale platitude of the meantime ......' we are all living in a great pale platitude, and we'd just better be thankful for people like Strachey."

It was a winter of discontent. For the Army there was slow, bitter, tedious fighting at Salerno, Anzio, Foggia and later at Monte Cassino. The Germans were firmly entrenched in the mountains, and few of the Allies understood the long drawn-out strategy they were forced to follow in the perpetual flogging, slogging trudge northwards to Rome and further. I wrote a note to Dipsy: "My God, are we ever going to get there? Let's pray things will be all right. Aren't we lucky to be taking part?" Eventually, however, the bitter winter began to give way to spring. The frozen snow, rutted and packed hard on the mountain tracks and roads, began to grow grey with mud.

The aircraft flying to southern Poland used three main routes: the first crossed Lake Balaton in Hungary and passed west of Budapest and over the Tatra mountains, the distance to Krakow close to 750 miles, that to Warsaw nearly 900. The second route was slightly further east, via Kotor in Yugoslavia, east of Budapest and into Poland east of the Tatras. The third lay still further east via Albania, a distance of 684 miles. For the crews it was dangerous, as weather conditions were often very bad and visibility down to nil, especially over the mountains, and there were always the night fighters and the flak to contend with.

The courage and enterprise of the Polish Resistance and of the Bods parachuted in to help them were responsible for the discovery in 1942 of the German V1* and V2 rocket installation and launching-pads at Peenemunde. As a result of the information they supplied, a bombing-raid was carried out, the success of which resulted in the development of these rockets being set back by many months. Later a V2 rocket came into the hands of the Resistance who, at the risk to their lives, managed to keep it hidden from the Germans, and this rocket was

* Vergeltungswaffe Eins, Revenge Weapon No. 1, 25 feet long with nearly 1 ton of explosive. The V1s killed 6,184 civilians and seriously injured 17,981. The V2s killed 2,754.

examined by two of the Bods, one a young engineer, who made detailed notes of every one of its 25,000 components. Not long afterwards this Bod was arrested and shot. Undoubtedly an unknown number of people in Britain owe their lives to the discovery by the Poles of the rocket installations and to the information about the construction of the rockets which they were able to obtain and pass back to Britain. If the bombing-raid had not caused a delay, these rockets would certainly have been launched against Britain much sooner than they were and in much greater numbers, resulting in appalling casualties.

The details of the rockets were sent out by cipher or by courier. A few of the couriers and some of the precious technical documents on the rockets were brought out of Poland by night in a small aircraft—an unarmed Dakota, fitted with two extra fuel tanks—which flew from Italy, a long and perilous mission, dependent upon very good weather conditions to enable the pilot and navigator of the aircraft to find the landing area. Every detail of the operation had to be planned and timed down to the last minute, for speed was essential if the aircraft was to land, on-load its passengers and cargo, and take off before the enemy arrived. Because of the very real risk of the enemy locating the landing area—the sound of the aircraft passing overhead was almost certain to alert every German patrol in the vicinity—the pilot had to be ready to take off at a moment's notice. The passengers would go aboard therefore according to a pre-arranged order of priority, to ensure that those with the most vital information would not be the ones left behind if he had to do so before everyone was aboard.

The Dakota was to bring out of Poland a sack containing all the drawings and technical details of the rockets, as well as several of the Bods who had information which was of vital importance to the Allies, and this sack with its precious contents had priority over the passengers, for it had to be brought back to Britain at all costs.

This mission, the third, almost met with disaster. It could only take off after eighty minutes of suspense because the landing ground was too small and soft. The

Dakota was loaded and off-loaded in an attempt to reduce weight, and as a last resort it was even thought that it would have to be destroyed by fire, but further frantic efforts were made by placing wooden planks under the wheels. Against all odds it reached base, and the information required by the Allies was handed on. The composure and courage of those participating—both the crews and the members of the Resistance in Poland—were the more remarkable in view of the great danger and tension.

Sometimes in Italy the British and Yugoslav Bods attached to Tito's military mission came up to the hillside hideouts and talked. They discussed Tito and the way he was uniting the people in the areas of Yugoslavia that had been liberated. Rougher than the Poles, the Yugoslavs were ferocious fighters; like the Poles, they were motivated by patriotism and took appalling risks. Wounded Partisans, men and women, came to the Adriatic coast; there were a great number of women amongst the Partisans, and they enjoyed complete equality with the men. They came from bitter, savage mountain country. Some had gangrene —I already had seen poverty and want, but I was now to witness ever greater suffering.

One of our friends had a twenty-first birthday and wrote a poem for me—

Ah, thank God for laughter without reason or result,
But to make the blue sea golden and the golden sea exult
And all the ardent sunlight, spreadeagled on the sea,
is a bright corridor leading your laughter back to me . . .

Another friend in the Rifle Brigade wrote: "I am not at all happy about you. You seem to be working much too hard and much too long. Has J. mentioned the local fauna? There are masses of small finches and warblers here. Greenfinches and goldfinches are frequently to be seen. I saw some siskins a few days ago, more wagtails, more tits, many types of larks, hoopoe, bee-eaters, practically every known type of hawk and buzzard and several types of eagles, and even ravens have appeared since I have been here. There is a quaint little animal called a wingill or wugill—a cross between a badger and a polecat—which lives in the sands and sometimes shows itself. Jackals live round about in the hills and I often hear them at night."

I replied:

"Your letters remind me of the sort of things that we too are seeing and meeting with. Among the many things which used to be described in letters from the desert were the cold nights and the quite unbelievably glorious sunsets and sunrises. They make up for an awful lot of other things, and I wonder in what other countries one sees such exquisite skies. Perhaps in Asia. And I wonder too whether we shall find them in the other lands that perhaps eventually we may reach. The birds we are more than conscious of. I wish I had time to go into greater detail, as you have. Certainly the jackals at night make quite a noise don't they?

The pressure, you know, has been with us really ever since the beginning and isn't all that bad. It's a challenge which we may not only enjoy, but would expect. What is far more important, is the gaiety and laughter, the singing, and even, at odd moments, the dancing. The stories, too, and discussions held on many different subjects . . . . and above all, there's so much else in this life that we are now experiencing, the faith which I can't really properly describe and never will be able to, the courage, the songs that we have been taught, and the endless discussions and talks on such a variety of subjects. It is as good almost as being in a sort of university lecture room, but in a more relaxed atmosphere and hearing it all from much younger people. I wish you were part of it and could listen with us, but doubtless you have occasions too in trenches and on mountainsides, on muletracks, in the back of trucks. It probably even reminds you of the poop deck and watching phosphorous out into the night, in convoy, and many other things.

Through Italy and the treacherous hard way up, every yard was defended by the Germans. Travelling through the country, the signs of inequality between rich and poor

53

impressed themselves upon me. From Naples to Rome to Florence and beyond we saw heart-breaking poverty, and on occasions we had a strange feeling that we were amongst neither friends nor enemies. I remember too in late May 1944 driving up Highway 6 past a village bombed mistakenly by American planes, killing Allied soldiers. The unburied bodies lay swollen in the sun and we could smell the sickly scent of death.

Reaching Rome just after the liberation on 4th June, we enjoyed the luxury of a bath and sleeping between sheets in a proper bed—an incredible sensation. We had an audience with the Pope; there were great crowds, and much singing and excitement in the blazing sunshine. Tim, aged twenty-one, an officer in the 10th Battalion Rifle Brigade, had a day's sick leave, and I was allowed to meet him: together we walked up to a village, explored churches and heard the Italians singing *Caro Nome, Home to our Mountain,* and other extracts from Verdi's operas. We listened, too, to the birds, and talked about the value of faith. As Tim left, I had a strong feeling that this would be our last meeting, and in fact he was killed on the 26th July. The following note came to me from Geoffrey, a brother officer:

> We were doing one of those beastly night marches and a dawn attack, and Tim was in the company on my left. I believe "high-ups" thought that the particular hills were unoccupied, but as usual they were wrong. Anyway, Tim's convoy ran into German machine guns and heavy machine gun fire. His platoon was sent round to the right towards us to get behind them, and got lost in the valley. After a lot of trouble, both convoys got on to their objectives and established the position, but nothing was heard of Tim's platoon which, it later transpired, had gone too far to the right—in fact they met some Germans on *our* right. Unfortunately Tim was leading. They heard some movement ahead of them. They challenged and the reply was "Italiani" which was followed by a burst of Schmeisser (machine gun fire) killing Tim, very badly wounding his corporal and just missing his platoon

sergeant. Later we found Tim's body where he fell. Mercifully he had been killed outright, and could not have known anything about it. . . .

"I believe so much," Dipsy wrote afterwards to me, "in not letting one's personal tragedies affect work or other people's lives; in knowing how those who have gone before would so hate one to mourn and not care for the better things in the world. But it's so hard to laugh and forget, even for five minutes—'Better by far you should smile and forget, than that you should remember and be sad'—but I think one does both."

Neither of us ever became accustomed to death.

During that summer of 1944, sorties into Poland continued—and the losses continued too. The effort was very great—169 sorties to Yugoslavia and Northern Italy were carried out—but though the surviving crews were weary, they were always ready to volunteer for further duties.

When the Warsaw Rising started during the afternoon of 1st August, 1944 there was dismay and also concern as to how help could be given. Night flying by moonlight to special dropping zones had proved difficult enough, but suddenly to be faced with the need for dropping large quantities of arms, food and medical supplies from a low altitude on Warsaw defied all description, encircled as it was by fires and hidden by smoke, with sectors constantly changing hands. Apart from flying hundreds of miles, the aircraft had also to contend with harassment by German fighter planes and anti-aircraft defences throughout the journey as well as over the dropping zones. British, Polish and South African losses were appalling.

The heroic rising, in which 250,000 individuals were killed, was suppressed by the Nazis sixty-three days and nights later. It is a time which none of us who had connections with the fate of this city can bear to recount.

In another note I wrote to Dipsy: "You once said my feelings on death and eternal life were well clarified. This I question. But what I have no doubt about is the ghastly frustration and hopelessness which face us whenever there are moments to think. The mere fact of so many people being killed hourly in the desert, in the jungle, in sub-marines, in the mountains, being shot down, in concentration and extermination camps or in Gestapo headquarters or prisons—they are all suffering untold hell for something which each believes in or hopes for. It's silly to boast about idealism. War is too bloody for an individual suddenly to become a hero—or to say good and brave things when he's tortured or dying. It's more likely to bring out the opposite—but each of us has to try."

Molly, another of my friends, was serving with the YMCA up in the line on the Senio river with the Divisional Machine Gunners of the Sixth London Division. During my visit to her, mortar bombs were thrown over and the Germans were very visible. It reminded me yet again of the smell of death and the whistle of shells from 88mm. guns in other places on the way. I had to get a lift to Senio and back, and on the way the truck stopped for the Tommies to "brew up" on a spirit stove from their rations of dried milk and tea prepared as a dissoluble cube. Noticing that I too carried my mug on my battledress, one Tommy said, "Watch out there that enamel isn't too chipped, lassie, and never borrow one, for it's V.D. you can get from this."

The characteristics of the men of different nations were very evident, especially under stress or tiredness. I recall one incident. There was a long convoy slowly climbing up and hugging the mountain road on one side while the truck that I was travelling in was (probably contrary to orders) coming down the other side of the road. Within minutes I realised from the driver's behaviour, his language and his manner of driving that he was "bomb happy." I persuaded him to stop and allow me to take over driving. A Welshman shouted from the convoy opposite: "You've earned the M.C. for this lot—he was a menace to the convoy." Mines had not been cleared from the road and there were signs along the edge "Beware of the Verges", with the usual unprintable sign or message underneath.

Dipsy received special permission to marry a pilot serving in the Lysander Squadron whom we had both known and admired for some time. The marriage was very short, for both were killed near Florence and buried on the banks of the Arno. The padre and another priest came over next day, and we all attended a short service, with the mimosa still alive in its tin vase, bearing the promise of spring and life. The impact of death again struck me. It seemed almost impossible to bear it without Dipsy, who had until then shared my feelings about death in the fullest sense, and I kept thinking it must be somebody else and that I could go and discuss it all with her still.

That night we saw in the dim light from the hurricane lamp Dipsy's battledress on the camp bed, her compass, her spare Army boots, Lyall's *Languages of Europe*, her well-worn English/Polish textbook and dictionary, and her hair brush which smelled of Chanel No. 5. On a scrap of paper I found the words: "When Thou hast a sorrow, tell it not to thine arrow, but tell it to the saddle bow and ride thee singing forth."

Into my mind came this poem, of which we had been so fond:

Look for me in England
On each oak and swan
When I am gone,
Pay the tribute of my glance
As if by chance
My shadow on the water stirred
The real surface with your own
Look on bud and leaf and bird
Not for yourself alone.

Hear for me in England
The music of the shires
By memory's fires
The whisper of the flame
Engraves your name.
Listen to the bells which spell
That name where echoes peal and stray
Beyond the valley and the fell
To us who are away.

Touch for me in England
Bark of elm and yew
The morning dew
Hands in your lap shall be
Cradles for me.
Your fingers on the pen reach out
Through words to mine, that trace
On sands and on the seas about
As if in braille your face.

From Dipsy's father, Brigadier Portman, I received the following letter:

> This is to send you my warmest thanks for all you have done for us, for your letters and your friendship for Diana. Your letters were the helpful and sympathising sort I wanted to have from Diana's comrades, and you managed to convey so much I longed to know, which no-one else could have; you made me very happy and almost cheerful.
>
> You were a jolly good friend to Diana and those you both served with and for. What a merry team you were; there can never have been such a unit in any other wars. I am afraid she never got my last letters, as scarcely any letters got through.
>
> I am terribly proud too that part of my old team, the London 56th Division (Black Cats) have done so well.
>
> Yours very gratefully,
>
> G.P.

Much later, when Dipsy's parents and I were discussing a headstone for the grave of their daughter and son-in-law, I suggested inscribing the lines: "Lovely and pleasant in their lives, and in death they were not divided."

CHAPTER 6

After A Famous Victory

In 1945 the conditions of—and for—relief work in the battle areas of Europe were very difficult. Communications were in a state of chaos, and everywhere around was to be seen the material wreckage of total war. With colleagues I continued to work through whole regions which proved that in calculated destructiveness man can far out-do any earthquake.

The relief units, severally and collectively, were tiny in relation to the problems challenging them. One of the first units was assigned to operate over the worst devastated areas of Normandy, and was then told to go from there into the Pas de Calais, Belgium and beyond, as might be necessary. We were to bring urgently needed succour to all who required it, regardless of age or condition, and to help all those suffering from hunger, disease, distress and strain.

General de Gaulle had given his blessing to the small unit to which I was attached—a rare occurrence, for he did not allow France, because of her pride, to accept help from U.N.R.R.A. (United Nations Relief and Rehabilitation Administration).

Even before this new journey began I had fallen into minor difficulties. The lorry I was told to collect in London was fully loaded, including amongst its "cargo" paraffin lamps and stoves, supplies of benzyl benzoate for the treatment of scabies, drugs for T.B. and typhoid, syringes, blankets and pillows. And with all this on board, the lorry broke down in Vauxhall Bridge Road. As he passed, a most untypical London taxi driver stuck his head out of his cab window, not to offer assistance but to suggest, rather luridly, that the lorry was past helping. However, with the aid of passers-by, I pushed it into the gutter, got

59

out the tools, replaced the sparking plugs, cleaned the carburettor and the petrol pump, and was soon off again.

Then I crossed to Dieppe, to find that there was nobody to meet me No map had been available and petrol was scarce, but I had been given the most implicit instructions to go on, having been referred, rather vaguely, to "the hospital near the Cathedral in Rouen". When I reached the ruins of the city in darkness and asked the way of a Frenchman, he replied wryly, "There once *were* several hospitals", and directed me to one of the few that had not been destroyed. There, to my relief, I found the other workers. They too had been despatched with the sketchiest of briefs, and, after a stormy Channel crossing in a tank-carrying craft, had landed well off their routes.

From the first moment when I decided to do relief work. I had wished it to be on just these terms—working with the people of the country, working for the ministries and local authorities and under their guidance; and the experience which lay before us is one which I shall never forget or cease to be thankful for.

The members of the teams were usually divided into twos and billeted in the simplest accommodation, thus sharing the conditions of the local population. Rouen was only the first of many widely dispersed bases for the Unit's mission, and my memory is of an almost continuous succession of drives, some short, some very long, so varied in their destination and nature that to attempt to describe them would be very difficult indeed. Yet isolated memories live very vividly in my mind, amongst them:

Driving by night in strange, ruined towns with no street lighting; after a while learning how to navigate by smell— the different smells of open sewers, choked drains, decomposing bodies not yet recovered from the ruins. The ruins themselves becoming memorable and useful as landmarks or signposts; the relics of a street lamp, of a charred wall, of a sagging roof truss; the shell of a church or a tall fragment of spire. Rightly even amidst these conditions the French Police insisted upon us passing a driving test in addition to fitting direction lights on the vehicle.

Tuberculosis was widespread, and efforts to bring it

60

under control were high on the Unit's list of priorities. But the menace of other epidemics was also great. This was partly because diseases that were less familiar, and for which the available antidotes were little known by the general population, had come with the survivors from concentration camps, in particular typhus, and associated illnesses.

All around the bodies of the dead still lying beneath the ruins were a potential source of infection. As everywhere in Europe, local authorities organised groups to search for them, and on occasion one felt obliged to help in this macabre operation.

My colleague was a nurse. At a General Hospital near Villers Bocage—in the lush country which had been the scene of prolonged and fierce fighting for the east flank of General Montgomery's beach-head—the two of us were based in what remained of a General Hospital. A thin partition divided our little bedroom from that of the obstetrician, and we were often disturbed at night by nursing nuns who came to his door to announce an imminent birth. Details of the girl or woman in labour were given in rapid French, but often the obstetrician was very tired and loath to get up, understandably enough, as sometimes he was called up nine or ten times in one night. The nuns would then appeal to the nurse and us to persuade him to come. If he had already fallen asleep again, we would try to rouse him tactfully, and if we did not succeed, would go back to the nuns for their assistance. The theatre Sister, named Agnes, I remember, had a beautiful face and a very remarkable serenity.

Before the devastation the hospital had had its own psychiatric department, but this had had to be moved to the block where the obstetrician, my companion and I were accommodated. So, in addition to the pleas of the nuns to the obstetrician, there were distractions from psychiatric patients. One, nick-named "Shaky Saul", was also suffering from Parkinson's disease, and was forever coming to our window with his friend "Leering Laurie", asking for mégots (cigarette ends).

During the first weeks we had to share a loo littered with

bins of dirty linen. It had no bolt or lock, and the patients, men and women, frequently came in to hold long conversations with us while we were in there.

There was a shortage of ambulances, and one night, when an emergency call came with no one else to help, I took Saul and Laurie as stretcher bearers. I remember having to go up a long flight of stairs to find the patient, and the consequent difficulty of getting her down to safety in their inexperienced hands without the stretcher being tilted.

On call with the women of the *Croix Rouge* (Red Cross) I drove a mobile clinic. In convoy the girls tended to drive fast, regardless of the pot-holes, and the locker doors at the back of the converted 3-ton van, previously used in the blitz on London, used to fly open until I secured them more firmly. Their leader was strict, and once rightly reprimanded me, asking me why I was not wearing the uniform correctly. I realised that it was not complete, as I was not wearing a forage cap and, having always taken a pride in my uniform (in all, I wore it for over 20 years), I felt ashamed and readily agreed that no uniform is complete without its appropriate headgear.

Morale was very high, and this was very important, for conditions were harsh. Amongst the memories I recall was sharing the roughest accommodation with eight girls of the *Croix Rouge:* we ate in a stable, and washed at a tap in the yard, and the only loo was a very primitive one which offered no privacy.

The girls were on a rota system with their ambulances, but they were not as disciplined as one or two of us thought desirable, partly because of the demands on their time. One night a call came and the girl whose turn it was to go out did not have her ambulance parked by the exit at the back of the narrow yard. At that moment another girl, who was sleeping in the rear of the van I used, lit a paraffin stove to warm up some cold tea, having come in late. In the darkness and the excitement of trying to get the ambulances reversed, the stove upset and the flames spread. We ran from the doss room to the pump in the yard only to find there was no water. However, between us we succeeded in extinguishing the fire by using the water in a jerry can which I always kept in reserve and by applying an old blanket to smother the flames.

There were dejected queues of adults and children to be vaccinated, and queues of sick people waiting for injections. We had to carry buckets of water and disinfectant to groups standing in the middle of open fields and dip children like sheep before they were sent to improvised or already overcrowded hospitals.

In all the places and hospitals to which the Unit was attached, we heard the same story—of suffering that could have been prevented or at least eased if only the right drugs had been available, if only the appropriate instruments had been at hand.

When there are too few beds available it is always very hard to decide between the rival claims of a terminal patient and those of an "acute" case for whom treatment, if an accurate diagnosis were to be made, might prove effective. It is harder still where proper facilities for diagnosis are lacking. "If only we could get hold of a microscope we could do blood tests . . . if only we had a lab!"

At Caen, the beautiful mediaeval town that had been almost razed to the ground, there were some nights when we had to sleep in a brothel. It was in Caen that I admired the gesture of a girl in her twenties, whose husband had been killed. A group of German prisoners had been detailed to help clear a small section of the debris. They told the girl they had little food and kept begging her to give them some, and she brought them her own small ration of bread, which they accepted. I did not admire the prisoners, who received parcels through the International Red Cross and had better rations than many of the French. Later, in Lübeck and in various other parts of Europe, I again saw the very people whom the Nazis had most tortured and humiliated offering food to German prisoners of war, and many German soldiers told me that during the campaign in Russia it was from Russians and Poles too that the German POW's had received help, in spite of their own indescribable suffering.

63

We soon developed a liking for the dehydrated bananas and powdered milk (sent out by the Relief Unit from England), and swapped our allowance of Camembert cheese for croissants. But often we ate potatoes, served on rare occasions in a chateau, on a separate plate as a main dish. There was also, occasionally, the limited luxury of a long French loaf to pull at. An important morale booster was a hairset for eight cigarettes. There was no shampoo, so very poor quality soap was used, and hair had to be dried in front of the open door of the oven. As in Poland, parts of Holland and other occupied countries, hairpins were scarce and if any were dropped they were always picked up from the floor. On a shop counter there was the occasional glimpse of a bottle of Dior or Chanel perfume, but at an exorbitant price—however, sometimes a kind hairdresser would let me sniff at an empty bottle.

During this period, for a very short while, I made one of my attempts to keep a diary. It survives on a few dog-eared scraps of restaurant paper. This extract is typical:

Long loaves, berets, clogs and black pinafores. Shawled figures through the market. Garbage tins, potholes and mud. Fat men eating cabbage and labourers drinking Calvados. Women in widows' clothes with sallow complexions, hair piled high. The clip-clop of sabots on the cobbled courtyard. Cupboards with costly cosmetics. The subdued voice of a woman offering forbidden goods. Selfish farmers, oblivious to want and despair. Black market butter and Camembert cheese, hake and crab sold on filthy barrows, hours wasted in idle chatter. Gesticulations and hand-shaking: "Ca va bien?" The prevalence of the bourgeois.

Fleas in the beds and tins of DDT. Water frozen in the jug and a threadbare carpet. Reckless drivers, oblivious of danger. Covered carts hogging the road, overcrowded hovels. Milk given out in shelled barns to crowds of curious children. Swastikas scrawled on buildings; slogans written overnight on walls. Germans detonating mines. Straw mattresses and small boys vomiting; the smell of vaccine. Tussels with corsets to get them undone. The smooth touch of benzyl on scabied skin. Cognac on lumps of sugar. Doctors, unshaven and distraught. Flacons in canvas bags and bubbling test tubes. Overcrowded rooms with windows closed and the squalls and screams of babies. The girls of the *Croix Rouge* in limp, creased aprons. Truckloads of the Boche driving to the docks. The noise and dirt of cranes moving. Field grey uniforms and gaunt faces under peaked caps. Familiar divisional signs on rusted armoured cars.

Midnight Mass in a martyred church. Bells tolling from battered belfries. Old châteaux and the sound of owls at night in overgrown gardens. A flying bomb site almost obliterated by nature. The expanse of solitary grass and rows and rows of little regimental crosses stretching beyond the eye's comprehension; Pte J. C. Hawkins, 1st Black Watch, X KIA 17.6.44.

The mocked defiance of a German 88 mm. still hidden in its camouflage. The strange, sad, shocked silence of these scenes by moonlight. Derelict landing craft. Seagulls crying. Torn clothing on barbed wire. Green mounds in mine-fields marking the place of the dead. POW's digging graves and lowering shrouds on stretchers. Notices that hang drunkenly from broken hinges in unexpected places: "Out of Bounds", "Water not drinkable", "Orderly Room—knock here before entering", "Rear HQ—DR's entrance", "Canadian Signals on Left". *Rauchen Verboten* (Smoking Forbidden).

The remains of twisted girders and the quiet solemnity of Bayeux Cathedral. The gracious movement of nuns in the cloisters chanting Benediction like bees buzzing on a summer evening.

Official meeting in flag-draped halls. Rats gnawing beneath floorboards. Cattle trucks marked "*pour 20 hommes*", human export for the Reich. Concentration camp survivors wearing dirty striped jackets. . . .

On the outskirts of Falaise the road was littered with evidence of the German retreat—smashed tanks and useless, twisted ammunition. In the middle of it a flattened Mosquito which had been shot down, *Just Jam*, a lucky mascot, glared in the sunlight on its side. A woman living in part of a small, damp cellar. "We'd seen the writing on the wall, but we never thought it would come to this."

There were people all over the country, living, like her, in corners of cellars and in very bad conditions. She symbolised millions of men, women and children in many countries, who, despite their circumstances, retained a supreme sense of courage and humour.

APPENDIX

Basic equipment needed for normal labour ward in 1945:
Hot and cold running water.
Labour bed with mattress, sheet, blankets.
Mackintosh sheets.
Newspapers, buckets.
Cots.
White rubber wellington boots for the staff.
Autoclave drums containing gowns, gloves, masks, caps and dressings.
Obstetrical forceps.
Bowls, syringes, suture needles and needle holders, scalpels, dissecting forceps, artery forceps, scissors, catheters.
Suture material.
Tubes to aspirate baby's air passages.
Nappies, safety pins.

Drugs:
Hyoscine—in preparation for Caesarian delivery if necessary.
Pitocin—to induce labour—intravenous fluid giving sets not disposable.
Ergometrine.
Vitamin K.
Lobeline.
Eye drops.

Anaesthetic trolley with nitrous oxide, oxygen, trilene and
  perhaps ether or chloroform.
Oxygen and mask for baby.
Potassium Bromide and Chloral Mixture.
Local Anaesthetic.
Heroin.

CHAPTER 7

Recall to Life

Because of you we will be glad and gay,
Remembering you we will be brave and strong;
And hail the advent of each dangerous day,
And meet the last adventure with a song.

And, as you proudly gave your jewelled gift,
We'll give our lesser offering with a smile,
Nor falter on that path where, all too swift,
You led the way and leapt the golden stile.

Whether new paths, new heights to climb you find,
Or gallop through the unfooted asphodel,
We know you know we shall not lag behind,
Nor halt to waste a moment on a fear;
And you will speed us onward with a cheer,
And wave beyond the stars that all is well.

Amongst the hardships and difficulties of the life we were leading, memories of books and poetry meant a great deal to us. Maurice Baring's poem *To Julian Grenfell*, written in memory of the poet who was killed in the First War, was one of my favourites, for it seemed to epitomise the spirit of those, a generation later, who were fighting yet another World War.

For the majority of the public the full terror of life in Occupied Europe was only to be known after the Liberation, but in S.O.E. we received firsthand accounts day by day, and later as we proceeded across Europe, were to see for ourselves the suffering that these atrocities had caused. It was a corroboration of everything that those who had entered or left these territories earlier had reported—incredible and sickening. Moreover, it involved many people whom we had known and cared about deeply, people who had been lost and not heard of again, caught or betrayed, taken to prison and herded off into cattle

68

trucks to forced labour, or, more usually, extermination and concentration camps.

Since the 1930s when I listened to stories from escaped Jews and others and heard well-informed people discussing Nazism, I had continued to be amazed that not more of the real facts of the Nazis' ideology and of their racial persecution was known to the public in Britain, the Commonwealth and the rest of the free world. Since 1933 a number of Germans, including the well-known theologian Dietrich Bonhoeffer and other courageous individuals, as well as members of the opposition parties, had tried their best to inform us all long before war became inevitable, but their warning voices had been silenced or ignored. It is a pity that so few people outside Germany read Hitler's *Mein Kampf* (My Struggle) which stated exactly and in detail what his intentions were. When he stated much later: *Even if we cannot conquer we shall drag the rest of the whole world into destruction with us* he had his mind bent on that choice of alternatives.

During the war, on the 31st May 1942, Bonhoeffer and his friend Pastor Schönfeld (Secretary of the Ecumenical Council in Geneva) met George Bell, the Bishop of Chichester, at Sigtuna in Sweden. Dietrich Bonhoeffer managed to make the journey to Sweden through the help of his friends in the German Foreign Office. Speaking for the German Resistance, Bonhoeffer asked whether, if they succeeded in overthrowing Hitler and his régime, the British Government would give some assurance of a willingness to negotiate peace. The Bishop put the proposition to Anthony Eden who consulted Churchill, but the overture was rejected. With the benefit of hindsight one might well feel that this was a tragic mistake.

It may be asked why this chapter is included in this book and my simple answer is that regrettably many people in different walks of life, irrespective of nationality, still do not realise the intensity of the suffering which others endured so that we might enjoy peace. It is written in the firm conviction that we are all responsible for each other. It is also intended as a reminder that we are still living in a world of injustice, appalling poverty and racial persecution.

Confronted as they were by the horrors of the camps they liberated in their advance across Europe, the Allied Armies had to help internees there as best they could. Although this was only part of our work, what we underwent there made an indelible impression on us; but even after so many years, many of us find it quite impossible to describe what we saw. When I am asked to talk about the experiences of the men and women I knew who fought in the Resistance during the War, or to describe the scenes I subsequently witnessed myself, I find that my own voice breaks as the memories come back to my mind. I also feel that I owe it to those men, women and children no longer here to speak for themselves, to depict those scenes as they really were, yet I know that I am not equal to the task. I wonder, too, whether the listener could believe that what I am describing truly happened; and so perhaps I may fall back on an extract taken from a doctor's diary, written at the time.

Dr. Michael Hargrave, now in practice at Wootton Bassett, was one of the medical students from London hospitals who went to Belsen ten days after the liberation of the camp to do what they could for its victims. In his diary of this experience he wrote:

"Brigadier Glynn-Hughes, R.A.M.C., Senior Medical Officer, 2nd Army, gave us an account of how, when conditions got completely out of hand in Belsen, the Germans decided to pass on the baby to us and so they asked us to take over the Camp. We agreed, providing that we also had an area round the Camp and that the bridges over a nearby river were left intact. This the Germans refused to do, and so it was decided to fight for the bridges, but it was agreed that there should be no firing into or out of the area round the Camp which they were going to give up. This worked in practice, although a few shells did land in the area. There was no actual fighting in the area, though the Germans did not completely evacuate it.

From the German sources it was learnt that the political (*Waffen*) SS were in charge of the Camp and they handed over to us on April 13th at 1200 hours, leaving only administrative officers and introducing *Wehrmacht* (Army) guards.

70

Brigadier Glynn-Hughes was the first of our people to enter the camp and he was followed by one battery of anti-tank soldiers consisting of 120 men.

That evening there was a riot over a potato dump. Some German guards fired at internees who were trying to get some of the potatoes. Several internees were killed. Glynn-Hughes told Kramer (the Camp's Nazi Commandant) that if there was any more shooting he would have one SS guard shot for every internee shot. There was no more shooting from the Germans. But what struck him most forcibly was that neither Kramer nor the German doctor responsible for health in the Camp was in the least ashamed about the Camp. He made them bury bodies, but all the time they maintained an air of dumb insolence.

Typhus was raging in Camp I. Inside the huts conditions were appalling: the dead and the living were lying together. Brigadier Glynn-Hughes personally counted twenty women living in an area of 30 square feet, whereas a soldier never, under any conditions, gets less than 45 square feet living space. There were piles of dead everywhere in the open, accumulated in a fortnight because the crematorium had broken down. Women were leaning against these piles of dead to eat their food.

There were about 10,000 dead lying around in the open, and the British soldiers hastened the death of about 1,000 more by giving them chocolates and their own rations. Seventeen thousand people died during March. Since the Camp's liberation, 23,000 had died.

The death rate in Camp I had now fallen from 500 a day to about 90-100 a day. There was no typhus in Camp II and its inhabitants were fairly fit.

One striking thing we noticed was the Camp smell. This was a hot, humid smell mixed up with the smell of burning boots, dirty clothing and faeces. Once smelt, never forgotten. We eventually came into the Women's *Lager* (camp) where the smell increased in intensity.

Hut 224 was painted the usual pink colour with the Red Cross which the Germans had the nerve to paint on each hut. We went into the hut and were almost knocked back by the smell, but we went on into one of the two main rooms. There were no beds whatsoever and in this one room there were about 200 people lying on the floor. In some cases they wore a few tattered rags and in

71

others they wore no clothes at all. They were all huddled together. In many cases one blanket had to cover three people. The floor was covered in faeces and soaked in urine, and the people lying on the floor were in just the same state as they all had extremely severe diarrhoea and were all too weak to move.

Next to each person was a tin can or old mug and various small pieces of bread which they were carefully hoarding up, this latter lying on the floor, and when they felt like it they took a bite out of it, irrespective of what it had been lying in. Their hair, hands, faces and feet were all covered in a mixture of dry faeces and dirt. At least three-quarters of them had hacking coughs and the other quarter were just lying there. Here and there a dead person could be seen between two living ones who took no notice of her at all and just went on eating, coughing or just lying, and these were all women whose ages varied from 15-30.

We had a look at one or two patients and they were quite literally just a mass of skin and bones with sunken eyes which had a completely vacant look. They all had bites and severe scabies and some had terrible ulcers and bed-sores the size of small saucers, with no dressings on them at all.

To my relief I found that on Monday, Hut 210 had been cleaned out by the Hungarians and equipped with double-tier bunks. There was a young Polish woman doctor in charge of it and under her were six Polish women nurses. One of the nurses spoke quite good English.

The floor of the hut was clean and the hut was divided into seven rooms. In one of these lived the doctor and nurses and the others were divided up into wards, and these wards were used for typhus, post-typhus and advanced tuberculosis. There were about forty people to each room and they were lying two to a bunk, i.e. four to each double-tiered bunk, which was hopeless over-crowding. I learned that there were about 260 people in the hut and that every single one, including the doctor, had either had typhus or was having it now.

After supper, an R.A.M.C. Lieut-Colonel gave us a talk on the clinical aspects of typhus: it was very good and much appreciated. He was interrupted in the middle to say that the Germans opposite the 21st Army Group had surrendered (hence V.E. Day). All very pleased.

Saturday May 5th

I went up to the office and asked Mrs. Crossthwaite if there were any huts without any students in them. She said there were plenty. I was given Hut 217 and decided I was definitely needed there. It was smaller than the others—30 yards x 7 yards—but it contained about 460 women. It was easily the most crowded hut I had yet seen. It was composed of one single large room with people lying, sitting and standing all round the walls and also in the centre of the hut: most of the people who were very sick were lying opposite the door and along the right wall of the hut. They were lying in roughly three rows, but were all packed together head to foot, so that there was absolutely no room whatsoever between the rows.

George Woodwark showed me round Hut 216, and it certainly was the worst. In many places whole sections of the floor were missing and you squelched down into earth and God only knows what else. It was hopelessly overcrowded and faeces were even more abundant than in the other huts. George said they had pulled several bodies out from under what floorboards were left, and I could quite believe it. Was jolly glad to get out into fresh air again.

One of the most impressive things about the Camp was a pile of boots which the Germans had taken off the victims before cremating them. I don't know how many years it had taken to build up this pile, but it was about 20 yards long by about 6 yards across and about 12 feet high. The shoes at the bottom were squashed as flat as paper, so you can imagine how may thousand pairs of shoes were there, and each pair had once had an owner. Though the Germans may have destroyed all the records of this Camp, this pile of boots and shoes provided more mute but absolutely damning evidence of the number of people who had died in this camp before the British arrived, for we did not add the shoes of the 23,000 whom *we* buried."

This is an account of only *one* camp, and by no means of the worst. Belsen, which was built only in 1943, was not listed as an extermination camp, as for instance Treblinka* where it was estimated that a minimum of 800,000-

* Casualty figures from F. Zabecki, Railway Station Superintendent.

1,200,000 men, women and children died—today there are less than 40 survivors—or Auschwitz with an estimated several million dead from over twenty-eight countries. Indeed, no book or film can recreate the unmitigated suffering.

All over Europe, but especially in the central and eastern parts, thousands of prisoners had been taken out on death marches as the Allied Armies advanced. In some camps, evacuated early in 1944, the sick were left behind, but in others thousands of them, too weak and ill to walk, were still marched until they dropped, and then shot and left by the roadside.

Each individual prisoner, regardless of age, had his or her own story of suffering. For all, it was an experience indelible in their minds, a memory that remains for ever. Though many wars have been waged since 1945 in different parts of the world, and oppression of one sort or another goes on, no comparison can be made with the calculated, deliberate *and official* extermination policy of the Nazis.

In her book *A Thread in the Tapestry* Sarah Churchill quotes a remark her father, Winston, made to her one night near the end of the War:

> "I do not suppose that at any moment in history has the agony of the World been so great or widespread. Tonight the sun goes down on more suffering than ever before in the World."

Of the many individuals with whom I have worked, it is almost impossible to single out anybody, but I will mention here very briefly Zofia Chlewicka. The Germans murdered her husband in October 1939, and she herself worked in the Polish Resistance until she was arrested on 15th December 1942 and taken during the night to the infamous prison at Pawiak in Warsaw. She was eventually transported to the extermination camp at Majdanek* right on the main road leading out of the city of Lublin. This is how she described to me one of her experiences:—

* 400,000 victims.

74

"Amongst the constant transports (prisoners in cattle trucks) arriving in Majdanek from different parts of Europe there were those bearing survivors of the Warsaw Ghetto Uprising in April 1943. I was working at that time as a nurse in Field 5—Majdanek was divided up into five different Fields and each contained 20 huts. Sinister parallel fences of electrified barbed wire surrounded each field and again the whole complex, and made a terrible impression on any passer-by. At the beginning of September of the same year we were transferred to Field 1. On 3rd November, after the early morning roll-call the blocks were locked (Blocksperre). Double lines of SS men and women encircled the camp and reinforcements stood in the watchtowers. From the top bunks we looked out of the very narrow high windows and saw double lines, column after column of Jews who were being marched along the long road outside Majdanek and on the perimeter to beyond the crematorium. No less than 18,000 people were shot during the course of that day. We all lived from hand to mouth, day to day, never knowing when the next batch of us might not be selected for the gas chambers. This was true even of the prisoners allowed to work as doctors and nurses in the Revier (hospital), though without any of the drugs and proper facilities. And indeed, at 4 p.m. on that day of massacre some SS men came to the Revier to seize our Jewish physicians and nurses. An appalling scene followed as we made pathetic attempts to protect them by giving them our own ragged white coats in the vain hope that they might be spared as essential medical staff. One of the nurses, Helena (widow of a doctor), a very fair-haired young woman came up to me and shook my hand. In the tumult she said quietly: 'Before I die, I want as one human being to another amongst thousands, to thank you and to say how I valued our working together as friends to comfort the sick and each other, regardless of our nationalities or religious beliefs.'

"During the second swoop the same afternoon the SS returned drunk and roared about, wrenching an odd thin blanket away from the sick and dying, and the night was bitterly cold. I asked one of the SS men when our doctors and nurses would return. He shouted at me: 'Never'.

"At the height of this uproar I saw a young 14-year-old girl silhouetted in the wide doorway of the block. She was

75

slim and beautiful in spite of having suffered from spotted fever: she had been alone ever since her family died. Turning to me she asked in a calm voice 'Do I look very pale?' Trying to comfort her, I said 'No, but why do you ask?' 'I am glad', she replied, 'because I do not want them to see that I am frightened.' Then she was taken away by the SS and the alsatian dogs."

Of the children in just one of the thousands of camps was written:

"One of us
Will teach these children how to sing again,
To write on paper with a pencil,
To do sums and multiply:
One of us
Is sure to survive."

These words were written by Doctor Karel Fleischmann in Terezin (Theresienstadt) an old fortified town in Czechoslovakia which was in part a "transit-ghetto" for Jews awaiting extermination and in part a terrible concentration camp for 77,297 known victims.

After graduating from secondary schools and medical college Doctor Fleischmann became a specialist in dermatology in Cĕské Budĕjovic, Czechoslovakia. He devoted his free time to art and also wrote prose and verse.

In April 1942 Karel Fleischmann was deported to Terezin where he worked as a doctor. Most of his pictures and two volumes of his poetry were preserved, thanks to the Resistance groups in the camps. In October 1944 he and his wife were transferred to Auschwitz where both perished in the gas chambers.

Some of the survivors met death in tragic circumstances just before liberation. On the 3rd May 1945, Captain Pratt of the British 11th Armoured Division liberated a group of survivors on the *Cap Arcona*, a 10,000 ton merchantman in Neustadt Bay, on the east coast of Schleswig-Holstein. Earlier some ships had been observed by the Royal Air Force; what the R.A.F. did not know was that the *Cap Arcona, Thielbech* and *Deutschland* were laden not with fleeing Nazis but with concentration camp prisoners.

The Nazis were making a last desperate effort to get rid of tens of thousands of internees from such camps as Sachsenhausen and Ravensbrück—some were driven to death in forward marches, while others were transported hundreds of miles in cattle trucks towards the Baltic coast with the intention of drowning them there *en masse*. Some prisoners from Neuengamme concentration camp near Hamburg were marched to Lübeck and then loaded on to the *Cap Arcona* and the other smaller vessels. The *Cap Arcona* was crammed with 4,700 people including Russian prisoners of war, Yugoslav partisans, members of the French, Belgian and Norwegian underground movements, and a number of German anti-Nazis who had survived ten or more years in Hitler's camps. Major Vaseili Bukreyev, head of the underground resistance organisation in Neuengamme concentration camp, describes what happened:—

"As the Allied troops drew near the camp, we planned a rising. I was elected leader. Our plan misfired. On April 24th the camp was evacuated and we were marched to Lubeck, and there loaded on to various vessels.

"On board the *Cap Arcona* we planned to seize the ship. We organised a group of former sailors. Not far from our vessel lay a number of barges. They were loaded with prisoners from Stutthof (near Danzig) concentration camp. In the harbour lay German U-boats.

"During the night of May 2nd we heard two huge explosions and frightful screams. The U-boats had torpedoed the barges laden with prisoners. Then on May 3rd British planes bombed the *Cap Arcona* and the vessel went up in flames and sank in shallow water.

"I jumped overboard and then clambered back aboard along the anchor chain. The survivors were only those who got back on to the ship. Those who tried to swim ashore were shot from German boats and by U-boat cadets who lined the shore.

"How many people were killed that day in Neustadt Bay? Probably 8,000. I waited on the scorching skeleton of *Cap Arcona*. In the evening a ship came alongside and announced that Canadian troops had reached Neustadt. A boat took us ashore. I was appointed officer-in-charge of repatriation and remained in Neustadt until August 1945."

77

In the afternoon of May 3rd, the British Liberation Army rushed ambulances to the scene and ferried those who reached the shore to the local hospital where they had to overcome opposition to get them admitted.

The "Canadians" who were reported to have occupied Neustadt were in fact troops of the British 11th Armoured Division. They did all they could for the surviving prisoners, their allies. Major Bukreyev, who took charge of the survivors was given British battle dress; others had to make do with requisitioned civilian clothes, or even with captured German naval uniforms. A few days later at an official ceremony a British squad fired a volley over the graves of those whose bodies had been washed up, and a bugle sounded the Last Post. The British officer whose job it was to care for the living and honour the dead was Captain Pratt.

I was later to come to know some of these survivors very well when I visited and helped nurse them in the hospitals. One of them had lost the use of his right hand, had suffered severe burns and his sight had been affected during the bombing. While in a state of semi-coma he repeatedly asked for his only son, Christopher. One day some Allied soldiers stationed with a brigade at Schleswig-Holstein were talking about this survivor and of how he had cried out for his beloved son. Someone heard them mention the name Christopher and wondered whether he himself might be the man they were referring to. He was! This led to a very moving reunion. Afterwards when his father reached England he wrote this letter:

Dear Miss Ryder,

I just want to share my joy of reaching Britain. It has helped me more than all the medical treatment. Thank you for your compassion and kindness—for all that you did for so many of us. Hope to see you soon.

George.

From the window of one of the offices in which I worked I could see the hull of the *Thielbech* which was sunk approximately one mile off-shore. In the late 1940s a

above:
In contact with Europe—
F.A.N.Ys in S.O.E.

right:
'This is Your Life',
televised over BBC
nationwide network 1956.
Sue Ryder with
Mr. Eamonn Andrews.
(Mrs. M. E. Ryder second
from left)

below left:
Jeromy and Elizabeth
with their parents at
Cavendish.

below right:
Presenting prizes to Nurses.

Warsaw, 1945 and 1965.

below left:
Sue Ryder in mufti (after joining S.O.E.).

below centre:
Cecylia Niesmialek (died of ulcerating cancer of the lip and who could only write the word 'drink').

below right:
Zofia Szachowicz, Prisoner No. 10111 Ravensbrück, previously imprisoned for work in the Resistance in Radom, Kielce and Czestochowa. After being selected for execution on 29th April, 1943, she sat at a bare table and shared crusts of bread with her companions, to whom she said: "There are thirteen of us here—it is like the Last Supper."

above: Young patients with cancers at Zielona Gora, Poland. (Mr. Siemieradzki on far right.)

French team brought her to the surface. They found many bodies. Some were identified by the metal discs which they wore.*

On the same shore some 9,000 people are buried in a mass grave. This grave is preserved, and on its stone the twenty-two nationalities are recorded.

The War was over at last. For those now returned from the battlefields, especially to devastated countries, the huge task of reconstruction was awaiting. Those who fell have never been better commemorated than in some lines attributed to J. Maxwell Edmunds, written on the British War Memorial to the 14th Army at Kohima in Assam:—

> *When you go home*
> *Tell them of us and say*
> *For your tomorrow*
> *We gave our today.*

In certain parts of Europe there were very many whose "tomorrow" did not bring the fruits for which they had suffered and fought.

I was only twenty-two then, but knew what dehumanisation was like: had seen what happened to people when everything, even their hair, was taken from them and their minds and bodies subjugated until some could only crawl on all fours or lie in silence.

It was summertime, the middle of August, with the sun shining and harvesting to be done. Everyone was celebrating the victory over Japan. People in London, as in all liberated countries, streamed on to the streets and there was a jubilant pealing of church bells. Two friends of mine, whom I had not seen since they had been fighting with the Grenadier Guards in the Italian campaign, telephoned me and asked me to join them at a party in London. Instead,

---

* Mummification of a few bodies had occurred owing to the cramming in, which had prevented total decomposition

I took the tractor out and spent the day working in the fields alone before returning to work on the Continent.

Geoffrey from the Rifle Brigade happened to come home just in time for V.J. Day (Victory over Japan, 14th August 1945). He wrote:

"Home on Leave! Marvellous! I arrived to find a civic reception committee waiting for me, masses of flags and a huge welcome home banner above the gate. The house was like a bear garden with everyone shouting, ragging, running and dog barking; Mama swearing because she couldn't be heard above the din!"

Reading Geoffrey's letter I felt it described a different world where some people (though certainly not Geoffrey) heard of the suffering but remained remote and unconcerned.

It was now time to ask whether the same urgent sense of unity and purpose that had carried us through to victory in War could be continued in peace-time, lest we should fail the generations who had died or the children who would be born in the years to come. We who were left were responsible for their future.

CHAPTER 8

The Boys

I first started prison visiting in France in 1945. It was here that I had witnessed the chaos due to a breakdown of all services and communications which left thousands of citizens with a total lack of purpose and resulted in some of them taking to crime. There had been no forward planning by UNRRA or other relief units; probably they had not foreseen the situation which arose, and when they were faced with it they had no trained workers to deal with it. There were, of course, some officials who took an interest in the local prisons, but they had to follow the rules laid down by their organisations and these were primarily concerned with the immediate relief of human suffering, the visiting of hospitals and helping with repatriation.

The great need for prison visiting, however, was quickly apparent, particularly in Germany, and I obtained permission from the Penal Authorities to enter the prisons there. My procedure was to ask at every prison for the card index of all prisoners, and then to go through every name—sometimes as many as eight hundred—making sure that I had those of all non-Germans and putting these down on my list. It was poignant to see sometimes on these prisoners' cards that the entry against "Previous Prison" read "Belsen", "Auschwitz", "Ravensbrück" or some other concentration camp. Their countries of origin were in Central and Eastern Europe and the majority of them were young. I realised that these prisoners, in an alien country and many hundreds of miles from their own families, would have no one to visit them if I did not do so. Thus, I felt that I could become a link—perhaps a vital one—between the prisoner and his family and the outside world.

In my experience, the cause of the lawless behaviour of the Boys nearly always arose from the atrocious conditions

81

during the War and the chaos of its aftermath. Hunger was a prime factor. I also discovered that reactions among the young criminals differed according to their temperaments. There were many who, because they had no work or purpose in life, raided local farms for food and clothing. They usually operated in small groups, and sometimes— although this was not always intended—shooting occurred.

There were also Boys who, having lost families, friends and everything in total war were at the end of their tether and decided to take personal revenge. Often it was known that former members of the Gestapo, the SS and the SA who were not on the list of war criminals for whom search warrants had been issued, were living in the neighbourhood; then some of the Boys would decide to take the law into their own hands and execute them.

There was a third group who, in the boredom which followed the excitement of the liberation and from lack of work and the discipline of routine, drifted into the underworld of the camps or hospitals. They were often accused of "black marketeering" or of comparatively petty crimes, but the sentences they received, if caught, were savage. A man who sold the scrap metal he picked up received a sentence of three years' imprisonment.

Some Boys lived in cellars; some were sick and in overcrowded hospitals; while others existed in miserable huts. Free food rations were available, but inadequate. Reactions towards them varied. There was one German farmer who, despite having had twelve members of his family killed during such raids, came forward many years later and offered to do anything he could to help the Boys who had not been executed. He understood their terrible plight only too well.

For my part, I tried everything within my power to reason and plead with the authorities on behalf of the Boys in prisons. Once sentence had been passed then, even if it had only been partly served, the prisoners knew they had no hope of ever being allowed to start life afresh in another country.

In the British Zone, military courts had in some areas been hastily set up, but they had not had any proper briefing about the background and circumstances of the Boys who came up before them. As a result they meted out sentences which were out of all proportion to the crimes. For armed robbery or for being in unlawful possession of firearms sentences varying from ten to thirty years were passed.

The military courts were succeeded by Control Commission Courts, whose personnel were often either ignorant or prejudiced. There were, of course, exceptions; some of the judges to whom I spoke, after hearing of the circumstances in which the homeless Boys were living and the tragedy of their lives, understood how they had come to fall foul of the law, and took account of it.

For the Boys who had not committed crimes, there were many problems to be coped with if they were not to be driven to crime. The greatest problem was preventing them from brewing 'Bimber'—a crude drink, sometimes based partly on methylated spirits, and sufficiently potent to kill or blind. There were gatherings, which the Boys referred to as "parties", to which I was often invited. I did not refuse, but explained to them that I was not going to be persuaded to drink 'Bimber' as I did not enjoy the concoction!

But the fact of being around was helpful—for instance, I might hear of a plan for a raid later that night, and could then say to them: "Look, there are better things in life than going out raiding. All is not really lost, and if we manage to keep our heads and our sense of humour, one day we may again see a more normal life." Sometimes when the 'Bimber' had not already got too great a hold on them they would drop the plan. But whether they did or not, it meant staying until very late to keep an eye on the Boys to prevent them from getting blind drunk. Though some of them inevitably would succumb, I remember especially the others who retained their dignity and sense of humour and helped to carry the helpless ones to their beds.

In spite of all the squalor, the great thing that came through was the humour and the singing. If there were some men in the party who said "Yes, we have survived so much, why shouldn't we manage to go on?", this would be enough to change the general mood; everyone would start to sing and an ugly scene would be avoided. In view of the prevailing situation it was remarkable that so relatively small a percentage of Boys came up against the law.

In the early days just after the War ended, the Allied Courts sat at numerous places within their own zone of occupation. The non-German prisoners were scattered throughout the different zones. During 1946–47 it was decided to concentrate the non-German prisoners in the British Zone at Schleswig, Hamburg, Altona, Werl and Hamelin—a considerable area. At Werl they were held in one wing of the prison and came under the British Governors, who were also responsible for German prisoners. The Governors and some of the British warders were greatly respected by the prisoners, who referred to them as their 'fathers' or 'uncles'. In the same prison were a few German war criminals, some of the Kapos (Camp Foremen) and some women who had served in the SS. This concentration of different types of prisoners in one place made for a very difficult situation needing careful handling. The tension was increased by the attitude of the former SS women, who were allowed to sit outside their cells knitting; whenever I had occasion to pass them on my way to visit other prisoners they would use foul language and shout insults at me. What I can never forget is their lack of repentance.

Father Wnuk,* a priest from Poland, who had been a prisoner in Dachau for many years, was appointed Chaplain at Werl. Once he said to me "I am almost at breaking point, having prepared thirty young non-German prisoners and given them the Last Sacrament before the death sentences are carried out." In the presence of Boys who were under sentence of death and to whom I knew that faith meant a lot, the prayer by Cardinal Newman called "A Meditation" was handed out. I had learned from both Survivors and the sick that God gives people

---

* (Father Wnuk continued faithfully in his work, with one assistant, until approximately 1951.)

special grace and strength to forgive, to overcome adversity and to win confidence:

THE MEDITATION

God has created me to do Him some definite service; He has committed some work to me which He has not committed to another. I have my mission—I may never know it in this life, but I shall be told it in the next.

I am a link in a chain, a bond of connection between persons. He has not created me for nought. I shall do good, I shall do His work. I shall be an angel of peace, a preacher of truth in my own place *while not intending it*—if I do but keep His Commandments.

There I will trust Him. Whatever, wherever, I am, I can never be thrown away. If I am in sickness, my sickness may serve Him; if I am in sorrow my sorrow may serve Him. He does nothing in vain. He knows what He is about. He may take away my friends. He may throw me among strangers. He may make me feel desolate, make my spirit sink, hide my future from me—still He knows what He is about.

An eighteen year old boy left the following letter for me:
"I am leaving this letter with my companion, for you to remember us. Please if you get the chance have the courage to read this letter to our friends. May I ask you to try and find my father who, as you know, has been missing since the Gestapo took him, and give him a copy too. I beg you not to let this letter out of your hands, and to say goodbye to everyone. Much as I would like to do so myself, it isn't possible, and I hope to be forgiven."

"We are taking leave of you for ever and of our beloved country. In a few short hours we shall be taken to the place of execution. Let us hope that somewhere there will be understanding for what we have done at this early age and in exile. We must die at the hands of our Allies for shooting the SS who killed all our families. We fought in the same cause, but this and the things which followed are all forgotten. We are leaving this world after receiving Extreme Unction from Father C."

Four Boys signed the declaration before being taken out to face a British firing squad.

Although I had never had the opportunity of studying it, law had always interested me. Later on, when the Allied Courts had handed over jurisdiction, it became a necessity to grasp as much as possible of German law, and I was instructed, usually during the discussion of cases, by German lawyers and Staatsanwalte (Public Prosecutors). *Up to the early part of 1949, the Legal Department of the British Control Commission, whose headquarters were at Herford, with branches in different parts of the British Zone of Germany, were extremely co-operative. They knew of the difficulty of trying to rehabilitate those whose sentences had been commuted. Many were repatriated to Central and Eastern Europe, but there were those who had lost not only their families but their homes too, because the villages or towns in which they had lived had been destroyed.

One afternoon, during a lengthy discussion, the British lawyer at Kiel with whom I worked, suggested that under a German law passed on the 9th April 1920 †sentences should be deleted from the Central Register (*Strafregister*) in Berlin. We both felt that if we were able to get some sentences deleted from the Register (after the appropriate application had been made and due consideration given), it would enable the people concerned to be considered by the immigration authorities and perhaps to start a new life in a country overseas. We pursued this objective and were sometimes successful. The Australian and New Zealand Immigration Authorities proved to be particularly helpful in accepting immigrants whose sentences

---

* On 11th May 1937 the law on passport-foreigner-police-registration and deportation was passed; this was followed on 1st October 1938 by an Order governing the deportation of undesirable foreigners. This in turn was followed on 28th April 1965 by the "Foreigners Law" (*Bundesgesetzblatt*, Part 1, page 507) which came into force on 1st October 1965.

† *Reichsgesetzblatt*, Part 1, page 507. This has been replaced by the Central Register and Education Register (*Bundesetzblatt* Part 1, page 243) which came into force on 18th March 1971 and 1st January 1972.

I had managed to get deleted. The British Army also proved responsive, and would offer civilian jobs to some of them. Productive work in prisons obviously prepares prisoners for work outside. It is an immense pleasure and relief for me to see those who—despite all the odds— have succeeded in getting jobs as waiters and shopkeepers (often as a result of learning English and other languages while in prison). Some of them, too, developed a great interest in painting, pigeon racing, boating or fishing.

In the French Zone I found that there were fewer homeless amongst the non-Germans and, consequently, that the French Courts were not faced with the same large number of cases. Also, as France herself had been occupied, it was easier for the French Authorities to understand the Boys' situation and to handle it. They carried out very few death sentences and were quick to realise that it was often necessary to commute sentences rather than let the prisoners linger indefinitely in gaol. The French concentrated their relatively small numbers of non-German prisoners at Wittlich, where they also had a few of the German war criminals whom they had arrested. Again it seemed to me most unfortunate that these two types of prisoners should be housed under the same roof. I have a distressing recollection of parcels weighing five or seven kilos being brought in for the war criminals by their relatives while non-Germans had no one except myself to fend for them or to visit them.

So far as the American Zone was concerned, it seemed that after the ban on fraternisation between American Armed Forces and the Germans had been lifted, the United States policy went to the other extreme. Their military and civilian Courts were as harsh as the British towards the non-German prisoners or harsher, and I was shocked to find that, having been sentenced to death, a number of the condemned Boys had to wait anything up to two years before they were executed or had their sentence commuted to life imprisonment.

In a certain prison, which was one of the largest in the whole of West Germany, there was a block which was openly referred to as the "death block". On one occasion, an American officer strode into this block brandishing a loaded revolver: this incensed the prisoners and almost caused a mutiny.

In some of the prisons where the Americans held non-German prisoners, their bureaucratic attitude and marked lack of compassion created a tense atmosphere. I vividly remember waiting to be admitted into the presence of an American official whose signature was needed on the list of prisoners I wished to visit. I spent hours in the office of his German secretary, and all the time could hear him talking in his own office; but I had to be patient and pretend not to worry about the passing of valuable hours —at least it gave me a chance to write up my notes. When eventually I was allowed in, it was to find him with his feet on the desk and hear unfriendly remarks about the dubious value of my work and presence in the prisons. Finally, however, I collected my signed list and started off on the long drive to the next prison.

On another occasion I succeeded in getting my list signed by the American Penal Officer only to find, on arriving at the next prison, that he had already rung up to say that my presence there was not wanted. As I did not wish to disappoint the Boys, who had been looking forward to my visit, I made myself as pleasant as possible to the German warders at the outer and inner gates and asked to be shown to the Director's Office. Whilst I was not very optimistic about the outcome of the interview, as I suspected him of being in complete agreement with the American officer, I thought it at least worth a try. I then discovered that it was the Director himself who had received the phone call, and realised that he was probably working in collusion with the American authorities. After much persuasion, he agreed that I could see some prisoners, but only those whose cases came before the German Courts; I argued that it was equally important that the American Court cases should be visited, especially as they had been told the date on which I would be arriving, but he was adamant in his refusal.

Undeterred, I returned to my car and, in the 'loo' of a local garage, changed into my old relief worker's uniform.

I then re-entered the prison and made my way back to the Director's office. The sight of my uniform seemed to have the desired effect and he let me through.

This type of obstruction happened on another occasion: having collected my list of prisoners, duly signed by an American official, I drove to the next prison on my list only to find that I was refused permission to visit. Again, the Prison Director was in collaboration with the American official. He came in with a red face, shouting at me, and removing the files from the table. Then he ordered me out under the guard of an armed warder and I was marched off to the gate. I decided that the time had come to ask for an explanation so, hoping Providence would tell me what to say, I drove back to the American official's office—a distance of over sixty miles. He was taken aback at seeing me. Politely but firmly I asked for a full explanation and said if he wouldn't give it to me I should go straight to the British Press with my story. I told him I did not consider this was the right way to behave to a person who was trying to do something positive amongst men who had lost all hope, were totally disillusioned and who, if further provoked, would become very much worse. I added: "Unfortunately I have never worked in your country, but I am sure that what is happening to me is not representative of the American attitude. One is already up against all possible odds; either we co-operate or we decide to differ, but you should not say one thing to me in the office and then, when I am on the road, go back on it. If I have given you reason for complaint, please say so; I would rather you were frank with me." His answer was that he did not consider it necessary for the non-Germans to be visited or to receive any form of welfare.

From time to time such deplorable behaviour continued, but at least this particular American eventually came to realise that I meant to carry out my work conscientiously and that I was not prepared to accept his adolescent behaviour.

My aim was never to prejudice the Boys' situation and so, whilst maintaining a firm attitude, I had to proceed with great coolness.

One day, approaching despair, I felt obliged to remark on this to the Head of the Penal Department at Bad Godesberg, an American colleague whom I held in high regard and respect. He himself was deeply affected by the injustice and told me just before he left his post that he had had to obey instructions from Washington, which required him to give preference to the release and re-habilitation of war criminals. He was very objective, tried against impossible odds to improve conditions, and made every attempt to persuade his colleagues to see the true situation; but in many cases he failed.

In order to review the sentences of non-German prisoners, the Mixed Clemency Board was formed, which held regular meetings at the main prisons to consider—and usually reject—the appeals made by these prisoners. In addition the penal officers themselves were given authority to decide appeals. Many of the German officials and warders had welcomed me from the start, looking upon my work as constructive and recognising it as a bridge between prisoners and the world outside. Some were even courageous enough to do their best to see that local conditions were eased for the victims while others followed the line laid down by the Americans.

In my meetings with the prisoners all I could hope to do was to listen patiently, hour after hour, to men of different nationalities—each one pouring out his troubles, grief, bewilderment and grievances. I tried to take a bit of the sting out of the situation. I realised at the time—and still do now, in retrospect—that both the best and the worst in human nature were exposed in those circumstances, and that tolerance and optimism were the qualities to which we needed to cling. It was not uncommon to have to visit between thirty and forty prisoners a day, but to each I tried to give as much time as possible.

Although it was not until 1955 that West Germany regained her sovereignty, the French, British and American authorities handed over judicial and penal powers to the Germans in 1949. At that time the non-German prisoners were kept in more than twenty small prisons scattered throughout the Land of Rhineland-Pfalz. This made the

90

work much more onerous, since it increased both the number of places to be visited and the distances that had to be covered. Generally drives between prisons in different parts of Germany were made overnight, but sometimes, if not able to finish my visits at one prison in the course of a day, I had to remain overnight in the vicinity of the prison and resume visiting next day. This meant that I had to try to find food and accommodation for the night; more often than not unsuccessfully. In the areas of Germany where there were existing hospitals, camps and canteens, however bad the overcrowding was—some with a total lack of privacy—there were always colleagues who would find me a bed or a mattress and share with me their meagre rations; but in other areas finding food and accommodation was a great problem. Enquiring at local pubs frequently brought an uninterested or negative reply, and this meant that I would have nowhere to wash or sleep or to write up my notes.

The monotony of prison life cannot be imagined by those who have never experienced it. The loneliness too is terrible. Indeed, in my own small way I felt something of it then—in some parts of Germany there was no-one in between prisons with whom I could share my thoughts and the pressures. Attendance at Mass whenever possible sustained me and gave me strength to try and cope with the situation.

In 1952 I was able to found the first Home for the Boys. This was thanks to the persistence of Ministerialrat Professor Doctor Albert Krebs, Doctor of Philosophy, Social Worker and later Governor of Untermassfeld prison, Thurigen until 1933 when he was dismissed by the Nazis. Between 1945 and 1965 he was in charge of the Penal Section (Ministry of Justice) in the Land of Hessen and Honorary Professor of Criminology at Marburg University. Doctor Albert Krebs is also well known for his writing. Professor Krebs became one of my closest colleagues whom, as well as his wife, I greatly admired and respected. They gave me hospitality and a bedroom in their own house, and occasionally would invite a released prisoner to visit them. It was Professor Krebs who helped find an empty hut on the outskirts of Frankfurt am Main, which was converted into a Home and a small office for non-German prisoners released into the chaos of those years. But, one Sunday when I was on the road, the Boys hung their washing too near the stove, and within an hour their Home was burned down. Their main concern had been to try to rescue hundreds of valuable dossiers and files that I kept there, but unfortunately the majority of these were lost.

After this disappointment Professor Krebs suggested that a disused prison at Bad Nauheim, a fashionable spa, could be converted and used as a Home. The prison building was surrounded by a high wall. Naturally enough, the idea of a Home for discharged non-German prisoners was disliked by the local residents, but at least it met, for a while, the great need for accommodation for Boys who had literally nowhere to go. Many were at the end of their tether—jobless, without identification cards or birth certificates; some were awaiting repatriation; others remained ever hopeful of finding their families. It was my task, together with the Warden, to attempt to get jobs for them, even though in those days in Germany jobs were at a high premium.

The attitude of the authorities at the *Pass-Stelle* (offices where identity cards and passports were issued) varied enormously. Some saw the need to issue passports so that the Boys might have a chance of finding work, security and a new start in life, but others stubbornly refused. Some declined even to issue the essential passports and national insurance cards, without which the Boys had no official existence. A further difficulty was that, according to the law, all persons had to be registered with the police, but in order to do this it was necessary to have accommodation. This presented yet one more problem because any form of accommodation—whether in a hostel or in 'digs'—was extremely difficult to obtain, the more so when the Boys had been released from prison. In several of the *Lander* it was fairly common practice to adhere to the 1938 Nazi Aliens Law (since revised by an Aliens Law passed in 1965). The so-called *Aufenthal-*

teverbot decreed that undesirable aliens should leave the country. In Frankfurt, Munich, Nuremburg and a few other cities the *Pass-Stelle* authorities actually suggested that I should take the Boys out of Germany in the boot of my car, adding: "We feel no responsibility for them".

Here was a dilemma which clearly called for patience and coolness—on the one hand the obstinacy of official-dom, and on the other the frustration and disappointment of homeless prisoners. For Poles and Czechs the nearest repatriation centres were in Berlin; but to get there they needed to cross East Germany, which they could not do without passports. No-one, sadly, seemed interested at that time, and there was virtually nobody else to whom these unfortunate people could turn.

There were grim scenes in the large cities and, in particular, in the bunkers, the air-raid shelters erected in Germany before and during the War. Some of them were used as doss-houses. One, at the *Ostbahnhof* in Frankfurt, remains vividly in my memory. Long before evening there were queues of both Germans and others trying to gain admittance for a wretched bunk bed and a bowl of soup. This was one of the many places I used to visit as often as I could, and the men—many of them very rough—were always respectful and polite and would let me go through to see the Warden and his wife who were in charge. Both were members of the Salvation Army and proved helpful colleagues.

The bunker was very dimly lit by the equivalent of 15-watt bulbs, and had no windows. Brawls were frequent, and the language was unrepeatable. Not infrequently I would find myself trying to separate two men or two gangs who were going for each other, or having to help lift a drunk off the floor. And all the while there was the noise of the queue shuffling up to the so-called 'reception' office, a kind of hatchway behind which were the ever calm members of the Salvation Army who tried to explain that there were no bunks left and no food. Everyone had to be put out by 6 a.m., and nobody was allowed to stay for more than two nights. The unfortunate Boys had no alternative but to work unofficially in the local markets, where they were always picked up by the police for not having passports or labour permits.

As this situation was repeated throughout most of Germany's large cities, it was little wonder that the after-care of released prisoners was a never-ending struggle.

The American authorities considered that this was not their responsibility, and in the neighbourhood of Kaiserslautern (in the state of Rhineland-Pfalz), previously in the French Zone, yet another serious situation had to be dealt with. Among units attached to the U.S. Army in France and Germany were the Labour Service Companies. These consisted of civilians of various nationalities, some of whom had had very chequered careers fighting with the Foreign Legion in the War, while others were the flotsam of Europe who between 1939 and 1945 had lost their families, their homes and all their possessions. Suddenly they found themselves discharged without papers, without proof of identity and with nowhere to go. Towards these men the U.S. Army Authorities sometimes pursued a ruthless attitude, forcing them to take to the woods. Known in the neighbourhood as the local "Mau Mau", they had to live off whatever food they could scrounge or steal.

In all my attempts to intervene with the U.S. Authorities at Heidelberg, I found only one officer who seemed to care. He made it clear that his position and career would be in jeopardy if it were known that he was ready to help, yet he was prepared to do so.

By that time there were between one and two hundred men who were likely to take the law into their own hands; I knew that they would have to be moved out of the woods and taken somewhere, but the question was where? Eventually I arranged with the friendly American officer for army trucks to be made available to carry the homeless away. Starting at short intervals, these were driven some hundreds of miles to the Headquarters of the Rhine Army at Bad Oeynhausen which took a minimum of nine to ten hours. It was like running the gauntlet for there was the ever present danger of pursuit. As for the American officer, he risked a Court Martial, for no American truck carrying non-United States personnel, could be allowed officially to leave the American Zone. Indeed, the U.S. Military Police—nicknamed "Snowdrops" because of their white caps and braid—were often hot on the trail.

At Kassel, a town bombed to destruction and still at that time largely in ruins, was an American hotel. Here I had to make sure that the truck was parked near my own vehicle, where I could be certain of finding and recognising it at night. I asked the Boys in it to promise that they would lie low and keep quiet while I went into the hotel to get boiling water for the flasks. This done we continued our journey, and before dawn made coffee in the woods on the outskirts of Bad Oeynhausen. It was then necessary to conduct each Boy separately to a loo, where he shaved, and afterwards take him to a British establishment where I explained the situation to an obliging British Major. Eventually these Boys were gradually absorbed into the mixed service organisation attached to the British Army, and to the best of my knowledge all made good: certainly I received some very touching notes from the Boys who had found some sort of security and a sense of belonging.

This work among the Boys involved attending Court on many occasions, sometimes in order to see the Judge before proceedings started and explain to him as best I could something of their circumstances. For the most part, however, it was a matter of just sitting in Court hoping to give some measure of encouragement and support by the mere fact of being there in person.

To the question that I am sometimes asked, "But wasn't this dangerous?", I can merely answer that I was threatened only once. Quite frequently in doss-houses, cellars and attics, camps and woods, I was breaking up fights and appealing to the Boys, yet I never came across disrespect from any of the different nationalities, I was never frightened, which perhaps sounds conceited, but I know fear: I am frightened, for example, of Alsatian dogs, which remind me of Nazi camps, and terrible scenes, and the prisons.

The night I was threatened (some years after the immediate post-war era) I had a suspicion that one Boy

95

was getting steadily more drunk and that he intended to commit a crime, although I was not sure whom he had chosen as his victim. He had threatened violence, both in the afternoon and that same evening. He had managed to procure more beer and liquor, and now said in a very tipsy voice that I should have got his repatriation papers through (which was true in so far as I had written repeatedly and telephoned to East Berlin, but to no avail). He was fed-up and frustrated.

I talked to him for hours. We cooked supper for him— he refused to eat it with the others. Suddenly he left the Home. The doors were locked, but he got back through a window, came up to my attic and said through the door: "Here I am, ready to make you cold". I replied that this would not lead to his immediate repatriation, and suggested that he go downstairs for some hot coffee, where I would join him. After several minutes he followed my advice and then, as I heard him go down, I walked to the Warden's room where I found his wife looking very white and frightened. We locked the door. Shortly afterwards a shot was fired and bricks were thrown through the window. The Boy then re-entered the Home, rushed up the attic stairs, and wrenched the door of my attic room off its hinges thinking that I was still inside.

I thought it prudent to telephone the police, only to be told that they were out on patrol and that we must wait. This we did—for forty minutes. Since the Boy was armed and very drunk, and was muttering threats, the situation needed cool heads. We spoke to him through the Warden's door. Eventually the local policeman arrived, and, in his presence, the culprit was asked to account for his behaviour. Because of the amount of alcohol he had consumed he was unable to give any coherent reply. I asked the police, for everyone's safety, to take him to the local police station, and although the policeman was very reluctant he finally agreed saying that they would release him at 8 a.m. next day.

When the Boy returned he had a bad hangover; I gave him black coffee and he was very apologetic.

There was also the night Gregory arrived. I was working

in my small office in Sandweg, Frankfurt am Main, on a day when there seemed to have been even more callers than usual seeking advice or assistance of one kind or another. Kenneth Brentford, who looked after the office for us, had left to return to his room in the city thinking that there would be no more visitors when Gregory appeared. He obviously had a long story to tell and spent the evening explaining that, because of what he had gone through in extermination camps and prisons, he had decided to kill a prostitute, or perhaps someone of whom he had at one time been fond. He showed me the knife and boasted that he also had a revolver. Since he was under the influence of drink, I made him some black coffee and kept him in the office until morning. I spent the whole night imploring him not to unlock the door and go off to carry out his threats. At one moment, he made an attempt to get out of the window and I had to struggle with him. As the hours went by, I tried to keep him occupied by asking his help with the filing or his advice on some of the letters, thus diverting his thoughts from his plans. By the time I was cooking his breakfast, he began to thank me for prevailing upon him not to carry out his threats.

Amongst those who in different ways have helped is Margaret, Princess of Hesse and the Rhein who since 1955 has given practical support and abundant moral encouragement. She is a prominent member of the German Red Cross. For a number of years she was Chairman of a small German Committee in Frankfurt, which did what it could to further the prison work in Hessen, in addition to which she provided overnight hospitality at her lovely house Wolfsgarten.

In 1954, Hannes Kramer, a young German social worker from Caritas, was appointed to take over the visits and after-care of the Boys in Bavaria and, until he was forced to give up through ill health, he relieved me of much travelling.

In Hamburg, my work has been made much easier through the personal assistance of Hanna Lenz, who has devoted a great deal of time to the task of dealing with correspondence and translations, but to find someone acceptable to the Boys and the Prison Authorities, to take over at least part of the prison visiting has not proved possible.

In the prisons Christmas is a particularly poignant time of the year, and I have always made a special point of visiting each one of them at this period. Until 1974, when a different system had to be introduced, volunteers were found to make up food parcels for each Boy, which I would then distribute individually. Making up these parcels was not an easy task, for in each state regulations as to the contents of the parcel varied, tins or glass normally being forbidden, and in earlier years at least the Authorities were excessively strict—to the extent once of opening an orange to see if there was anything inside! In addition, it was not always easy to ensure that the lists of Boys were complete and up-to-date and that no one was missed out.

In one of the large prisons in Hessen, where there were more than 800 German and non-German prisoners, the German Director invited me each year until his retirement to attend the Christmas Eve Service. It was at the same time a ceremonial and a moving occasion. As the only woman present, I was invited to walk with the Director from his office down the spiral staircase from which fanned out the three wings containing the prison cells and at the bottom of which were gathered the prisoners waiting for the service to begin. By the staircase itself was the Christmas tree decorated and illuminated with plain white candles, in front of us the prison orchestra, which always included some of the Boys, and on all sides of us, gathered round the staircase, the huge crowd of prisoners, gaolers and other officials. Everyone would take part in the singing, and both the Director and the Prison Chaplains in the address which they gave, would offer me a welcome and a word of encouragement.

In another prison, in Baden Wurtemberg, I was invited by the Director to attend Mass in the prison chapel. Amongst the Boys here was one who refused to talk and insisted on everything being put in writing. Even here in the chapel, where we could not see each other, we would sit exchanging notes. It seemed strange in such a setting, but

somehow I think that it contributed towards his rehabilitation, for gradually I was able to win his confidence,
saying that it would be much more practical if he would
agree to speak; and eventually he did.

My own spirits were revived and uplifted by the life and
example of Dietrich Bonhoeffer who himself was so long in
prison and made so great a sacrifice in the cause of truth and
freedom. His books, especially "Letters and Papers from
Prison", and his prayer "Who am I?" are particularly
inspiring.

WHO AM I?

Who am I? They often tell me
I stepped from my cell's confinement
Calmly, cheerfully, firmly
Like a squire from his country-house.

Who am I? They often tell me
I used to speak to my warders
Freely and friendly and clearly,
As though it were mine to command.

Who am I? They also tell me
I bore the days of misfortune,
Equably, smilingly, proudly,
Like one accustomed to win.

Am I really then all that which other
    men tell of?
Or am I only what I know of myself?
Restless and longing and sick, like a
    bird in a cage,
Struggling for breath, as though hands
    were compressing my throat,
Yearning for colours, for flowers, for
    the voices of birds,
Thirsting for words of kindness, for
    neighbourliness,
Tossing in expectation of great events,
Powerlessly trembling for friends at an
    infinite distance,

Weary and empty at praying, at thinking,
    at making,
Faint, and ready to say farewell to it all?

Who am I? This or the other?
Am I one person today and tomorrow another?
Am I both at once? A hypocrite before others,
And before myself a contemptibly woebegone
    weakling?
Or is something within me still like a beaten
    army,
Fleeing in disorder from victory already
    achieved?

Who am I? They mock me, these lonely
    questions of mine,
Whoever I am, Thou knowest, O God, I am Thine!

Throughout the thirty years since I started visiting
the Boys the deepest impression has been made
upon me by the fortitude they have shown. Although they
have been through the most appalling suffering and
difficulties, many of the Boys manage, in some incredible
way, to remain almost unaffected by this. One of the Boys,
who had been in Belsen and various other camps, said to me:
"You know, people can get used to anything if they have
no alternative." To the present day there remains the most
remarkable courtesy and good manners amongst the Boys.
On their side the Boys regard me as their 'sister'—I am of
their generation—and to some of them I am even 'Mum'!

This work has also shown me that in life one must never
generalise; whether it was in the hospitals, the prisons or
the Pass-Stelle, or with the police, the authorities, or the
Staatanwalten (public prosecutors)—I hope I made an
honest attempt not to react to provocation or indignation.
I did my best to restrain my feelings, otherwise there
would have been a complete breakdown of any hope of
reconciliation and of any working relationship. After all,
the authorities did not have to accept me. . . . it was easier
for some to say the things they did, but throughout the 130

prisons visited regularly, it was really an experience I would never regret. Tiredness, frustration and sorrow were there for much of the time, but, on the other hand, there were many individual directors, warders and officials who, although they did not have to do so, went out of their way to be welcoming and co-operative. They seemed to recognise my difficulties and predicament, even though by offloading their own problems they perhaps took up valuable time; and, if some of them ate their sandwiches and drank their coffee in front of me while I had not eaten for hours and were uncouth—well, one came to terms with it.

Inevitably for anyone who becomes involved in prison visiting, to however small an extent, the question of penal reform and the prison system arises. With the necessity for capital punishment I do not and cannot agree. But how to cope with murderers, those who resort to violence and robbery, is a huge problem to which no one can fully know the answer.

It goes without saying that we must discharge our responsibility towards the public and recognise that there are certain seriously malajusted individuals who, either because they were born with delinquent tendencies or because they are psychiatrically disturbed in some way or they are fanatics, must be prevented from coming into contact with the public and be put into a place where they can receive treatment and learn also to give something back to society. But there are some people for whom no psychiatrist can do anything, and one has to accept the fact that they will always be a danger.

Personally I do not believe in allowing such individuals to be at loose in society, because they can constitute a danger or potential danger; but we must be realistic and understand that simply locking up a person out of the way does not always provide a solution. Is not the provision of more treatment, more productive work, more social workers and more psychiatrists a part of the answer?

The ignorance of the public is profound. An increase in the severity of the punishment does not necessarily produce results. I think the judiciary and the police are put in an invidious position.

Violence begets violence and I am generally against arming the police; it brings to my mind riot situations in which each side becomes trigger happy. Yet with armed robbers one should be very firm indeed, and bring them face to face with their victims, if that is possible and they have survived. If a sound scheme could be worked out whereby the offender be made to pay a part of his earnings to the victim or his family this, in itself, would not only give some slight form of compensation but such a scheme would give them a better sense of their responsibility to society. One should try to make them conscious of the evil they have committed. We know that some choose crime to avoid work. Penal reform is right and humane. Unless you try to redeem a prisoner he will come back into society the worse for having been in contact with other offenders, for he may have learnt many other crimes from them rather than have been educated into better ways. The penal system should be so ordered that it creates a positive atmosphere, and the State and Society should be made to try and enforce moral standards.

APPENDIX

In one of my annual reports to the Ministry of Justice in the Land of Hessen, I referred to the words spoken by Winston Churchill as Home Secretary in a speech he made in the House of Commons in 1910:

"The mood and temper of the public with regard to the treatment of crime and criminals is one of the unfailing tests of the civilisation of any country. A calm, dispassionate recognition of the rights of the accused, and even convicted criminal, against the state; a constant heart searching by all charged with the duty of punishment; a desire and an eagerness to rehabilitate . . . tireless efforts towards the discovery of creative and regenerative processes."

In this age of widespread violence these words may seem difficult and too generous to accept, but the principle they lay down seems to me to be supremely important. So, I would like to add this postscript on my prison visiting, because it has involved a great deal of effort and taught me much. The work is complicated by the variety of bureaucratic systems operating in the different Länder. It would be simpler if there were a National system throughout the Federal Republic. Nobody could have been more helpful in the last few years than Dr. Per Fischer at the Chancellery at Bonn and Dr. Wagner of the German Red Cross.

It is difficult to describe the position of the prisoner, his dilemma and the necessity for respecting the dignity of the individual and his potential contribution to society.

As mentioned before, the care of the non-German prisoners may be divided into five aspects:

1. Actual prison visiting.
2. Visits to those released and to others who have been repatriated.
3. Appeals on behalf of others wanting to return to their countries of origin.
4. Those who cannot be repatriated and have nowhere to go.
5. After-care.

Several are recidivists, but, even so, we cannot judge them by any average yardstick. Usually they have no roots in the country of their captivity: no fixed abode other than their jails; and have long lost touch with whatever natural home they ever had.

It is difficult for the long-term prisoner to keep alive hope for the future when he is serving a "life" or a long sentence and has already been in prison for a great number of years and has to a large extent lost contact with the outside world.

In general, there seem to be three different attitudes of mind among those whom I visit:

1. Those who, regardless of the odds against them, remain optimistic, positive and actively interested not only in their immediate surroundings but also, through the media of books, newspapers, foreign languages, television and radio, in the greater horizons outside the prisons. They maintain a normal contact with the wardens and authorities.

   No effort should ever be spared to offer these individuals even greater possibilities for extending their thoughts and interests. Hobbies must always be encouraged and discussions during visits. Sometimes their adaptability, even in their fifties, is remarkable.

2. There are those—probably the majority—who have mentally deteriorated and for whom society is now sour and unobtainable, since they have become so introverted that they

103

have no wish to take their places in the community. They may abuse the chance if they were allowed it. Isolation and imprisonment only increase their bitterness. Only treatment and trust (two essentials, but difficult to put into practice) could perhaps restore the confidence of someone to whom almost everything is the same. I can only reiterate that in my opinion it is positively bad to confine anyone like that in a community so large, but at the same time so uniform and restrictive, that he simply cannot preserve, still less expand, his own personality. Also, regrettably, a few cannot work— they have periods of deep depression and spend their days reading—one or two occasionally paint with materials which I provide. For other prisoners, I have always found that once an opportunity has been given to them to learn a profession or trade they have usually responded. Nowadays there is much unemployment, and this means that a percentage of the prisoners are inevitably without work.

3. The not-so-hopeless or ill person who might yet become a good citizen, and who might remain "on the level" given the right opportunities.

With regard to *Repatriation*—Judging from those who have already been repatriated, this solution seems the most logical and is usually the most successful. Visits to repatriated individuals also cost money and involve a lot of driving, which I do myself.

After-care—The importance of the Foundation's small Home at St. Christopher's near Celle cannot be over-stressed, nor for that matter can the problems of handling a small number of men of different nationalities, backgrounds and personalities, particularly in view of the inevitable tendency amongst one or two to seek refuge in drink.

It is most rewarding to meet one of the Boys who has faced up to his release and made a real success of it. His pride in his job, perhaps a happy marriage (a much sought after goal), his new sense of security, and his ability to communicate the joys and benefits of these things—in all this one finds a comforting assurance that one's labours have not been in vain.

The obstacles and the disappointments are not to be underestimated, but the number of Boys redeemed speak for themselves. Comparing the many hundreds whom we were originally trying to retrieve with the very small hard-core that remains today, I am conscious that everything possible should be done to rehabilitate these too.

CHAPTER 9

A Corner of Suffolk

After I had for some years worked with and for international relief units, they withdrew—the Red Cross in 1949, because of heavy commitments elsewhere, and the Guide International Service in 1951, when they had exhausted their funds—and I decided to continue the work on my own. Those were very difficult days, with no funds and no certainty of any support. I led a frugal life shared with those who faced uncertainty, sickness and disappointment most of the time, and they told me that they felt I was one of them.

At this stage I was working in different countries, and my activities consisted largely of prison and hospital visiting and the provision of medical aid and the Holiday Scheme for people who were ill or suffering. One Home had already been founded on the Continent, as mentioned in the previous chapter, and it was hoped to establish others in Britain and in different parts of the world.

I received some support from Britain for this work. One of our earlier supporters preferred to remain anonymous, sending regularly 5/- and 10/- notes with a written message, "from a Suffolk housewife". The difficulties and struggles of those early years are hard to describe, and no doubt it is equally hard for others to believe and appreciate our problems.

Through all the years of relief and social work, including nursing, I continued to be reminded everywhere of the Bods in S.O.E. and of the desire which had arisen in me of perpetuating their spirit of optimism, courage and sacrifice—and that of their people too—by founding a Living Memorial. I have mentioned this before, but considering the importance of the fact in all I subsequently tried to do, I feel that I should repeat here my desire to commemorate the millions lost in both World Wars by providing relief from suffering and insecurity of all kinds through personal contact and service, restoring dignity to the humiliated irrespective of age, sex, race or religion. By these means I hoped to contribute towards the building of a better world, one in which peace might be established, however hard the struggle and endless disillusionments.

The work I was doing in the prisons and hospitals of Europe grew so quickly that by the time I returned to England on leave in 1951/52 I had decided that it was necessary to form a small committee and to register the Living Memorial with the Charity Commissioners. In this way the Sue Ryder Foundation as it is today was born.

After my father's death in 1942 our house at Thurlow, together with the land, was sold. My mother remained there with her many varied activities, plus war work, until 1946, when she moved to the village of Cavendish, ten miles away. The wrench of leaving Thurlow with all its memories and the community of this and the surrounding villages was very great and we found it sad not to be able to stay there.

The house to which my mother came to make her new home was originally a farmhouse and contained five bed-rooms. It is reputed to be over 300 years old and has some beautiful Tudor bricks and timber beams, which we later exposed, but it was very damp, without heating except for coal fires in a few rooms. Originally there had been 50 acres attached, but when my mother came the garden consisted of two acres.

My mother continued to lead a full and very busy life, and parallel to this she offered me every kind of encouragement and strength. Despite rationing, too, which lasted until 1954, she sent me food parcels for distribution in the different countries where I worked. Moreover, she gave talks in a wide area, having a great gift for public speaking, and thereby the work—part of which she had seen during visits to the Continent—gradually became known in Britain. It was through her friends and contacts that the first postal orders had come in.

In 1953, the Foundation having been established, with the help of a small legacy, credit from the bank and much optimism, I bought the house in Cavendish where my mother was living to serve as the headquarters of the Foundation and as a Home. My mother herself later moved to a smaller house in the lovely village of Clare, but she continued to help with the running of the house in Cavendish and took a most active part in the building up of the Foundation.

She had always been heart and soul behind me when in 1945 I first started relief and social work, and ,later, in 1952, when the international organisations withdrew, she was as convinced as I that the rest of my life should be devoted to the relief of suffering. Without her constant encouragement my tasks would have been twice as difficult —until she became disabled at the age of 85, she worked tirelessly for the Foundation. Apart from countless other activities, she ran the clothing stores at the Home, writing hundreds of letters of acknowledgment by hand.

There were many other people who helped in those early days and continued to do so as the work expanded. Of all these unselfish and generous individuals it is very hard to single out anyone specifically, but I feel I must mention the name of Harold Ince, the Honorary Treasurer. He and his wife, Dorothy, both lived in the village—she was a graduate of Girton College, Cambridge and an enthusiastic producer of plays performed by the local Dramatic Society. Harold Ince was a keen musician, sang in local choirs, served for over 40 years on the Parochial Church Council and was very active in many other sides of village life. He had his own tailor's shop in Clare. As Honorary Treasurer of this Home for 22 years he will always be remembered by the Staff and Bods with love and great affection. No one could have been a more loyal or devoted worker, never sparing himself during evenings or weekends. He will also be remembered by countless people for his punctilious work and determination to deduct the maximum discount on settling every account. Nobody was spared! Late one evening he came up to our room bearing an envelope marked 'Urgent'. On opening it I found a note from him and attached was a sketch of the village cemetery. He was asking me to mark my plot by the morning! Moreover, he believed that we should make a block-booking so that eventually all the Bods and Staff should be buried together. The amazing thing about Harold Ince was his moral courage and the way he continued right up to the end, despite his 86 years, to apply himself with conscientious devotion to the interests of the Home. He was also well-known for his oratory and ability to express our feelings: for instance, when a member of the Staff left or one of the Bods returned to Poland, he would give an impromptu and most moving message of thanks. To our grief he was knocked down by a van and died 12 days later on 23rd January 1975.

The building at Cavendish was plainly too small for our purposes even at the outset; in addition it had no central heating, and the pre-war Esse Stove (brought from the still room in the Hall at Thurlow) badly needed to be replaced. Nevertheless, the house was furnished with the help of a friend who owned quantities of dilapidated second-hand and antique furniture (which had to be renovated), and volunteers wrote in from many parts of Britain and abroad offering their services. Soon we were being helped by a large number of people, including nurses, carpenters, several part-time secretaries and two honorary treasurers. When I was not otherwise occupied, I enjoyed taking my turn at cooking, scrubbing and nursing, for I found it relaxing as a change from coping with office work. Everyone worked together as a team, and, knowing how short funds were, many people insisted on paying for their keep.

No sooner had the house been acquired by the Foundation than the first groups of patients arrived. They were referred to us by almoners (Medical Social Workers), physicians and local authorities, and they enjoyed the informal atmosphere of the Home and its large garden: able-bodied patients took great delight in helping with the gardening and with the decoration and conversion of the house. The previous owners had had an obsession for green paint not only in nearly all the rooms but also on most of the floorboards. This of course had to be removed. In those days the kitchen was the heart of the Home, possibly because of its central position and its warmth. It was the gathering place for everyone, both at meal-times and in the evening, when, in addition to typing, discussions with patients and staff took place there. These lines of Edna Jacques come to mind:—

I like old houses that are weather-stained,
Whose doorsteps sag beneath the weight of years;
Old walls that echo back with softened tone
The laughter that we knew, the sounds of tears . . .
Old homes that breathe of peace and quiet hours
That we in happy dreams may see again.

During the first few years the Home became a place of curiosity and callers dropped in, especially on Sundays, often bringing clothes and gifts with them. On one particular evening, as supper was being prepared, no fewer than four coach loads of visitors arrived to be shown round. When they stopped to admire the supper, I asked whether they wanted any refreshment, and was slightly taken aback when they gladly accepted the invitation. There was a shortage of crockery and cutlery, but, by frequent washing up, the problem was overcome.

Visitors are often surprised by the informality and atmosphere of the Home, and though it is functionally not easy to run because of its low doorways and unexpected corners, one is aware of its past history and of the many people through the centuries who have lived here. It was reputedly a convalescent home for missionaries in the last century, and a charming description has been given of them going out for walks on Sundays with their parasols. Today, on each door of the rooms and offices there is a plaque with the name of a flower representing the colour of the room. Our bedroom is called Dawn and my office Speedwell.

The national press took a great interest, and later, much to my embarrassment and surprise, I was confronted by the television programme *This is Your Life*, of which I had never heard. Although I have a personal dislike of publicity, it is, however, most useful to focus attention upon the needs of large sections of the community, both here and abroad.

A Chapel was made by converting and enlarging the

original box-room and garden shed, and oak pews were made and donated in commemoration of certain individuals. The oak itself was donated by a company in Bury St. Edmund's and the pews made up by a carpenter in the village and others by our tradesmen. In time we hope to get more pews of the same design for the Chapel. The main altar is of Cornish rock. The candlesticks were carved by hand by one of the supporters. On the right-hand side of the Chapel there is a small room with a statue of Our Lady where people can retire to say their prayers in more privacy if they wish. In here at Christmas we have a tree illuminated with plain white electric candles and on a table below the communion rail stands a small simple crib. On 24th December every year a bouquet of flowers is sent anonymously from Liverpool with the message "In loving memory." Between the Chapel and the sacristy is another very small room used as a confessional, which has on its walls two full-size reproductions of the Holy Shroud of Turin. The altar bell was found on a battle-field during the First World War. It is hoped one day to have an organ and a roll of honour. Mass is said in the Chapel every Sunday and on Holidays of Obligation and Feast Days, usually by priests from the Augustinian Priory at Clare, and priests who are themselves survivors of the Dachau concentration camp come to stay at the Home. Every year Christmas Midnight Mass is said by Father Rorke, who was a prisoner of war of the Japanese.

Two prayers hang inside the Chapel, one was found on a scrap of paper near the body of a dead child in Ravensbrück. It reads:

> *O Lord, remember not only the men and women of goodwill, but also those of ill-will. But do not only remember all the suffering they have inflicted on us, remember the fruits we bought thanks to this suffering, our comradeship, our loyalty, our humility, the courage, the generosity, the greatness of heart, which has grown out of all this, and when they come to judgement, let all the fruits that we have borne be their forgiveness.*

and the following we composed:

110

left:
Sue Ryder Shop,
Shaftesbury, Dorset.

middle:
Interior of
Sue Ryder Shop.

below left:
Helpers outside the
Sue Ryder Shop, High
Wycombe. Bucks, with
the Founder.

Sue Ryder Shop,
Crawford Street, London.

Sue Ryder Shop,
1 Launceston Place,
London.

above:
1957—The beginning at
Raphael, India.

above centre:
Several years later.

left:
Sue Ryder with Sister
Monika in Yugoslavia.

O most Holy Face of Jesus, who in Thy bitter Passion looked down with such mercy from the cross for the salvation of the world, look today upon us all, poor sinners. Grant peace and eternal rest to all the departed, but especially to the millions known and unknown who died as prisoners in many lands, victims of the hatred and cruelty of man. May the example of their suffering and courage draw us closer to Thee through Thine own Agony and Passion, and thus strengthen us in our desire to serve Thee in the sick, the unwanted and the dying wherever we may find them. Give us the Grace so to spend ourselves for those who are still alive, that we may prove most truly that we have not forgotten those who have died.

Bless us continually with the awareness of Thy presence; give us humility, gentleness and unselfishness in all our work for Thee; dispose our hearts never to refuse what Thou askest through Thy inspirations and commandments. Compass us about with Thy holy angels and grant that at the hour of our death they may lead us to Thee in the splendour of eternity. Amen.

When the Home began here, and for several years after, Cavendish had a railway station and regular service of trains on the branch line from Cambridge via Sudbury to junctions with the main London line at Marks Tey and Colchester. This, of course, was most useful, and the sudden, permanent closure of the branch line in 1967 was a cruel blow to the Home, to many of its patients, supporters and visitors, and to the general population of the Stour Valley.

There have been various crises and emergencies at Cavendish during the past few years, such as the flood of 1968, when the Stour rose and filled the house with water to a height of eighteen inches, some hundreds of pounds of damage being caused. Thanks to the initiative of the Staff and Bods and the help of the local Fire Brigade the most disabled were quickly rescued and taken upstairs although the lights had gone out. Within 30 minutes they had also managed to remove to safety all the card-indexes and most of the furniture. They did this under the most difficult conditions by using lanterns and torches. Regrettably we lost 10 beautiful national costumes from different countries which were laid out in an oak chest. Vigil was kept up throughout the night and after the tide of water had subsided a lot of mud was left behind. There was a further threat of flooding after heavy rains in the autumn of 1974. Nevertheless the house has continued to serve as headquarters of the Foundation, and over the years further extensions have been added to provide more accommodation for patients and staff. At present the building at Cavendish harbours the offices of the assistants, the General Office—where five secretaries work—the office called the Treasury, the office of the personal secretaries, and the Appeals Office.

In addition to the resident and non-resident secretaries, very valuable assistance with the office work is given voluntarily by the "weekend" secretaries who travel from London or further afield to help in whichever way they are needed. For the past fourteen years volunteers have also helped with the cooking, attending according to a daily rota (which is currently thirty strong), and preparing lunch for everyone in the Home; some of these volunteers have long distances to drive to the Home and others bring delicious dishes with them. I should like to pay tribute to Sheelagh Crawford and Honor Penton, who since the outset have organised and been responsible for the weekly rota of voluntary cooks. This is no easy task with the inevitable loss through people moving or being without transport, and they would like to see their numbers grow again. Very much of the work done for the Foundation is voluntary, and paid members of the staff work for the smallest wage they can so that only a small percentage of the money received by the Foundation is spent on administrative costs. The services of Mrs. Edna Swan, Chairman of the Home Support Group, and Stephen Wise, Chairman of the Home Committee, have been incalculable.

We have always been extremely aware of the beauty of the garden, and it is delightful on Saturday afternoons or summer evenings to hear Jeromy and Elizabeth playing games there with Bods and members of the staff. Our gardeners and tradesmen have made several improvements recently such as the small fountain, bridge, and summerhouse at the end of the pond. We are always delighted to receive bulbs and herbaceous plants and gifts for the old greenhouse.

In the wing of the main house there is a room packed to the ceiling with gifts made and given by patients and voluntary helpers, including toys ready to go to the Sue Ryder shops. Wherever possible, both in Britain and abroad, work therapy is encouraged amongst the Bods and children in the Homes. Items such as trays, stools, knitwear, dolls dressed in national costume, and many more made by the patients are sold to raise funds for the running of the Homes.

There are nearly one thousand voluntary helpers who knit cardigans for the patients of all age groups. Some of them have been doing this for years—the oldest knitter is 96—and, for some, it is their prime interest in life. Those who cannot afford to buy their own wool and patterns are supplied by the Foundation. Knitting is also undertaken for the Foundation by schools and clubs.

In another room, parcels are put into coloured sacks for distribution to the disabled overseas. Then there is the clothing store, which for many years was looked after by my mother and her friends, working in an unheated storeroom and keeping meticulous note of the thousands of items donated. Unbeknown to Mama somebody had put a notice in the magazine announcing that the Foundation would welcome wedding dresses. In the midst of the influx one of the Boys who was helping Mama had yearned in vain to be married, so for him it was made worse to be surrounded by nearly 400 dresses, veils (some accompanied by bridesmaids' dresses too) and the situation was almost too much for him in the unheated store. In the midst of this added activity a worried mother wrote to say that in her enthusiasm, after reading the notice, she had posted her daughter's wedding dress and please could we now send it back. She described it as being made from wild silk with a tulle veil and sprigs of orange blossom. For hours Mama with the boy searched, selected and sent various wedding dresses nearest to the description, but to no avail. So Mama finally hoped that a small gift would help to smooth things out. Today the work of handling the daily arrival of parcels and gifts is done by Survivors and by young voluntary helpers who come from Poland for six to twelve months. They work very hard dealing with the many tons of clothing and other articles which arrive from different parts of the world.

In the film unit 16 mm. documentary films on different aspects of our work are edited and slides are sorted. Many months, sometimes several years, are spent on the making and editing of a film.

In the Christmas Card Room, which becomes a hive of activity many months before Christmas, five helpers make up and dispatch between two and seven hundred orders a day. The cards, tags and gifts are selected by members of the public, who are asked to vote for their favourites from a wide range of designs at least 17 months ahead. The effort involved in getting the right designs and dispatching the orders can never be over-estimated. Once in the very early stages of the Christmas Card business an overprinting order was placed by a Harley Street Specialist. It was dealt with very promptly, but he rang me up to complain that the type did not match the printed message on the card. He quite rightly scolded me, and I learnt a bitter lesson, and subsequently all orders for overprinting were scrupulously coped with by the Carmelite Sisters.

It is at Cavendish too that we compile and send out our annual magazine *Remembrance*, which first appeared as a newsletter in 1957, but is now a magazine of 32 pages, containing photographs and articles on all aspects of the Foundation's work.

Preparing the copy to be sent to the printer is a task involving comparatively few people, but by August a certain sense of urgency begins to build up as the Post Office van comes to collect the thousands of envelopes, which have been addressed and sorted for months beforehand, and take them away for franking. Trestle tables and chairs are lent by the Memorial Hall in the village, and

114

then the work begins with the arrival of 70,000 copies of *Remembrance* from the printer. A chain of helpers hand the magazines in through the window and stack them in the drawing room where they are subsequently unpacked and put into the franked envelopes by volunteers working in shifts. These envelopes have then to be sorted by counties and tied up in bundles of 25, in return for which the Post Office allows us a most welcome rebate of postage. The dispatching of a magazine is an horrendous task, and it is frustrating when hundreds of copies of *Remembrance* are subsequently returned to us because the persons to whom they were addressed have either died or did not notify us of changes in address.

The Home is an important part of the house at Cavendish registered to cater for 33 physically disabled or psychiatrically disturbed patients, who are looked after by two full-time State Registered Nurses and a staff nurse, assisted by volunteers. These patients (affectionately called "the Bods" in memory of the Bods of S.O.E.) live together in the community; before they came here many of them, as already mentioned, were living on their own, unable to cope with life through loneliness or lack of care; others were blocking hospital beds, and they came to Cavendish through applications made on their behalf by social welfare workers, physicians and local authorities in Britain. From the beginning we have close ties with the Bods, living together as a family.

It is hard to single out anyone from the many Bods who have lived with us, for all in their own way have contributed to the community, however sick they were, and their characters and personalities would be hard to describe, but I cannot resist mentioning a few names.

Edward was our Librarian. He had created and built the Chapel at Flossenberg to the memory of 24 nationalities.

"The Colonel", having won the D.S.O. for his part in the Resistance in France, was a much loved person. He died with great dignity of a cardiac disease.

Then there was Bubie whose room looked out over the pond and God's Garden, as he described it. He did the glazing of the prints for the Photographic Section and kept

115

a record as well of all envelopes he addressed to new people who wrote in for information about the Foundation. In the evenings he enjoyed playing the piano. His mind was an encyclopaedia and even his merry remarks about "fantastic news", "a marvellous meal" could be heard in different parts of the building. After long drives from various places he would say to me: "Now do go and soak yourself in a warm bath". Bubie died of TB and chronic rheumatoid arthritis after great pain which he bore nobly.

Phyllis is another brave person. She was completely alone and has suffered from hypo-thyroidism ever since childhood. She breathes with great difficulty and bears her suffering with cheerfulness.

Living with the physically handicapped is generally easier but here having a percentage of psychiatrically disturbed individuals means that even more time must be given to listening to and discussing their ideas, complaints and problems. We remember too the individuals from various parts of Britain who have turned up unexpectedly, including the alcoholics, drug addicts and the woman who had been a nurse but had a breakdown and sat counting the blades of grass on the lawn.

It is important that the handicapped should be integrated into the community and not relegated to a shadowy half-world where they have no interests or occupations apart from their ailments and the television. Being handicapped, after all, does not disqualify one as a human being, but merely acquiring "a new technique of living" as we call it.

Perhaps one might add a word of advice to all well-meaning people who come into contact with the handicapped. Although it may seem to be an act of kindness, never complete a sentence for someone who is slow of speech, or attempt to do anything for a handicapped person which he is capable of doing himself albeit much more slowly. A small point, but of great importance to people who are trying to lead normal lives.

We are fortunate to live in the midst of the village and thus feel a part of whatever else is going on. The Home is easily accessible and the ambulant Bods enjoy doing their own shopping and going for walks and therefore do not feel isolated or cut off.

Throughout the year there are builders and tradesmen living and working here, some who apply their skills to maintenance of this Home, some who go forth from here to work elsewhere, as has already been mentioned. At times there were several tradesmen with the same names and so nick-names were given. Many have left particular memories as a result of their hard work. For instance. "Long John" restored the rosewood piano by stripping and french-polishing it.

As is always the case in life, there are differences of opinion and temperament, but to the outsider it is astonishing and altogether delightful to see how naturally, easily and enjoyably the Bods, the staff, the tradesmen and volunteers—of many nationalities and age groups—come to terms with one another, the routine, the disabled, and with whatever they can make of life in this corner of Suffolk.

CHAPTER 10

Partnership

In February 1955, Leonard Cheshire invited me to visit his new Home for the disabled at Ampthill. It was a cold bleak day, and as I had a coli infection I did not have much inclination to go, but I felt it would be rude not to keep the appointment. The journey along familiar roads brought back memories of war-time days and nights at Tempsford Station—the blackouts, the signals, the changing huts, the briefings, driving the Bods to the aircraft, watching the take-off and waiting for the crews to return.

I had not heard of Leonard Cheshire. Neither of us knew about the other's work, for during the War I had been immersed in Special Operations Executive, much of the time overseas—indeed until the early fifties—and I was therefore out of touch. Originally he had won fame as a bomber pilot. He became at twenty-five the Royal Air Force's youngest Group Captain and won the Victoria Cross, the Distinguished Service Order three times over and a Distinguished Flying Cross in the course of more than one hundred bombing missions. To quote from the official citation, he acquired "a reputation second to none in Bomber Command for his sustained courage in the face of enemy action". He was the man responsible for the low-level bombing and destruction of the Gestapo headquarters in Munich.

Leonard Cheshire and William Penney were the two British observers at the dropping of the Atom bomb on Nagasaki. The Allied leaders were placed in a cruel dilemma. It is right to mention here—because the event is so often taken out of context—that the only alternative to the bomb would have been to fight it out to the last man, taking island by island over a vast area and invading the Japanese mainland. Estimated casualties were two million Japanese and one million Allied lives. Meanwhile a minimum of 175,000 Allied prisoners of war and civilian internees were lingering and dying in terrible conditions worsened by the appalling climate totally cut off and without help.

After the War Cheshire was at a loss to know what to do. He tried to establish a community on a Christian Socialist basis, which failed, but out of failure grew a series of Homes for the disabled, confined then to Britain, known as Cheshire Homes, of which Ampthill was already the fifth.

In 1952 he became ill and tuberculosis was diagnosed. In the next two years he underwent four operations (two stage thora) at Midhurst Sanatorium facing up courageously to sickness and pain. During this time, he was obliged to delegate to local committees the task of running his four existing Homes, which involved some difficulties, for he was reluctant to delegate—but actually it gave him greater freedom of movement and opened up avenues of expansion which otherwise he would not have had. He had splendid encouragement from his father, the international jurist Professor G. C. Cheshire.

At Ampthill that afternoon he talked to me about his work and showed me over the house. Both of us were totally involved in our own work and animated by it. I told him a little about my small international Foundation and about the Bods, and I explained briefly to him the aims of the Living Memorial. This was new to him, but it was clear that both of us worked and built up our respective Foundations without funds and on faith. Apparently after this meeting Leonard said he had a feeling he had met someone with whom he had an affinity. "I could not define it," he said to others, and added, "but it made a vivid impression on me."

We had established our respective organisations long before meeting each other; the Foundation on the one hand and the Cheshire Homes on the other had each developed its own positive and distinctive character and individuality. I had as a child always hoped and intended to take up nursing and social work, and my mother had the greatest influence on what I intended or hoped to do with my life, quite apart from the War.

119

The work done by the two charities also differed. The Cheshire Homes were intended mainly for the physically handicapped, including the young disabled, whereas the Foundation cared for a wider range of age groups, in addition to operating a Holiday Scheme and doing social and relief work and prison visiting. Each organisation had, however, been established for the relief of suffering, and to that extent their general purpose was the same. Later I became a Trustee of the Cheshire Homes and for years attended the long, lively Trustee Meetings on Saturdays at Market Mews in London, giving whatever encouragement I could to the handful of Trustees about taking on more properties and opening new Homes. In the early days there were grave decisions for us to make. Later Leonard Cheshire became a Councillor of my own Foundation.

Thereafter we met at intervals at Staunton Harold in Derbyshire where two or three Bods came with me to help the many others restore the large and lovely house. Leonard also accompanied me on a few of my drives to the Continent, but it was in India that we really got to know each other, ultimately getting engaged there.

In 1957 I went to India for the first time, arriving from Moscow, where I had gone for further discussions concerning the repatriation of Russians still in German prisons. I flew via Tashkent in a Russian plane, seeing the beauty of a part of the Himalayas, and landing in Delhi.

Leonard met me at the airport and together we travelled through the country by train and bus, often suffering considerable discomfort in the heat, but getting to know it and at least some of the individuals among the anonymous millions. I was deeply impressed by the vastness of India with its teeming masses of people and its many different languages. The poverty and suffering haunted me, and what I saw was often appalling, but I grew to admire the way in which the people put up with their sufferings and with the dreadful natural calamities that so often ruin their lives; and I admired too their willingness to share even the little they had, their friendliness and helpfulness to others, and their attempts to improve their situation.

Together we visited the various Homes Leonard Cheshire had founded in India with the Indians who made themselves responsible for raising the money either to convert a building or on occasions to construct a new one. This they did independently of outside support and were responsible, too, for raising the funds and covering the maintenance of the Homes. Later we travelled in *Ezekiel*, a secondhand ambulance bought in Malaysia and shipped to Calcutta, where it was renovated and serviced voluntarily by the Indian Army. Taking it in turns to drive, we covered several thousands of miles, to Jamshedpur, Burnpur, Allahabad, Lucknow, Agra, Delhi and finally to Dehra Dun. The distances were great, Calcutta being nearly a thousand miles from Delhi. Travelling rough, we appreciated the hospitality which was warmly offered by the locals and friends wherever we went.

Near the city of Dehra Dun in Uttar Pradesh we found a site of some thirty acres which seemed to us suitable for a joint venture. This site had been offered to Leonard by the Government of Uttar Pradesh, and the two of us visited it together, bicycling there across the dried-out bed of the Rispana River.

Here we determined we would create a centre which in time would care for many different kinds of people in need —mentally handicapped children, spastic children, healthy children whose parents, because of illness or poverty, could not care for them, and cases of leprosy. It was to be named *Raphael* after the Archangel of healing.

In February 1959 Leonard Cheshire and I became engaged. This was a step we had to think very seriously about. The work had meant my life, and nothing I felt should or could change this. How in the future could one combine both marriage and work? This posed a grave question. Moreover, even in normal circumstances, marriage inevitably brings great responsibilities—I had always felt that it was a gamble. Furthermore, the implications are so serious that it is wiser to remain single and work than to run the risk of an unhappy marriage. Comparatively few people prepare themselves for sharing literally everything and then being equal to the task.

121

Before any announcement was made, the following note, signed by both of us, was sent to colleagues, supporters and friends of both Foundations:

Before the news should become public, we want to let you know personally that we are engaged, and plan to get married in the near future, quietly and abroad. In doing so we assure you that our sole aim is still the good of the work and to help those who are sick or in need, whoever and wherever they may be, but that together we feel strengthened and better equipped for all that lies ahead. During the last few years, as we have gradually seen and appreciated each other's work, we have come to realise not only how many opportunities of giving assistance were missed, but also how much remains to be done. We believe that with God's grace we can now help each other cope more adequately than we have in the past, and wherever the work may take us we always look forward to keeping in personal touch with each of you. We do hope that our intention will receive your approval and that you will give us your blessing.

We were married by Cardinal Valerian Gracias on the 5th April 1959 in his private chapel in Bombay, which in 1966 Pope Paul used during the Eucharistic Congress. It was a very simple wedding, as we meant it to be, attended only by a handful of close friends, and took place after my return to India from working in Poland and Czechoslovakia.

After taking part, in the humid heat, in the reception given by local supporters and patients at Cheshire's *Bethlehem* home on the outskirts of Bombay, we left on the 36-hour train journey back to *Raphael*, the joint centre we had started at Dehra Dun, and where we took part in modest celebrations with the staff and patients.

The demands made on us were to be as heavy after our marriage as before, but in future we would be able to bear much of the burden together. Significantly enough our married life began with a joint undertaking, a tour of Australia and New Zealand, where we were to give talks on our work in India and elsewhere and to raise funds for it.

Before leaving, however, we tried—despite the intense heat—to spend three days peacefully together in a simple hut on the banks of the river Jamna, cooking over a camp fire and drawing water from the river, seeing the everyday life of India continuing in the distance—the boats passing on the water, the people washing themselves and their clothes—and hearing at night the beat of drums in the neighbouring village. But even here our solitude did not remain undisturbed for long: on the second day we were awakened by the noise of three hundred children who had arrived on an outing, and soon also an Indian family of six came to take up residence in the small hut where we were staying.

From India we flew to Singapore to visit the local Cheshire Home near Changi, and from there to Sydney to begin our first tour of Australia and New Zealand. To our astonishment the acting Prime Minister of Australia lent us his house and the use of his den and car. Then we returned to Britain to the Foundation's Headquarters at Cavendish. Here we had our base in one room of the house. In this room we lived and worked, our children were born there and it was their nursery, and today it still forms part of our home. Several years after our marriage an adjoining room became available, which is used as an office/study. Our children, Jeromy, born in 1960, and Elizabeth, born in 1962, each has a small bedroom near our room.

Both Jeromy and Elizabeth were delivered by the local district nurse, Sister Collins, assisted by Miss Knapp: they were midwives of the old school, whom I respected and liked, and they also used to enthral me with tales of their experiences. I was able and anyway preferred to keep working normally until a few hours before the children were born, and shortly afterwards responded to the cables and correspondence. One Support Group who had planned their Annual General Meeting expected me to attend this in any case. There was great rejoicing throughout the Home when the births were announced. The joy of having a newborn child in our midst created a new happiness, especially to those who had lost families or had been

123

denied them. The children were christened in the chapel at Cavendish in ceremonies attended by the Bods, relatives and friends.

For seven years after the birth of the children Kitty (Catherine McGrath), a State Enrolled Nurse from Cork, helped us to look after them. She tried to ensure that the one room home did not become, in her words, "a transit room or rather like a main railway station". Kitty remains a close friend.

Jeromy and Elizabeth are growing up as part of a family which comprises not only us but also everyone else— whether Bods or staff—for whom Cavendish is "home", and at no stage in their lives have they or the Bods felt different or separated from each other. It has given them an awareness of other people's needs and taught them at the same time that the sick and handicapped are human beings with the same feelings, hopes and fears as theirs differing only in the fact that they have to adapt themselves to living with their disability. Like us, both children are extremely sensitive and feel very deeply about other people.

One of the essential things which still divides my husband and myself, however, and will of its nature continue to do so, is the work of our respective Foundations, which occupies much of our time and entails long journeys, separating us from each other and from the children. We dislike these separations intensely but we have tried to accept them and to build a happy family life around them. As Mother Teresa told us years ago in Calcutta, marriage would mean more sacrifices, but we would be the better for it. Sharing problems has made all the difference to both of us. Our feelings are best expressed in the following prayer we composed together:

> To Thee, O my God,
> Who art infinite Love,
> Yet Who hast called us to be perfect, even as Thou
>   art perfect:
> Who so loved the World,
> That Thou didst give us Thine only begotten Son,

And who hast thereby given Thine all, Thine
everything:
Who emptied Thyself of Thy Glory,
And became obedient unto death,
Even the death of the Cross,
For us:
To Thee,
We surrender our all, our everything,
To be consumed by the unquenchable fire of Thy Love:
We desire to love Thee even as Thy own Mother loved
Thee,
To be generous as Thou only art generous,
To give our all to Thee as Thou givest Thine to us:
Thou hast called us, O Lord, and we have found Thee,
In the poor, the unwanted, and the suffering,
And there we will serve Thee,
Unto death.

Amen.

CHAPTER 11

India

There are sounds, sights and smells which evoke and bring a country or place to the mind instantly. Within the confines of a few pages one can recapture only a few impressionistic memories to illustrate the immensity and diversity of India.

Over-crowded trains; cooking on trains; steaming heat rising from the ground; moments of wondering how and where to escape from this oven-heat; bitterly cold nights; people sleeping on pavements; scraggy dogs scrounging for scraps amongst the garbage; the sound of waves lapping on the coast; the grace of women carrying water or bricks on their heads or combing or plaiting their long sleek hair, or winding brilliant saris round their bodies; the greeting *namastes* with folded hands;

The jiggling and jangling of horse-drawn tongas; twinkling lights; changing a wheel by candlelight on the road; ticklish warmth in 90°F; notices at Delhi Airport— *In case of any grievance contact the Assistant Collector. No anonymous complaints:* the sign *Blow horn please* on lorries; the chowkidar (watchman) and his whistle at night; the savour of chapaties cooked over a simple fire; tooting of hooters; relief at the caress of water and rain; thronged and raucous bazaars; maize, rice, bananas, swarming flies, occasional mosquito nets; the chirping of crickets or cicadas at night; the haze rising everywhere at sunset from innumerable family fires; ubiquitous and penetrating dust; tropical storms; shouts of children; staggering loads carried or pulled by men, women or emaciated buffaloes;

Holy men in silent meditation; innumerable migratory birds in the hill stations; mainahs with their cheeky chatter; spontaneous *salaams* from all and sundry; the powerful

126

scents of frangipani blossoms and bright marigold garlands; the disciplined bearing of the Indian Services (men and women); the strong and prevailing smell of curry and spices—appetising to many, so unpleasant to the few; the howling of jackals at night; the stark contrast between the human ant-heaps of bustling cities and the fatalistic calm which broods over hard-working villages; camels plodding on the wayside; the delicious taste of succulent mangoes and refreshing papaya; eternal snow on the distant Himalayas in their lonely majesty, in contrast to the littleness and transience of men.

A pandemic problem which in India affects us directly is the continual movement of people from the country to the cities and towns. Many uproot themselves or drift away from the country because of the poor soil conditions, lack of water, or because their tiny plots of land cannot support them and they hope vainly that by moving they may find work in a city. It is tragic to find whole families or even whole village communities who have done this, only to find themselves living on the pavements or in shocking huts unfit for human habitation. Intense heat makes such an existence almost unbearable, and it is particularly awful to witness the exhaustion of the sick, most of whom know there is no relief. During the rainy season (if the monsoon does not fail) the huts are frequently washed away.

There are usually two ways of approaching Dehra Dun —by train chugging through the night from Delhi, or by road. The road runs fairly direct for 130 miles through villages and the cantonment towns of Roorkee and Meerut before climbing into the forest-clad Siwaliks. From these the road drops into a broad plateau and so into the city of Dehra Dun.

To find the Ryder-Cheshire Centre one must leave the city and, on its outskirts, cross the dry bed of the Rispana river. Just beyond the river, against the blue haze of the

Himalayan foothills, one sees through the sal trees a group of white buildings. This is *Raphael:* here we have a leprosy colony, a Home for mental defectives, the Little White House for destitute children, a hospital with a TB wing, and a school.

At night the glittering lights of Mussoorie, a famous hill station, watch over them from its mountain ridge just north of them.

For us the establishment of the Centre was a big project, all the more ambitious because we had no money to invest in building. Undeterred, however, we decided to make an immediate start. With others, including a few of the leprosy patients, we helped to clear the site of bushes and undergrowth, after which tents were bought and set up, and in these handicapped children were soon being cared for by two nurses who had come from Britain, local *ayahs* (nannies) and a cook.

Not long afterwards Ava Dhar, the widow of an Indian civil servant, offered her services as Secretary-Administrator, in which capacity she stayed on at the new settlement until forced through ill health to retire. Ava Dhar was a remarkable person. Shy and reserved, she had the capacity to create beauty in the simplest surroundings. Before she started her long working day she would go out to collect wild flowers with which to decorate the office. An admirer of Pandit Nehru, she was liberal-minded and often spoke warmly of the positive contributions which Britain had made to her country in the past—in particular the judiciary, the civil administration and the railway system; and she shared with me an interest in medicine and history and a love of poetry. For many years she had worked with the Red Cross.

Ava Dhar was a quiet administrator, and if at the start she sometimes lay awake at night wondering whether there was going to be enough money at the end of the month to pay the wages and the bills, she quickly adopted the view held by us that financial security is not to be achieved at the expense of refusing admission to the Centre to applicants for whom such refusal would mean certain death. She always believed wholeheartedly that *Raphael* must not be just a hospice or a shelter in which those who cannot fend for themselves may be protected, but that its objective is to offer a new life and a sense of purpose to those who previously had none.

Sadly in 1966 Ava Dhar developed cancer and had to give up her work. In a letter written after she left and shortly before her death she says: "It was a terrible wrench to leave *Raphael* in this way. I had a long, last look to bid farewell. The children, patients and Sisters and the leprosy patients were standing together along the bank waving until we were out of sight. It was a heart-breaking moment."

In her simple white sari Ava Dhar had for many years been a lovely and reassuring presence at *Raphael*. Barbara Coleman, an Australian, who had worked with her wrote: "To those for whom she worked, the individuals both at the Centre and nearby, to those who came to her in their distress and learned of her extraordinary compassion, this loss must seem irreparable."

The Centre is run by a governing council whose chairman is Lieutenant General S. P. Bhatia. He was Director General of the Armed Forces Medical Services, comprising Army, Navy and Air Force from 1960-62. Eventually he was head of the Medical Services of the Air Force and Army. On his retirement from the Services he became the Government of India's first Commissioner of Family Planning.

In the course of fifteen years all the units that had been planned came into being, but their needs will always remain great.

The *Little White House* is so named after a Polish folk song. Here we have seventy healthy boys and girls whose parents cannot look after them because of poverty or illness—a few are orphans. Some were brought by relatives who walked for miles to reach the Centre. The maintenance and education of each child costs £80 a year. Often when they first arrive they are shy and sad, never having had the opportunity of playing with a toy or knowing where the next meal was coming from. Some of these children are educated in the home, while others go into

Dehra Dun and to a Boarding School at Sadhana. In bringing them up, the staff aim first and foremost to show them that they are loved, and to ensure that they are equipped to cope with life when they are grown up. The eldest are training in general nursing and midwifery.

When we stay at the Centre and share in the daily lives of those who live there, we have the opportunity of listening to them and exchanging ideas and thoughts. The children always greet us by saying "Hello Mummie, Hello Daddie". They enjoy and respond to the opportunity of being educated, and it is delightful to hear what each of them plans to do in the future, even the five year olds eagerly join in a discussion about learning a trade or profession. Their wishes, like all children, are diverse and probably cannot be attained, but it is wonderful for both the Sponsors and ourselves to see them grow and become useful members of society. It is also a proof that, however humble the background, a child can develop and make something of his life providing he is given this chance.

The Ava Vihar Unit, which cares for the mentally handicapped, has patients whose ages range from three years to fifty, many of them severely retarded and in need of specialised medical care. This is the unit that has the longest waiting list. In time we hope not only to increase the accommodation in this unit, but also to classify the patients according to their particular needs and to provide better care.

Pamela Breslin, the Australian teacher who started the school for these patients, arrived in 1960. She needed faith and patience and skill; but with the minimum of facilities that she had at her disposal she was able to evoke a response from a few children and to introduce calm and discipline into their lives. She taught them to identify colours; she helped them to cut out patterns, to recognise nursery rhymes and to sing simple songs. When she left she was succeeded by Indian teachers.

The children's disabilities and backgrounds vary considerably. Among them is a deaf and dumb boy who, although mentally retarded, has learnt that some people can be kind. Another boy, who is blind, can hear music in the wind, Then there is a Muslim girl who had had to mother two other children: she was found begging in the street, demented as a result of ill-treatment, but she is now one of our regular helpers. One little boy stumbled in by himself with nothing to identify him but the name of the Ryder-Cheshire Centre scrawled on a piece of paper pinned to his shirt.

The Leprosy Unit at the Centre cares for 112 burnt-out cases; this means that, while the disease has been arrested and the patients are not infectious, as a rule they are suffering from severe mutilation. Some have lost their fingers, some their toes, and if they have stumps left these are devoid of sensation. Others have lost their eyesight or suffered some other severe disability. Injections are administered and drugs given under the supervision of a medical adviser, while a medical orderly treats the patients' hands and feet which are often badly ulcerated. Loss of sensation in their hands makes it difficult for these people to learn trades which will enable them to be independent. Nevertheless, many have overcome this obstacle and are now weavers, spinners, cobblers, painters or tailors; the head shoemaker of the group has attended a special course to enable him to make shoes for the leprosy patients whose feet have been deformed.

The Leprosy Unit consists of small, single-storey cottages, where each couple or family have their own simple room and a verandah on which they can cook their meals. There is also a dispensary. Many of these individuals were originally reduced to begging as they had no means of employment. Some came from the mountainous area of Tehri-Garhwal in the foothills of the Himalayas, having left their families in search of treatment.

It is believed that three million two hundred thousand people in India suffer from leprosy out of an estimated ten million eight hundred thousand in the world. The disease is not hereditary, and the treatment for it is now so highly developed that the medical authorities believe that if a great world-wide effort were made to combat it, this shocking affliction might be brought under control.

Leprosy is a cruel disease and there is much ignorance and prejudice about it. One of the worst problems is the fear it causes. People generally believe leprosy is contagious, but medicine has proved that it can only be passed on after prolonged and close skin-to-skin contact. Many who do develop leprosy become outcasts and consequently beggars. Leprosy causes more deformities than any other disease. If a huge, sustained, international, long-term effort could be mounted, more mobile teams might be organised to detect and to give treatment, thus saving untold humiliation and despair to millions.

What is being done at *Raphael* is a single very small attempt to deal with this terrible illness, but it is hoped that it may make its contribution towards inspiring and convincing others. Instead of people thinking of the victims as permanent derelicts, dependent upon charity, it is only fair to say that many of them prefer the dignity of work which gives independence. In the context of our task the words "aid" and "charity" have become devalued by misuse and abuse and prejudice. In a neighbouring Colony with which we often exchange visits, Agnes Kunze—a social worker from Munich—has proved in the last eleven years that the most deformed leprosy patients are willing and able to produce textiles for export.

Whereas the progress of malaria has been largely arrested, thanks to W.H.O. (World Health Organisation) and others, cholera and typhus are unfortunately still very prevalent, and it is also common to see smallpox and the havoc it brings. We carried an entire family stricken with this disease from their single room to our ambulance, but four out of seven died.

From amongst those who either arrived on our doorstep, were found locally, or had managed—despite their state of health—to walk miles the following individuals may illustrate the plight of millions.

Brijender has a badly disfigured face and right eye and his neck was twisted giving him a very crippled appearance. He was then sixteen. One day when helping to clean out the storeroom he burst into tears, having discovered a tattered piece of blanket which had been his only possession before. Brijender has had surgery twice in Delhi and this has effectively corrected the contracture of his neck; skin grafting has also helped to improve the appearance of his facial skin and eyelids. He also received a full course of anti-tubercular drugs. He liked and enjoyed the idea of having a "home" and gradually became of great assistance to both the hospital staff and the helpless patients, giving them their meals, taking them to the bathroom, etc. He also started to learn cooking and tailoring and proved very quick at the latter. In 1971 he attended a tailoring school, but unfortunately his application for obtaining an apprenticeship has not met with success. So he works as a ward boy and boards out privately in our accountant's room.

Dhani Ram comes from a village in the Simla hills. He has tried to work as a cook but had a poor resistance to infection, developed pulmonary and intestinal tuberculosis and while in our hospital also developed an appendiceal abscess. He was then seventeen and spent fifteen months in the TB ward before being discharged. He is on our list of follow-up cases and received domiciliary treatment for one year.

Krishna was born on 1st February 1961. Her mother died of leprosy and her father, also a leprosy sufferer, is completely blind. When Krishna first came to us she was very solemn, shy and seemed reluctant to play. She is now in Class 8 and though she does not find her studies easy she works hard and hopes to become a teacher. She is a very pretty, pleasant looking girl, even-tempered, with a calm attitude towards life. One of her greatest thrills, which is shared by the other children, is participation in producing concerts which includes miming, acting, dancing and singing.

One of those who came to *Raphael* in 1959 is *Baisakhi.* She had badly deformed hands and feet and poor eyesight. She always enjoyed, despite her handicaps, a happy disposition and liked being in charge of the workshop. During the past few years she has worked as an ayah in our hospital and insists upon only receiving rations, accom-

modation, drugs and twelve rupees per month. When Anne
Young, an Australian nurse—who had previously worked
at *Raphael* for seven years, before taking a specialised TB
course in London—started visiting the poor in the
surrounding area of the Centre and then opened a clinic at
Tehri, Baisakhi volunteered to be her assistant. They are
complementary to each other. Anne, having learnt Hindi,
thoroughly enjoys the company of Baisakhi. They are fearless travellers, going on public buses for miles and miles
into the hills, visiting people in isolated villages who are
too weak and sick to get to hospital. When they do reach
them, many patients are in an advanced state of tuberculosis (both acute and chronic) and then very little can be
done. But as this work develops we hope to be more
effective to these men, women and children by either
giving them treatment in one of the clinics plus domiciliary care or alternatively continue as before and attempt
to get them to the hospital at *Raphael*.

The scenery which stretches for hundreds of miles is
magnificent in its grandeur, and on the twisty roads one
meets various hill people—they have fine faces and are
always friendly—with their herds of goats and buffaloes.
Not infrequently there are landslides when transport has
to be abandoned. The jeep proves invaluable, though the
travelling is still tough. Wherever they go—and in the past
particularly when they have had to use the buses—
Baisakhi takes full opportunity of using her lively personality in telling all and sundry about our work and the
clinics.

I have mentioned the clinic at Tehri, but would like to
add a short note on what it involved for Anne and her
companions. From Dehra Dun it is a journey of seven and
a half hours by bus, or five hours by jeep. On arrival they
have to have a thorough wash, and then decide on a
practical order or precedence for patients, trying to see
first those who have been waiting longest, or who seem
particularly ill, or who have to return quickly to work.
They have a routine for examining each patient: weight,
temperature, pulse, blood pressure, respiration, lung
capacity, sputum, E.S.R. (Erythrocyte Sedimentation rate),

haemoglobin, etc. Then comes the treatment by free supplies of Isoniazid and Thiacetazone tablets, or B.C.G. (Bacille Calmette Guérin) vaccines, or whatever is available and necessary. All this adds up to a heavy day's work, and afterwards they sometimes go on to another clinic at Dharolti.

Owing to the potential size of the Centre and the needs we did not feel it fair to leave all the fund-raising to the Indians, the more so as there is a local Home in Dehra Dun anyway. Consequently during our first tour of Australia and New Zealand we asked for support from these countries. This aim has been achieved in no small measure due to the interest and generosity of countless people including very many school children who become sponsors for individual children or adults at *Raphael* and thus feel a special responsibility for them, receiving in turn reports and photographs to keep them in touch. These sponsors are joined by others who are willing to undertake raising capital funds for the approach road known as The Causeway, the greatly needed tube-well—which we hope may overcome the acute shortage of water—and extensions to the Little White House and other units. During the past fifteen years specially selected nurses, occupational and speech physiotherapists have come—mainly from Australia and New Zealand—usually for a period of two years or more. Each volunteer working at *Raphael* receives, in return, board and pocket money, their work in the different units complementing that of the Indian staff. This now includes a doctor, dispenser, a medical administrator, a Housemother, and three full time teachers for some of the children in the Little White House. We have sometimes had nursing sisters from Spain.

In 1961, on the Feast of Divali (the Festival of Lights) the Prime Minister, Pandit Nehru, visited Raphael, and to welcome him the pathway to the Centre was lit by dozens of flickering lamps. I was impressed by the personalities of both Mr. Nehru and his sister Madam Vijay Lakshmi Pandit. I admired their conversational gifts and wished I could have listened to them for hours. Madam Pandit has

135

lived in Dehra Dun since she returned from the Diplomatic Service and is a stimulating visitor to the Centre.

A bi-monthly report gives my husband and myself, wherever we may be, a vivid account of the growth and consolidation in India of the Ryder-Cheshire Mission for the Relief of Suffering. The term "Mission" has been used deliberately in connection with the Centre because it comes from the Latin word "missio" which means "sending". It was chosen to stress to those who participate in the work that they must look on themselves as being "sent" to those who are in need.

This Centre is not the only enterprise in India with which the Foundation is associated. With the help of a number of Indians we established in the early 1960's the Sue Ryder Medical Aid Foundation in Bangalore, which provides relief for the sick and the poor in their huts and in the slums. In Madras in the South of India there is also a Ryder-Cheshire Foundation Centre which provides training and work for leprosy patients.

The Indian Committee which is responsible for the running of the Foundation's centres raises its own funds: as well as receiving individual donations they also organise functions of one kind or another, including concerts, sales and parties.

In 1972 the Foundation collected or was given sufficient Green Shield Stamps for a van to be acquired; and it was shipped out to Bangalore for use by the medical aid team. Having their own transport has enabled this team to bring help to many more people, for formerly they had either to walk to their patients' homes or to rely upon public transport.

When I visit this team I accompany the doctor and nurse on their rounds. To be in the field and witness the stoic courage of those people who live in appalling conditions and privation and who know they have nothing to look forward to is a very humbling experience. It is a world apart and one doesn't really want to leave them.

I just wish that those people, near and far, who criticise or make light of the efforts of people in India to help those in need could come with me to see for themselves what it is like. The sheer size of the sub-continent, the physical differences of climate and of soil, can in themselves cause many desperate material problems from which we in more temperate climes are protected. I wonder whether these critics would do as well if they found themselves in a similar situation, and whether they would show the same patience and endurance. As in many other developing countries extended family ties in India remain strong. The Indians show a willingness to help themselves and strive towards self-sufficiency. Of course it is true that there is passiveness and fatalism, but where there are people to organise and take the lead, results can be seen. Whatever may be thought of their civil hospitals, their military hospitals would be a credit to any nation. The solution of the country's problems lies with the younger generation. With idealism, far more organisation and enthusiasm, a great deal could be accomplished and more improvement brought about despite the extremely serious population explosion with all the consequences, including lawlessness.

While more could and should be done by the different countries for the underdeveloped ones—of which India presents the greatest challenge—I believe that the contribution of the West should not be exclusively financial. What our Foundation seeks to do is to render personal service, and so to show to the people we are trying to help how they can help themselves. If the dangerous gulf between the rich and poor nations is ever to be bridged it is not just a question of spreading the world's wealth more evenly; the quality of life in the developing nations must also be improved, but this can best be done on a very personal level by individuals directly involving themselves, even though this may be at a distance. In our small way this is what we hope to achieve, but we realise that our effort is painfully small in relation to the immensity of the task.

137

The average visitor or tourist, understandably, is not only appalled but confused by the experience and shock of the sights which meet him. What I have mentioned in these pages are our own personal experiences, which must in turn be related and harnessed to the goodwill and determination not only of the Indians but of humanity elsewhere. If we all despair, then nothing can be done but to quote a Chinese proverb: "It is better to light one candle than to curse the darkness."

CHAPTER 12

Hickleton

For eight years the Foundation's Home in Suffolk had cared for the disabled, including patients from hospitals, but there were long waiting lists. Many required care, attention and affection in a Home with something close to a real family atmosphere, in addition to their need for qualified nursing staff adequately supported by other workers, including volunteer helpers.

It was in these circumstances that Hickleton was acquired.

Hickleton Hall belonged to the Woods of Hickleton and was the home of the family's best-known sons, the first three Viscounts Halifax. The second Viscount (1838-1934) was for many years the foremost layman in the Anglican Church. He worked so eagerly for a close rapport with the Vatican that in many minds, friendly or hostile, Hickleton became almost synonymous with the reunion movement. The village church—part Norman, part Perpendicular, and close to the Hall—had been filled by the family with emblems of their ecumenical interests.

The son and heir of the second Viscount, a Viceroy of India and wartime Ambassador to the United States, returned to Hickleton in 1946, where he found the house and the estate looking worn and neglected. During the War the house had been requisitioned by the Army, and in 1940 served for six months as Headquarters of Corps Commander Alexander (later Field Marshal Viscount Alexander of Tunis) when he was responsible for the defence of Lincolnshire and the East Riding of Yorkshire, while the grounds had been turned into a camp, first for German prisoners of war and later for displaced persons. The family decided reluctantly that they could no longer maintain the Hall, and they leased it to the Anglican Sisterhood of the Holy Paraclete, who used it as a school until 1958-59 when they returned to their senior school in

139

Whitby. The Hall then stood empty for some 18 months until I saw it on one of my searches for new Homes and "fell for it". Its potential was great, its flaws offered a challenge and the purchase price was modest.

Very little seems to be known about the Hall's origins. Nikolaus Pevsner puts it at "about 1730", with additions which probably date from 1775, but there are remains of a reputedly much older house.

In its heyday Hickleton was a great place for gatherings at Christmas when the family held huge parties for retainers, villagers and neighbours from all around. Indeed, in the autobiography of the late Earl of Halifax, *Fullness of Days*, there are vivid descriptions of the Christmas celebrations. As recently as 1933, when the second Viscount's son came of age, there was a luncheon for tenants and neighbours in the stable yard which was attended by a thousand people.

I first saw Hickleton Hall, which lies off the A635 in the West Riding of Yorkshire, in November 1960: it was shrouded in Yorkshire mist and half hidden by the heavy, sodden branches of very beautiful trees. Accompanied by Mr. Mutch, Lord Halifax's helpful agent, my mother and I toured the house by torchlight. Three staircases led to a long passage underneath the main rooms on the first floor. The rusted commercial-size cooker and the flagstone floors reminded me of my childhood—of the scrubbing and the old black iron ovens.

I could see the possibilities of the house, if some walls were knocked down and a few rooms linked. I could also foresee the large kitchen with its high ceiling being converted into living accommodation by putting in a floor and a false ceiling. The worse the state of a place, the more I feel attracted to it because of the sheer enjoyment of working with other people in restoring it, especially when it is beautiful.

The house had to be ready in six weeks to receive its first patients. Accompanied by Beth, who was looking after Jeromy, then a year old, I moved into two rooms in the stable block, and from time to time my husband came to join us. A voluntary secretary from Wombwell sat at a portable typewriter sending out letters of thanks to supporters and new friends in the area.

Word went round the neighbouring villages and towns that help was needed at Hickleton Hall, and within days the rooms were filled with well over a hundred people offering their services, a few of them even accompanied by their young children, who provided added distractions. A good many stated that they could decorate, but many were inexperienced. Knowing that the renovations and decorations should be done to a high standard and for the long term, it called for a fair amount of tact to explain to inexperienced but enthusiastic volunteers that the colour scheme for each room, which was typed out and pinned up on the wall (with a copy kept in the office) must be adhered to, and that paint-brushes must always be cleaned after use and then left to stand in turpentine. In some rooms plastering and painting proceeded to the accompaniment of transistor radios blaring out at top volume. Hadfields a paint firm in Surrey supplied the paint at well below trade price, and other firms were equally generous.

There was no hot water in the Hall and the boiler was out of action—as were many of the loos. Throughout the house water had to be heated in kettles, but in the stable block there was a small water heater, and cooking was done on a primus stove. The only furniture in the house—a table—stood in the middle of the large library but offers of furniture came from far and wide, much of it in very good condition, and including some antiques as well as 30 harmoniums and 75 double beds!

Dr. Ken Jackson was the first Chairman of this Home's Committee. Both he and his wife, together with Mr. Tom Siddall, the Honorary Treasurer, were to give many years of long and devoted service: they appeared unexpectedly one day in the temporary office in the stable block and offered their assistance. Dr. Jackson described it as a home which might never have started—"and, indeed, it never would have", he adds, "without the unshakable faith of those concerned." Then a local supporter came to talk to me, presenting a donation of five pounds, and asked what the priorities were. When I answered, "A builder", she returned within an hour with a local decorator from Doncaster who, greatly to his astonishment, found himself taking off quantities of paint (i.e. measuring the quantity against the area to be covered). For the next six weeks he was at the house virtually every evening and all weekend, helping to co-ordinate and supervise the large army of enthusiastic volunteers.

Just as in Poland the rebuilding of churches and cathedrals was considered to be a priority, so here at Hickleton I felt that the Chapel should be restored as soon as possible. The Honorary Treasurer may have looked a little surprised when he was asked to buy on credit a red carpet to cover its bare concrete floor, but he ordered it nevertheless. Two men from the Pontefract Undertakers Co-operative came forward to renovate the panelling and decorate the very high walls. The cross and candlesticks for the altar I found at a bargain price; by coincidence they had been used in a film about a Japanese prisoner of war camp. Near the door of the Chapel a text was discovered: "In the beginning was the Word and the Word was with God and the Word was God. All things were made by Him."

The kindness and willingness of the local people was overwhelming, perhaps encouraged by the knowledge that I had been born in the county. Some offered lorries to bring the furniture to the house, while miners from Thurnscoe and Goldthorpe came straight off their shift to work at Hickleton. There was a great sense of unity and friendship, and many sang as they worked. I was reminded of my childhood in Yorkshire by the perpetual coal-dust and memories of Scarcroft and of the West Riding came flooding back to me.

The drawing-room and Lord Halifax's study were converted into bedrooms, while the dining room was renovated and decorated by British Ropes Company. The lovely cornice and moulded ceilings were decorated in white (as in the other rooms) and the walls were painted in Wedgwood blue. Within the six-week target we had set, the house was ready for the first residents, with most of its 70 rooms renovated and decorated.

142

Loading 'Elijah' prior to the journeys.

'Joshua' in Poland and Czechoslovakia.

A typical team of tradesmen with Sue Ryder.

Dr. Kowalczewska with the younger girls at Konstancin, Poland.

Barbara talking with Sue Ryder at Radzymin, Poland.

A corner of the Workshop at Konstancin, Poland.

Today Hickleton Hall provides accommodation for between 50 and 60 residents, and includes a few flats for married couples and others who can cook for themselves; and more are independent: if their dependence decreases, they are cared for. The idea is that those who live there should enjoy both independence and care, or, in the case of the more severely disabled, dependence without loss of dignity.

The Home is autonomous, and has been run faithfully over the years by a local House Committee who are responsible to the Foundation's Council. Members do not consider themselves merely as a management committee, but take part in the day-to-day running of the Home by giving services voluntarily and by sharing all problems with the staff.

Molly Trim, the Housemother, calls it a community: "We set out to live a shared life," she said, "and with some it was to be a very deep sharing indeed." A New Zealander and formerly a novice in a religious order, she has served the Foundation since April 1962. Talking of the patients, she said she could never fully realise their suffering. "I aimed at giving them warmth and good food and at getting to know them. It was sometimes a humbling encounter. They always know you better than you know them because they realise how life works. They have seen life in the raw, experienced terrible pain and they also know what makes people react and tick."

Miss Trim had already learned about community living from missionary work among the Maoris. "They understood the individual," she says of them. "They had an outgoing joyfulness and ease. Some had time for everything. If they wanted to learn from someone, they shared his life with him, talking to him and gradually getting to know him. It was an exchange of personalities, an exchange of the essence that lies at the heart of people. The individuals here, like the Maoris, couldn't be bothered with superficial relationships."

But, as with people in all situations in life, they were very different in temperament: while some showed great patience and tolerance, others were far from saintly.

Some had lived close to death in hospitals, and the experience had not enriched them. Some were embittered, some distorted, some broken down. For many independence was not a goal but a threat to be avoided at all costs. Each and every one of the individuals, the physically handicapped as well as those with psychiatric disturbances, received the affection and care they deserved.

After so many years the people have begun to settle down and to carve out for themselves some kind of acceptable pattern. Of the original patients over 30 have died, but there is never an empty bed.

Sister Elizabeth from Dublin worked at Hickleton for eight years. Later the nurses were joined by Win and Linda, who are young and say they have learned more there than anywhere else. They realise that this is different from hospital work. "The patients aren't like ordinary people. Sometimes you get annoyed when they're difficult—but then you thank God that you can work."

Local cooks, Mrs. Dawes and Gladys Chambers, come in to prepare lunch, and patients and staff eat together in the dining room. The resident staff are supported by a large number of local staff who live in the neighbourhood, for voluntary help is encouraged too and the unaffected cheerfulness of these helpers and the contact they provide with the surrounding towns and villages are a vital element in making the patients feel part of the local community.

In each room I enter when I visit, there is news. People tell me their hopes and fears; I hear about their diet, their illness, their concern at being incontinent, and memories of their homes.

S.P. has severe multiple sclerosis: he prays a lot and he is always interested in news brought by visitors.

H.C. lies on a spinal carriage: she has Potts disease (T.B. of the spine) and disabled hands, but in the privacy of her room, she does lovely embroidery.

In another part of the house Irena and Eugen have a self-contained flat. He is the handyman and works as a member of the staff. He was only 15 when he was sent to Auschwitz, and both were liberated from Bergen Belsen, but they are the only Survivors at Hickleton. "Here it is a different life", Eugen says. "I have a car and a garage, and when I have my days off I can do what I want. I am at home here, and when I go to the pub for a pint of beer, people come and sit down and talk to me. They ask me how I am. When my wife goes out she likes being called 'Luv'."

As is generally acknowledged, there are still gaps in the service for the handicapped and those who, for a variety of reasons, cannot care for themselves.

But even if the state were in a position to do much more than is the case at present, there would always be a need for private initiative to complement the official services. There are at the moment many thousands of children and adults in Britain in need of care and, when possible, rehabilitation; and for an organisation to be effective it is necessary that it establishes priorities. The Foundation sees as its main task in Britain the care of cancer patients and the mentally handicapped, although not to the exclusion of other physically handicapped people.

In response to the requests made of it, and in order to supplement local authorities in attempting to cope with the existing needs, the Foundation has always wanted and striven to provide more Homes. The searches throughout Britain for property and sites have, over the years, brought many disappointments, but we are ever hopeful of founding more and reaching greater numbers of those who are waiting.

CHAPTER 13

Stagenhoe

During the time that I was doing relief work on the Continent, I was deeply impressed by the sufferings I witnessed and moved by the conditions in which the sufferers were forced to exist, the lack of privacy, general over-crowding and bad living conditions, all worsened by the severe winters. Many seemed too to face extraordinary personal tragedies and sickness. I remember a typical example, a woman who for years had shared a room in a large block, separated from the others only by a blanket—her husband used to help me with my correspondence and typing. She was sitting on the lower part of their bunk bed cutting one of her few dresses into shreds and saying, "I can't take any more. The noise and the misery around me and all this has forced me to do it." As I witnessed scenes like this I felt increasingly the wish to give these individuals a change of environment, even if only temporary, and a holiday, which the majority of them never enjoyed.

With the help of friends in Denmark the Holiday Scheme was created in 1952 for the sick and the survivors of the concentration camps. The Danes were very generous with their hospitality and invited their guests to stay in their own homes for periods of up to three months while they relaxed. Although Denmark may appear on the map to be a small country, it seemed quite a large area when I helped to deliver and collect both the survivors and the sick.

The sight of large tureens of delicious soup, real coffee, butter spread liberally on rolls and varieties of bread, and fresh ham and bacon was unforgettable after the frugal life to which we had grown accustomed.

The Danish Holiday Scheme was a short-term arrangement, but those involved felt it should be continued, though possibly in a slightly different form. Because of the distances involved and the language problems, it seemed

146

preferable for the visitors to stay together as a group, not with individual hosts, as had been the case in Denmark, and moreover it appeared a good idea for them to spend their holidays in a country which had been spared occupation by the Nazis and had thus remained largely unscarred.

While the Home for permanent residents was being established at Cavendish, I was therefore also looking for a suitable large house in England which could be used as a Holiday Home. This was not to prove as easy as I had hoped, partly because properties were becoming increasingly difficult to find and expensive, but also because of the type of house for which I was looking. The purpose of the Holiday Scheme was to offer the Survivors the chance to forget—even if only briefly, for a minimum of three to four weeks—something of what they had endured, and to try to compensate to some extent for what they had missed—to give them the opportunity to stroll through peaceful villages and meadows, visiting art collections, enjoying outings, and above all living in surroundings which would be conducive to happiness and peace of mind. Consequently it was not just four walls and a roof that were needed, but a house that by virtue of its architecture and atmosphere would provide the right setting.

At that time many period houses and historic properties were lying vacant in different parts of the country, and the Historic Buildings Council were in a number of cases making efforts to find purchasers who would renovate and preserve them, but it is a sad fact of this post-war period that so many such houses have been lost to the Nation for one reason or another. It is always easier for man to destroy than to create. Although I found at least two period houses within reasonable reach of Cavendish which, though in a state of dilapidation, would have proved suitable, I was not able to acquire them.

At this point my mother and her acquaintances came to the rescue by obtaining for me the lease of the empty wing of a large period house in Long Melford. The lease was only temporary and a great deal of hard work was needed to make the wing habitable, but once this had been done it served as a Centre for Holiday Groups for eleven

147

happy years, and over 1,000 Bods stayed there. The visitors came mainly from Poland, as it is in Poland that most of the survivors of concentration camps are alive today.

Mama especially realised how much details, though possibly unimportant in themselves, can contribute towards the general effect of a welcome. She would for example line the drawers of the rooms with white paper and find gay velvet coat-hangers, and we made sure that the Bods had matching towels, bedspreads, and flowers in their rooms. Friends would also do lovely flower arrangements in different parts of the Home, while Dr. Grace Griffiths and members of TOC H made sandwiches for the outings and the return journey, and others would invite the visitors into their own homes for a few hours or for a meal.

Fatigue and their own disabilities did not prevent the Bods taking a very deep interest indeed in each day's programme. Diaries were often kept, and it is moving to read years later, of the different activities, people and places which afforded so much pleasure. The joy they took in small things which for them were part of a once-in-a-lifetime visit made those of us around them feel humble as we ourselves were inclined to takes these same things so much for granted as part of the English scene. In particular they found visits to Cambridge, with the Colleges and the Backs, Oxford, London, Norwich, Windsor and Runnymede moving and enthralling. Other groups had the opportunity of visiting Devonshire, Cornwall, Manchester and Gateshead and thus deep and lasting friendships were forged between the two countries. These visits helped them to forget, temporarily at least, their own terrible experiences and sufferings, but unhappily their memories were long, and it was not unusual to hear somebody walking up and down during the night or in the early hours of the morning, unable to sleep, or to hear them cry out aloud in their dreams.

Birthdays and name days were always remembered on the last evening, when the helpers served supper by candlelight, and presents were exchanged.

Before the Lease of this Home expired, over 90 agents had provided the Foundation with details of other properties, and some 60 were inspected, most of them in various stages of disintegration, but for one reason or another none was suitable, usually because they were too small. One house, the former home of the poet Julian Grenfell, was discovered only as the demolition men moved in. By the time the lease of the Suffolk house expired, no alternative property had been found, and there followed some anxious months of searching more and more urgently. Amongst those who helped to carry out surveys, was John Adams, the Foundation's Honorary Architect for 17 years—a man who shared our sense of humour and who made up practical jokes on the spur of the moment.

Then at last, more by chance than anything else, I discovered Stagenhoe, a house with 33 bedrooms and nine acres of garden situated a few miles outside the town of Hitchin in Hertfordshire. It was almost a dream house, and though the purchase price was far beyond anything that the Foundation had ever contemplated, I felt that we must somehow try to aquire it.

The history of the estate surrounding Stagenhoe can be traced back to the Domesday Book. The original mediaeval house was burnt down in the eighteenth century, and the existing Georgian house built on the site in 1740. Improvements were made by the various families who owned it, and a third storey was added in 1879; Sir Arthur Sullivan rented it in 1885 while working on *The Mikado* and *The Golden Legend*. During the Second World War the house was used as a maternity home for evacuees from London, some 2,000 babies being born there, and after the War it was for many years a boys' preparatory school, but when the Foundation finally bought it in August 1969, it had been standing empty for over a year and was sadly neglected.

The house is extremely beautiful: a central hall gives access to drawing rooms, a library and a morning room, all with sash windows overlooking the terrace, lawns and fields on the west side, which sweep down to where there was formerly an artificial lake. A wide staircase leads to the upper storeys. All the rooms have large windows looking out over rolling fields of wheat and barley and the wooded hills surrounding the property. Behind the house are the remains of the stables and a series of walled gardens and orchards leading past the hothouses to the Dower House: in the days when ten gardeners were employed there, it must have been a lovely sight. It was in this beautiful garden that Her Majesty, Queen Elizabeth the Queen Mother, played as a child with the Bailey Hawkins. They especially enjoyed cricket on August Bank Holidays, with the return match at The Bury—the Bowes-Lyon's house.

Because of the delay in completing the purchase of the property, we were left with very little time in which to get the house ready for its first occupants. These were the 45 members of a group whose holiday would have had to be cancelled but for the generosity of the Rotary Club of Weybridge, Surrey, who on hearing of the situation offered them hospitality and accommodation. This was only for a limited period, however, and in order to make the long journey from Warsaw and back worthwhile, it was essential to have Stagenhoe ready by the end of their stay in Weybridge, which meant that we had only ten days in which to prepare for their arrival.

In a way it all seemed something like a repetition of Hickleton, except that the damage to the house was not as great, and the fact that it was August made it easier to live rough. But against this it was the holiday season, and though there had been press reports about the acquisition of the Home and the work involved in getting it ready, not many callers came from the district. Happily we had at that time three or four young volunteers from Yugoslavia and Czechoslovakia, as well as two Polish survivors of Auschwitz and Ravensbrück who had come to assist. This small team was augmented by two English teachers, one of them the Housemother Dorothy Rodick Smith, and a former member of the French Resistance now living in this country, and immediately began work according to a schedule which had been drawn up in advance. Many of the loos did not function, parts of the electrical wiring were in an unusable condition, and the kitchen was out of action, so that the cooking had to be done on two calor gas rings set up in the dining room. The team included tradesmen who went up on to the roof to clean all the chimneys and a carpenter who moved systematically through the house repairing sashcords and doors. For a time it was thought that no plumber would be forthcoming, but finally he arrived—at eleven o'clock one night.

In the first hours of work at the house everyone was absorbed in the general activity, and it was some time before we realised with full force that Stagenhoe lies in the flight path of Luton Airport and the package-tour season was in full swing. At times the volunteers had to shout to make themselves heard. Until the office was established on the quieter side of the house it proved somewhat difficult to make oneself heard properly on the telephone, especially when urgent calls from the Foundation's tradesmen came in from places like Prague and Warsaw and one had to discuss technical problems with them. Then I had to turn my attention to sorting out another crisis which cropped up when we learned that the shipping company and the docks had refused to accept five lorry loads of building materials required for the Foundation's Homes abroad; but in spite of this it was for me personally a happy time, even if occasionally a little hectic—partly because of the humour and spirit in which the volunteers worked, and partly because one could see the results of one's labours. A well-wisher offered some very old rugs and carpets, but these were in a somewhat shocking state and had to be hung from trees (as the grass was so long on the lawns) and beaten before being cleaned and shampood.

At one point I composed in a few moments the following letter purportedly from me to Lord Throgmorton:—

"Thank you very much for your most welcome donation and encouraging letter about Stagenhoe. I am glad you have heard of our progress there and I am quite overwhelmed by the offer of your own house at Throgmorton. It seems to be in a lovely position by the sea and your gift of such a valuable property is indeed generous. May I ask whether you would permit our Honorary Architect and Surveyor to look around?

You mention that the roof has bad patches and that the problem of erosion on the north elevation will necessitate a full survey.

At present our hands are rather full with different aspects of this work, including the new, as well as the old Homes. Throgmorton would certainly be more than large enough. It was considerate of you to tell me the number of bedrooms etc., and if only 37 out of 54 were in use during the past ten years, then I can believe we will face a lot of renovation. The question of wiring and installing the plumbing system to the house must, of course, be thought over very carefully. We are always short of electricians and plumbers.

The patients and staff enjoy the seaside when given the opportunity of being nearby, and I am sure we will all appreciate your kindness and generosity."

On a scribbled note from John Adams there were two words .... 'Oh no!'

But there came a further letter from the non-existent Lady Throgmorton:—

"Dear Miss Ryder,

You will have heard by now from my husband about our dream house at Throgmorton. Oh, how my heart aches for it and you, for it is so vast and so precious. Can you use it?

Amongst many things I must mention immediately are the underground cellars which lead to the cliff's edge and have a fascinating haunted story, but I will tell you about it in greater detail when you come over. Meanwhile, I expect you will be sending your loyal architects and surveyors. I know my husband expects them, and I *think* if they tell him of your desperate needs that he will offer one or even two of our small Reynolds. So you must explain to your architects and surveyors that they must admire the paintings and particularly the ones of the Deer and of Rosemary, Duchess of Duckford (she was fifth cousin to Dickie, whom you may remember).

Forgive me for disturbing you like this—until our next meeting.

Very sincerely,
Emy Throgmorton."

152

John Adams checked in Debrett's Peerage, and found no Lady Throgmorton, and when he failed to locate the area in the A.A. and R.A.C. book he rang us. He took it very well indeed.

One morning at breakfast, Pete, the Chippy (carpenter) and others asked me why the Foundation could not form its own Removal and Renovation Team for service to the public? We refrained from carrying out this idea.

Each day seemed to bring something unexpected. News that the Foundation had purchased Stagenhoe brought an influx of commercial travellers to the door, and seeing the size and the potential elegance of the house obviously made them believe that we were a wealthy organisation. The quotations they offered for various jobs matched up to this supposed wealth: the cooker could, for example, be repaired for £600, and the lift restored if £1,500 could be raised. At the announcement one day that "another man has arrived to see you" I assumed that it would once more be a commercial traveller and was somewhat taken aback to find myself greeting a man dressed in black shirt and shorts. He introduced himself as Father O'Leary, a Catholic priest from a nearby parish, and he wondered whether he and his group of Venture Scouts could be of any assistance. They certainly could! They proved as good as their word. Father O'Leary returned immediately with his young Scouts and nine lawnmowers and attacked the neglected lawns surrounding the house.

The final problem was the furniture. Local wellwishers donated a refrigerator and a sewing machine, a policeman brought a bath he had discovered on a rubbish heap, and the Foundation's Support Group in Hatfield contributed the outsize saucepans that were needed. Personal friends offered a large quantity of furniture that they had collected especially from sales, and stored in two barns. However, one of these had been flooded and the other proved to be the home of a number of birds, so that the state of some of the furniture left much to be desired, in addition to which the furniture movers had forgotten to bring the ends and springs of the 60-odd beds. To save additional expense a farmer offered to fetch the missing items with

153

one of his corn lorries, but with an unusually early harvest this was not immediately available, and on the very last day, with everything that they had to do, the volunteers were faced with the task of matching up over 60 sets of bed-ends with the springs and then finding mattresses to fit the resulting frameworks. We managed to meet the deadline, however, and had 24 hours to spare. Then, 15 minutes before the bus from Weybridge drew up before the front door, a local friend arrived with a small domestic calor gas cooker, just sufficient, with the existing two rings, to keep the temporary kitchen going until the main one had been fully renovated and the proper stove installed.

Since the first group arrived at Stagenhoe up to the time of writing, 1,483 Bods and others have benefited from a stay there. Individuals wishing to come apply through social workers, physicians or their own Survivors' associations. Each is interviewed, and from the resulting list of recommendations—on which there are 4,000 names—a choice has to be made. The small committees in the different cities and towns of Poland find it extremely difficult to be fair. The criterion by which they decide is not strictly defined, but broadly speaking priority is given to those whose part in the Resistance was particularly notable or who suffered the most, whether in concentration or extermination camps, in solitary confinement or in the ghettos, due attention also being given to their present circumstances and state of health. Priority is also given to young handicapped people, and those who have suffered in some special way.

The organisation of the Holiday Scheme is in the hands of voluntary caseworkers, many of them are women physicians who themselves spent years in different prisons and camps, and read medicine, often as a direct result of their experiences.

Pani Zofia, who has already been mentioned in a previous chapter is the principal (unpaid) organiser, with her daughter Hania. Together with their colleagues they work very hard during weekends and evenings both in Poland

and in Britain, travelling on public transport to visit those on the pending lists and assisting in all possible ways to enable six or seven groups, consisting of 34 to 40 individuals, to come over each year, the only limiting factor here being the availability of funds.

The groups travel by railway, receiving a special reduction in price because their number is over 25. The German Red Cross board the train twice and provide them with refreshments during their journey through Germany, and when the group reaches Brugges, the Foundation's Supporters in Belgium are responsible for welcoming them and showing them round. At Zeebrugge they embark on the car ferry for Dover, where they are met by the Foundation's bus. The Emigration and Customs Authorities are informed beforehand to avoid delays, but for many the journey itself proves extremely exhausting, and often a doctor or priest accompanies the group. By the time they reach the Home in the early hours of the morning tiredness is very apparent.

For the members of the groups the visit to this country proves an unforgettable experience. They find it hard to take leave, and we who have witnessed their warmth and affection are moved too by the poignancy of the leave taking especially as they often sing. Each group is quite different, and as the group leader says a few words which express the feelings of his or her group, we realise each time the spirit they express, exemplified by their courage, dignity, and humour. Their gaiety and laughter have often filled the house, yet the experiences of each one of these Bods would not only reveal unlimited depths of human suffering but untold heights of selflessness and love. The gracious Georgian house with its reminders of past wealth and privilege provides an unexpected background for these people who have experienced such incredible hardship and suffering.

On their return to their country they not only give talks on their visit, but also write most moving letters to say how much the experience meant to them. Perhaps one young girl may be allowed to speak for all those who have been enabled to visit Britain in this way. "My dear Mamusia,"

155

she wrote from Poland, addressing me affectionately as "Mother":

> Thank you very much indeed for the vacation. I will remember it till the end of my days. I did not know your country except from books and from what my father has told me. The English were so hospitable and honest and seemed to love us. I admired the neat little houses and gardens and the beautiful fields of barley. Your country has not been invaded for a thousand years. We listened to Benjamin Britten, we visited the British Museum and the National Gallery where for the first time I saw original works by Raphael, Leonardo de Vinci and Michelangelo. To us the 25 years since the Occupation have proved a great and wonderful challenge. We have raised entire cities from ruins, we have educated the present generations, and now a few of us have had the chance to forget the pressures of life and therefore really to enjoy a holiday. The visit was like entering a fairy tale. I will not forget to pray for you.

It is our intention that in the future the Holiday Scheme should continue to be international, and include those who are housebound and have never had the chance to travel or to see the places they have dreamt about. Relaxation in new and beautiful surroundings should not be confined to the able-bodied and those who can afford them.

Apart from providing accommodation for holiday groups, the house at Stagenhoe has also acquired other functions, however. It is registered with the local authorities as offering Part 3 accommodation for 57 physically handicapped patients suffering from many various disabilities including Parkinson's disease, hemiplegia, muscular dystrophy, cerebella ataxia and mutliple sclerosis. At present there are some 20 British patients* staying there, in addition to which young disabled from all parts of Britain are taken in here to convalesce, or to give their families a much needed break from nursing them.

Stagenhoe has also acquired a new role as a conference

*From some hundreds in the past.

centre. Since 1972 the various conferences held there have included one for sixth formers from local schools, one for the Duke of Edinburgh's Gold Award Scheme, and a meeting of Anglican Bishops.

If funds can be raised for an extension, a new wing and a chapel will be built in the style of the original house, which will provide individual rooms for 40 more persons. We hope that this historic house will continue to be a home and a meeting place for people of all ages, nationalities and creeds, and give its residents not only stability but also a purpose in life.

CHAPTER 14

A Bag of Tools

At the time the Foundation was registered, a handful of colleagues served as a committee, but as it expanded a greater amount of organisation and co-ordination obviously became necessary.

At present the source of all authority for the Foundation is its Council, which meets quarterly in London, and consists of men and women drawn from different walks of life, including the legal, medical, business and teaching professions, each offering his or her own individual skill and experience in a voluntary capacity, working together for the good of the Foundation and having its aims deeply at heart. I find it hard to express my feelings but I cannot let this opportunity pass without paying tribute to Mr. H. Sporborg and Mr. J. Priest, Chairman and Deputy Chairman and all other members of the Council for the unfailing help and support they have offered me throughout the years. A great deal of the burden has been borne by them.

The expansion of the Foundation's work during the past twenty years has greatly increased the amount of organisation and administration required, but our policy has always been to keep administrative costs as low as is humanly possible, without thereby impairing the efficiency or effectiveness of what we do.

In spite of this, money is, of course, a constant problem, and like everyone else we have been greatly hit by inflation. Postal expenses for Headquarters alone amounted to £5,580 in 1973. At the time of writing a folding wheelchair, for instance, costs £29, a hoist £119, and aluminium crutches £3.85. The Holiday Scheme costs approximately £45,000 per year, and to build an average Home (if the site is given and the services and road are paid for) roughly the same amount is required. Local Authorities and Area Health Authorities pay the maintenance fees once the building,

158

renovation or conversion of a Home is completed, and these are used for the medical and nursing care of the residents as well as the care and education of the children, but they never completely cover the full costs, and the Foundation has to raise the rest. The exact sum involved varies from Home to Home, and no generalisation can be made.

At the beginning we did not know where and how funds could be raised. When one of the building companies with whom we were trading very kindly offered to take out a life assurance on me as a means of ensuring payment of their account in the event of something happening to me, I was, however, prompted to further deep thought about the question of fund raising.

Despite the great difficulties and uncertainties we have encountered, I have always believed that the funds required for the Foundation's work will somehow be forthcoming; but on the other hand I equally believe that we must ourselves make every effort to raise these funds. Incidentally, I really dislike the word "money" and I remember in particularly poignant surroundings a woman doctor in Poland telling me never to worry or wonder where it was coming from because it was God's money. During the past twenty years almost every form of fund-raising has been thought of and explored: sporting events, such as a race meeting or a football match between a British team and an equivalent team from the Continent; art exhibitions, fairs, concerts by choirs, musicians and dancers, shops and stalls; deeds of covenant and legacies; sales of Christmas Cards and the Foundation's annual magazine; flowers and flower festivals; coffee mornings and the sale of handicrafts.

Above all, however, we count on the individuals both here and overseas who from the start have faithfully sent their postal orders and small cheques, usually after saving up or making some real effort. Frequently when the Foundation has been without funds, especially at the beginning, it is these unseen people upon whom we have depended and whose letters and messages accompanying their gifts have meant so much. I quote only a few:

159

Dear Sue Ryder, Have just had a lovely holiday, so here is £5 as my thanks.

Dear Miss Ryder, I had a nice surprise this morning when I received a cheque for £25 from my Premium Bond. I thought you should share in the money and am enclosing a cheque for £3.

And from a little boy:

Dear sue Ryder I have heard about your story and your Adventure it is very exciting and I like it and I have herd about you saving peopl's live's and saving peopl in the war that get shot and badly hert and I know lot's of poor peopl and I hope that they are being looked after and I want a book and that is what the 5p stamp is for. Love. Stephen,

There are other donors, too, whom I have been privileged to meet personally. I remember vividly an elderly disabled woman sitting in her wheelchair in a small and dreary room in London. During the course of my visit she said: "There is so little I can do, but I know a bit what it is like to suffer. Please accept these crumpled notes which I have saved. I give them to you for the work with my love. I don't want thanks, it means everything for me to do this."

Of the various ways in which the Foundation tries to raise funds, only a few can be described in greater detail. I have chosen to give here descriptions of the Appeals, the concert tours, auctions and the Shops.

Through the courtesy of the BBC I have been allowed to make two appeals on behalf of the Foundation—one by radio in 1963, which brought a response of 14,000 letters and over £18,000 in donations, and the second by television in 1966. Writing in her diary about the first of these appeals Mama said: "When Sue was asked what target had been in her mind before the week's good cause she said 'I don't think I've got one, but *hope* for a miracle', and the miracle happened."

The T.V. appeal itself proved to be exceedingly hard work; what I wanted to say had to be condensed into 3 minutes 36 seconds, and we had to cope with the technical difficulties which arose in the shooting of the film.

After the appeal every member of the staff at Head-quarters, Cavendish, and all the Bods who could help, volunteered to work in the Appeal Office, where the tables were cleared and adding and numbering machines brought in. The first mail brought sacks of letters, but little did we know that this was to go on for seven or eight weeks non-stop, and though we had hoped and prepared for a large response, we had never expected such vast numbers of letters. As a result we had to appeal to the Carmelite Sisters (who were responsible for our printing) and stationers in the area for further supplies.

Assembly lines were established, one being made responsible for slitting the envelopes and passing them on to the second for opening and writing up in the card index, after which they were passed on to the then Appeals Secretary, Joy Griffith Jones, and myself for reading, marking and separating into different categories. Anthony Green, whom we called *Green's Bank*, totalled on a machine after each letter and card had been numbered, and the donations were made up into bundles of twenty for the Bank. They in turn had to bring in extra trestle tables and staff from other branches, who worked in their cellars writing hundreds of receipts. One of the highlights of these days was when my mother came to the office window from the Store with a small paper parcel bearing no name and address, which was found to contain £460 in pound notes!

During the weeks following the Appeal, work went on until past ten or eleven at night, when everything would be carefully packed into boxes, which were then labelled and carried upstairs to our bedroom for safety, where they remained for the night. Next morning the cycle would begin again, with three-hourly announcements by Green's Bank giving the latest news of the grand total, which added to the excitement. The automatic typewriter *Freddie*, a gift from the Friden Typewriter Company, was in operation for more than fifteen hours a day, and added its clatter to the atmosphere.

Before the actual Appeal I had signed 40,000 letters, and afterwards each of the 18,000 donors had a letter of acknowledgment, which was also signed personally. A total of £43,000 was most gratefully received by these means.

The concerts and concert tours arranged by the Foundation have in their own smaller way been no less successful. In 1966 Benjamin Britten and Peter Pears gave a fine and memorable concert in aid of the Foundation at Blickling Hall in Norfolk, and in the following year a group of professional musicians from Poland offered to make a concert tour of the British Isles as their contribution in aid of the Foundation, performing works by Chopin, Puccini, Donizetti, Wieniawski, Verdi, and other composers. All gave their services free and waived their annual holidays in order to make this tour.

A concert tour was a new venture for us, far more ambitious than anything hitherto attempted, which involved finding suitable concert venues up and down the country and forming a committee in each place to organise publicity, sell tickets and arrange hospitality for the artistes and those accompanying them. Most of this work fell upon a small team, including Douglas Rapkin my Appeals Secretary, who worked tirelessly planning and making preparations for the tour.

As far as possible, the concerts were arranged geographically in order to keep mileage to a minimum, but this, of course, depended on the availability of suitable premises. Cathedrals, churches, theatres, public halls, schools and a number of private houses were chosen as locations, some of which were offered free by their owners or curators, and in every instance hospitality was provided privately or by the courtesy of a hotel manager. The warmth of the welcome offered by these hosts and hostesses was to prove a source of great comfort and encouragement to the group during an extremely strenuous tour (on an average three to four thousand miles are covered), and, moreover, it left them with many happy memories of their first visit to Britain. This personal contact not only gave rise to a number of friendships which have lasted ever since: the artistes were also ambassadors presenting their country to the Foundation. Many of them spoke either English or French, so language was not too much of a problem, and in fact sometimes caused a great deal of amusement!

At a few of the places arrangements had been made for the whole party to stay in the same building, and these occasions were great opportunities for practical jokes. A tour such as this is very arduous, with its constant packing and unpacking, long drives and continually changing circumstances, and fun and laughter are essential as a means of relaxation. At one convent, for example, two of the artistes decided after the concert to change the name tags on the rooms occupied by the rest of the party. I retaliated by inventing at the last minute a new concert for the next day—which, needless to say, did not perturb the artistes in the least, but at times on the tour their tiredness was obvious and they were always concerned with rehearsing and practising.

In 1969 three more professional musicians volunteered their services, one of whom was the brilliant young violinist Konstanty Kulka. Reviewing a performance in London, the music critic of the *Daily Telegraph* wrote that the "virtuosity and brilliance of tone" displayed by this artiste "were in themselves enough to make this one of the notable events here in Wigmore Hall for a long time."

The results of the original tour by the concert group were so heartening that a second tour was arranged, which took place in 1969 as well, and a third concert group visited England in 1972, also giving performances in Bruges and Waterloo.

The 1969 tour began at Chelmsford, going as far west as Cardiff and Cornwall and as far north as Aberdeen and Banff, so that it can almost be said to have covered the length and breadth of Britain. One of the Foundation's patrons, Sir Arthur Bliss, Master of the Queen's Musick wrote a foreword to the programme and Benjamin Britten, another of our Patrons, sent a long greetings telegram conveying his warmest wishes. H.R.H. Princess Anne had graciously agreed to attend the final concert at the Queen Elizabeth Hall in London. At the last moment she was prevented from coming by the death of her grandmother, Princess Andrew of Greece, but when she learned of the disappointment which this had caused, she gave the group the honour of receiving us in a private room at Buckingham Palace. As a schoolgirl at Benenden she had helped to carry in the luggage and sell programmes when the group performed there during the first concert tour.

In more ways than anyone could ever have anticipated the tours have proved both memorable and successful.

Financially they raised some £10,000 for the Foundation in all, but perhaps more important still, the large and varied number of people they reached, with the attendant publicity in the press and on radio and television, did much to make the work of the Foundation known to those who hitherto had been unaware of its existence.

In the first place the success of the tours is of course due to the artistes themselves and the organising committees, but special mention must be made of Sir George Clutton, who was one of the Foundation's staunch supporters. Before his retirement from the Diplomatic Service he had been British Ambassador to the Phillippines and Poland. Sir George travelled with us as Cultural Adviser and Road Manager, sharing the difficult conditions under which the artistes lived and worked, and remaining cheerful in his manner and meticulous in his work despite all difficulties. He died in 1971 of a coronary thrombosis, and is greatly missed.

The artistes had two programmes for the concerts, one for concert halls and the other for churches and cathedrals, but the last item was invariably one verse and the refrain of Dygar's *Dobranoc* ("Good Night"). For this Sir George would call us on to the stage individually by name, both the artistes and myself, and we would all sing it together.

"We drove home through the snow singing and feeling the better for having heard the artistes and bearing witness to their gaiety and courage," reads one of the many tributes received from friends and strangers after these concert tours, while another runs: "It was an occasion not to be forgotten because of their grace and dignity."

Others expressed their feelings spontaneously in speeches made after the performance, of which the following is an extract:

I would thank the artistes not only for the pleasure they have given us tonight and for the work that they are doing for the Foundation—which exists for the relief of suffering, of which they know more than most—but particularly I would thank them for being a living proof that evil and cruelty not only failed to destroy their courage but failed also to destroy their love of beauty.

To the parents of the younger members of the cast, I would express our gratitude that they have handed on to their children not bitterness and hate as they might have done, but a love of beauty, a joy in living and a desire to serve others.

It would be very difficult to single out any individual artiste for special mention; but audiences everywhere were particularly moved by Maria Bielicka's rendering of Schubert's *Ave Maria*, the song she had sung to the sick and the dying in the camps at Majdanek, Auschwitz and Ravensbrück. And there was a particularly moving concert as well when the group performed at Allington Castle on the evening of the Olympic tragedy at Munich, the Great Hall lit only by a log fire and six candles symbolising the Jewish faith.

I have many memories of these concert tours—of the unfailing cheerfulness and comradeship displayed by the artistes on all occasions, the great friendliness with which we were received everywhere, the unforgettable music, and—very especially—the lovely settings in which the concerts so often took place: the small theatres, with their fine acoustics and intimate atmosphere, the churches and the beautiful private homes—memorable was especially our first sight of Traquair House in Scotland, the lovely tenth century home appearing before us suddenly as the sun broke through the mist, while at Saltham House, near Plymouth, 150 candles illuminated the room in which the artistes performed. Perhaps one of these homes may be allowed to stand for all: Bramham Park, near Thorner in Yorkshire, where Mr. and Mrs. George Lane-Fox received the artistes in their beautiful Queen Anne house, and not only made all the necessary arrangements for the concert itself, but with their committee also prepared the most delicious buffet supper which was served to performers and audience.

The concert at Bramham took place under the crystal chandeliers of the Long Gallery at the back of the house, with its mirrors reflecting the light and family portraits by Hoppner, Lely and Kneller looking down upon the gathering. Outside the tall windows the rose garden and the lawns stretched out, fringed with old trees and yew hedges, and the beauty of the house, the sense of continuity and tradition, and the deep feeling of peace and tranquillity, provided a truly fitting setting for the music. Unhappiness and suffering seemed far away, and we who were privileged to experience that beauty and that peace could only pray that we might one day share it with all who are in such need of it in the world today.

Another strenuous tour of Britain and Belgium was subsequently undertaken by the Ivo Lola Ribar State Dancers from Yugoslavia, a group of forty-one performers the youngest of them only eleven years old accompanied by eighteen trunks of National costumes. From these beginnings the concerts and other similar functions have become a regular feature of the Foundation's fund-raising and cultural activities. It is hoped that further concert tours will be arranged, but in future we would prefer to remain in the same house for at least two nights at a time to radiate from that base and spare the artistes unnecessary fatigue.

For many years the Foundation held an annual Christmas Fair, which rotated among various East Anglian towns and usually ended in an auction. One year a professional auctioneer offered his services at Ipswich. He was young, very able and energetic and proceeded to arrange everything most efficiently. Several thousands of people were circulated with the news, and an advertisement placed in *The Times* headed "Moving House". A retired Army Colonel took charge of the operation as co-ordinator, and soon had been written to and rung up by countless individuals offering furniture of every style, type and size. In order to cut down the cost it was decided by the Committee that we should try and persuade carriers returning empty from jobs in different parts of Britain to collect the goods—but in some cases, having given prior warning, they reached the donor's house only to find that it was impossible to get the gift out of the cellar because of its size!

Several months before the event the auctioneer stood up in the drawing room at Cavendish and announced to the Committee that he wished to have Georgian silver and good antiques on his list and that everything offered should come within that category. We were rather taken aback, and did our best to explain to him that we were unlikely to receive antiques of such a kind!

In the last fortnight local barns were sought as store rooms and the front lawn at Headquarters was covered with every imaginable item which had been donated to us. One load even had to be sent back because the Auctioneer did not think it good enough, but it was sold in the shops. Very bad weather added to our problems. The auctioneer and his colleagues worked solidly from the Friday until the Tuesday once the assorted gifts had arrived, and over a thousand items were received, which had to be made up into lots and catalogued.

On the morning itself the hall in which the auction was to take place had been transformed. At the beginning bidding was slow, but it went on non-stop until the evening, when my mother was handed an account for over £20 because the auctioneer had taken the disapproving shaking of her head over the initial slowness as a bid, and had knocked down to her a box containing some very rusty forks and similar useless items! But the auction was a great success, and the Foundation made some £800 in all.

Auctions and fairs are, of course, occasional events. Full and part-time shops however, have with the years become very much part of the Foundation's way of life.

For a long time I had thought that market stalls and

shops could play a most useful role in raising funds, drawing attention to what we do and selling some of the things made especially to benefit the work of the Foundation. When the idea was first mentioned, the Committee and staff met it with mixed feelings, as we had no professional training or experience in running a shop; but within weeks an offer of premises on a main pedestrian thoroughfare in London came in and the rent was paid for. Danuta, one of my secretaries, was always willing to try her hand at anything that might be required of her, and as she had the gift of organising quickly and efficiently, she set upon what some might have considered a difficult task. The premises themselves were dilapidated and unattractive, but they were situated in a rather poor part of London, where the people, both adult and children, quickly discovered that they were able to turn to the shop and to the Foundation for assistance. After great efforts on the part of Danuta and other members of the Foundation, the takings in a good week had, within a month or two, reached £20.

In the early days the Shop had to be stocked from our store at Headquarters, and when I went to a meeting in London I always tried to stop there on the way with a load of clothing and bric-a-brac. The butcher next door had offered his support and said that, when necessary, the Manageress could call on him for help or use his telephone for local calls. On one occasion we were removing bundles and cartons of clothes from our van when the butcher appeared on the scene and said to my husband, "The last time we met, Sir, was on a Station in 1942. I didn't know you were in this trade too now, as well as Miss Ryder!"

It was not long before our second London shop opened, this time in Knightsbridge, in premises scheduled for demolition, but lent to the Foundation meanwhile for what turned out to be a period of two years. This shop and a former wine shop adjoining it (likewise lent rent free) were also in a dilapidated condition, but though the cellar was too damp for storage, some hard work by willing local helpers and boys from St. Joseph's School near

Peterborough soon had the rest of the premises cleaned, renovated and ready for business. The Foundation's name was painted on the fascia by a decorator who said that two of the letters were out of line because his hand trembled every time a double-decker bus thundered past where he was working on his ladder.

Within a month or two of our starting in London other Sue Ryder Shops—part-time or permanent—had opened up and down the country. At present there are about seventy in Britain alone, one near Brussels, and a thriving shop in Perth, Western Australia.

Of the Shops now operating in Britain the majority are run either on a completely voluntary basis or with Manageresses who are paid a small allowance. Every effort is made to see that the funds raised go directly to the people for whom they are intended. A large number of them sell donated goods, including bric-a-brac, books, pictures and clothing, bnt many also carry a large stock of gift articles, some of which are designed and made by the Bods in different Homes. The Shop in Launceston Place, W.8., is a gift shop, and in the Cotswold stone cottage which houses the Shop in Shaftesbury the helpers sell textiles and small antiques. All these Shops are well patronised by people looking for wedding, birthday or other gifts.

I try to visit the Shops at regular intervals: those in the main cities I visit once a year or every eighteen months, the others whenever I can manage it. If it can be arranged, a visit to a Shop will be followed by a meeting of the local Support Group to which the public are invited and during which the work of the Foundation in general and of the Shop in particular is discussed.

Each Sue Ryder Shop has its own history, its own collection of stories both funny and moving, and its own personalities among the customers—such as the men who come in to exchange their own worn-out shoes for a better pair without paying anything; and even, on occasion, to exchange their socks as well. There are other incidents one could mention too, like that of the enthusiastic Manageress who disposed of her husband's best suit, just back from the dry-cleaners, for a few pounds. There has been much weeping and laughter over the cleaning and tidying-up, the pricing, the selling and the window-dressing.

I do not think it would be possible to explain the amount of effort, time and devotion which has been given regularly and willingly by literally hundreds of people—probably thousands—all over the country. Usually they come from ordinary homes: housewives—young, elderly and middle-aged—who themselves have families to care for, young people and school children. At the Shops they have scrubbed floors, cleaned, cleared, sorted, priced and served, having walked from their homes or travelled there on buses, sometimes changing several times to reach their destination, in all weathers, throughout the year, year in, year out.

I remember the occasion when I received a telephone call from a "Mr. Snooks" who said that he thought his wife had decided the Shop took priority over their marriage! Trying to draw on my experience as a social worker, I suggested that perhaps the matter could be talked out by the husband and wife themselves, as I felt it would be unwise for me to come between them—especially as I had not been approached by the wife!

This was an isolated incident, for where there have been husbands or other men in the background, they have normally been most willing to lend a hand. It may have been a bore for them to have to lug things up and down stairs—and steep stairs at that—or to do other kinds of hard and demanding work, but somehow they have usually smiled at the end of it, if not at the start. We don't find that men always enjoy serving as shop assistants, but they usually play their part behind the scenes, and often take on the duties of the honorary solicitor, treasurer or chairman.

In addition to the work these Shops have done for the Foundation, both directly and indirectly, they have in practice also served a most valuable purpose in bringing people of all ages and from all walks of life together, promoting goodwill and acting as a tangible link within the community concerned. In particular the workers in the Shops have very often been able to give help and advice to those of their customers who are lonely or in some kind of trouble. The Foundation is most proud of this un-official but useful form of social work carried out by the Shops, and hopes that it will be continued and extended in the future, in addition to the other, more conventional forms of activity.

I tried to sum up our feelings about the Shops in the course of a talk that I once gave in an area where the Foundation's Shop has had to move to different premises no fewer than four times since 1964. "Being back here with you," I said, "one feels at home. We think of those who are not with us because of illness or because they have moved away from the area. In our thoughts also are our friends the customers, among them the old, the lonely, the sick, the young students, the pensioners, the man who uses us as his library, occasionally a young and frightened unmarried mum, or an unwanted child who looks for a toy, hand-made by one of you. We think too of those who have worked with us but who have gone now to a brighter and happier world.

"On behalf of those for whom we work—the disabled and the sick, wherever they are, whether in this country or further afield—we would like to thank you, your husbands and friends, and many others who lift and repair and collect, and to tell you how much we depend on the service which each of you is giving and has given for many years. Although you may not meet more than a few of our patients, they know that you have them in your prayers and thoughts and in your daily actions, and I hope that God will bless each of you in your lives and in whatever you do, and that our goodwill will increase and bring greater service in a wider area."

The foundations of the Living Memorial have been laid and the building operations have started—but they must continue to try and meet the desperate needs in the world. We hope to go on making our modest but ever increasing contribution to the universal task of relieving human suffering, assisted by the kindness and generosity of our supporters.

Isn't it strange that Princes and Kings
And clowns that caper in sawdust rings
And ordinary folk like you and me
Are builders of eternity?

To each is given a bag of tools,
An hour-glass and a book of rules,
And each must build, ere his time is flown
A stumbling block or a stepping stone.

CHAPTER 15

Poland—Ruins and Rebuilding

This colourful country, so often misunderstood, known to comparatively few and because of its geographical position subjected through its long history to attacks from its more powerful neighbours, is one with which I have been closely associated for over thirty years. With its tradition of folklore and strongly marked regional culture, Poland, thanks to the fierce spirit of independence of its people, has never lost its resilience and determination to resist, despite frequent invasions and several partitions, and has emerged as one of the most interesting countries in Europe. Between 1939 and 1945 it lost six million of its citizens, and a very high percentage of its wealth and physical assets. The central and North-West part of the country is a flat plain: the North-East has an undulating landscape dotted with many small lakes and in the South stretch the Carpathians and Tatra mountains range upon range for 818 miles.

Nothing impressed me more in Poland than the extraordinary devotion and skill with which the Poles have rebuilt their devastated cities, towns and villages. The initial work was done by people (including many of the young, with bare hands) who suffered from shortages and privations of every kind. Much of the labour was carried out by teams of volunteers, and everyone irrespective of age and status took part. The devastation was daunting in its immensity, but at the same time challenging in the opportunities it provided. In Warsaw alone some seven hundred and ten out of a total of eight hundred important historical buildings were reduced to rubble. They have been patiently and lovingly reconstructed in every detail, whether the style was Gothic, Renaissance, Baroque or Neo-Classical, including the sculptures, relief work, mural painting, fixtures and decorations. Fortunately complete sketches and inventories of every valuable

173

building were preserved in hiding or in foreign archives. In some cases an old church or palace was restored according to its original design with later accretions omitted so that the reconstructed Old City (Stare Miesto) now looks more like its original self as the nineteenth and twentieth century houses were not rebuilt. An up-to-date and most striking example of such reconstruction is the rebuilding in every detail of the Royal Castle, under the supervision of Professor S. Lorenz and his team.

To visit the Old City now is a most poignant experience. It is floodlit at night and only pedestrians and horse-drawn carriages are permitted so that one hears the clip-clop of hooves providing an old world atmosphere with young and old strolling through the squares and streets. This is in itself a contrast with the recent past.

Similar restoration has taken place in Gdańsk, Wroclaw, Bialystok, Poznań, Szczecin and other ruined cities with results of which the Poles are justly proud.

The other aspect of Poland which moved me profoundly is its strong religious life. Since 966, when it first received the Faith, Poland has been a deeply religious country, the Catholic Church with its tradition and teaching cementing and uplifting the people throughout those long centuries of oppression and struggle, and linking them to the millions of Catholics throughout the world. The hundreds of churches destroyed during the war have with great effort and sacrifice been rebuilt by the authorities and people, in most cases exactly as they were before their destruction, and today are always open and usually crowded with worshippers coming and going. In the larger ones, certainly all those in populated areas, as many as ten or even fourteen Masses are said or sung on a Sunday, with great crowds of people attending and thousands walking to church dressed in their best clothes, some in national costumes—the young girls looking very cheerful with bright bows or ribbons in their hair. On weekdays Mass is also well attended, and people on their way to work will call in for Holy Communion, or on their way back stop for Benediction—a custom that is still preserved in Poland; the scent of incense comes out into the street.

174

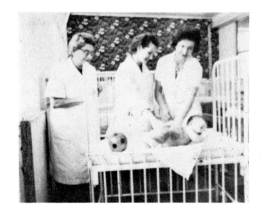

Sue Ryder working with
Dr. S. Dimitrijovic (a
paediatrician) and Dr. Olga
Milosevic (Medical
Adviser) in Yugoslavia.

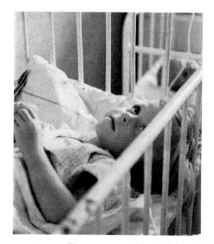

Two young patients dying of leukaemia, on the right with his mother.

Amongst the children at
the Little White House,
Dehra Dun, India.

Joy Griffith Jones and
Angela Wakeford with
Sue Ryder in the Appeals
Office.

Dispatching
Remembrance in the
Drawing Room at
Cavendish.

Sue Ryder receiving a
cheque from the boys
of Bryanston School,
Dorset.

From left to right are the
Revd. C. D. McWilliam,
Master of the School's
fund-raising efforts, the
Headmaster (Mr. F. G. R.
Fisher), Rob Weisberg
from U.S.A. and Richard
Quarshie from Ghana
(Head Boy).

Members of the
Campsmount Karate
Club presenting the
author with their cheque
following a sponsored run.

One cannot help being struck by the fervour and concentration with which people pray, and it is noticeable, too, how many young men and women there are in the congregations. On the main feast days, at Easter and Christmas, the churches are filled to overflowing so that it is usually impossible to enter unless one arrives early, and Communion is even distributed outside in the street or square, and the people always kneeling. Corpus Christi processions are held all over the country, from early in the morning, and in the months of May and October special devotion is paid to Our Lady, the many wayside shrines being decorated with flowers and ribbons: groups of people can be seen praying together or saying the rosary, even by torchlight as the daylight fades. Then at the end of May and beginning of June hundreds of small boys and girls, the former in dark suits, the latter in long white dresses and veils and with wreaths in their hair, walk through the villages and towns to receive their first Communion, each holding a candle. Pilgrimages are popular, particularly amongst the young people, including the children, and the shrine of the famous Black Madonna in Czestochowa has more annual visitors than Lourdes. Thousands of the pilgrims travel hundreds of miles on foot.

Although in the post-war years the church has been under surveillance—indeed Cardinal Wyszynski spent some years under house arrest—it would be unfair to overlook the help which the church has received in its rebuilding programme. Equally it would be very untrue and totally unfair to underestimate the amount of voluntary assistance and fervour which ordinary people have given to the rebuilding of churches.

Warsaw has a garrison church dedicated to Our Lady, and it is safe to say that Poland has more Party members who attend Mass and have their children baptised and married in church than any other Communist country. Although the state does not give religious instruction, children are allowed to be given it by priests. In this way Christianity is imbibed by the younger generation, and, as already mentioned, young people make up a large proportion of the congregations. It is indeed remarkable that despite the influx of many rural Poles into the new industrial centres, this important demographic and social change has not led to any falling off of church attendance. It would be unrealistic to ignore the grave shortage of churches in the new housing areas. Efforts are being made to try and build another thousand churches.

No-one can imagine how hard the Poles have had to struggle during the past thirty years: on the left bank of the city of Warsaw there was scarcely a single undamaged building. Warsaw especially suffered as did no other European capital. Heavily attacked by air in September 1939 it experienced two further tragedies in the course of the war. The first was the destruction by the Germans of the Warsaw Ghetto, the name given to the district inhabited by Jews whose numbers were monstrously swollen as Jews from other parts of Poland were crowded into its narrow confines. Every inhabitant of the Ghetto had been murdered or deported by the end of April 1943 in circumstances which defy all description. The second tragedy was the rising of August 1944. The S.S. repressed the resisters killing and maiming them in a way which was with unimaginable ferocity. Hitler's telegram to S.S. and Police General von dem Bach ordered that Warsaw should be razed to the ground. The total death role in Warsaw by 1945 was about eight hundred thousand, and when rebuilding began early in that year about a quarter of a million bodies were found under debris and in the sewers. Everywhere amongst the rubble were handwritten notices, some unbearably poignant. Two may stand for hundreds:

> "Am searching for my son Wladyslaw Grott who was one year five months old on 7th August 1944. In Chlodna Street a German took him away from his father and gave him to some unknown woman. The boy had fair hair, dark eyes. He was wearing two shirts, a blouse with blue and white stripes, and a dark blue sweater. Please inform Wladyslaw Grott, 51, Radzyminska Street, Apt. 9, Warsaw-Praga."
>
> "Will buy any book, in Polish or foreign language, fairy tales. Also shoe polish, shoe laces."

An estimated total of 85 to 90% of the city's buildings and services were destroyed: there was no water, no electricity, no telephone service and no transport. As the railways were not functioning there was no contact with the rest of the country. Men and women struggled to work in schools and hospitals with roofs open to the sky. Many of them walked miles to work day after day from homes that were beyond the suburbs.

The Nazis thought they had dealt Warsaw and indeed the whole country a mortal blow, but they reckoned without the spirit of the citizens: this they could never extinguish. Amidst the ruins of their beloved cities and towns the courage and determination of its people burned fiery bright. They had a passionate optimism, patriotism and lack of self-pity. No fewer than 35,000 mines of different kinds, 17,000 unexploded bombs and 41,000 shells had to be cleared by the sappers in Warsaw, in addition to 100,000 that were later discovered. The progress of the sappers could be followed by the appearance of the words "Checked—no mines" which were scribbled in the frost on the walls of demolished or gutted houses.

The standard appearance and size of the flats—especially the high rise—which have been built since 1947 throughout the country are usually criticised, but the outsider cannot easily realise the acute difficulties of attaining the right building material nor the pressures under which everyone continues to struggle. Landscaping and parks are a must and give privacy where it is sadly lacking.

During the course of my work, friends and acquaintances who themselves were architects and engineers invited me to attend their meetings and so I got first hand knowledge and saw for myself the huge problems they faced. I also remember the words "Warsaw Lives" scrawled in the dust on my van.

Fourteen miles out of Warsaw is Konstancin, a well-known health resort where, amongst the pine trees, two simple Homes built by the Foundation are scenes of much suffering, but also of a great deal of courage and hopeful activity. As one opens the door and senses the warmth of the atmosphere, there is a sound of voices, laughter, noises from the workshop and the room where lessons are in progress; feet trailing slowly along the corridor on crutches and wheelchairs being pushed. In winter the trees, loaded with snow, seem very silent and have a beauty of their own. In summer the smell of pines and of the grass in their natural surroundings gives a feeling of tranquillity and peace.

These Homes care for girls and young women suffering from rheumatoid arthritis and at present have 56 residents between the ages of ten and thirty-four. Three of these may serve to represent the many hundreds who have lived there or are there still.

Krystyna was sixteen when she came to Konstancin weeping with pain, her hands and feet being swollen with arthritis. She had been living with her parents in a damp dilapidated house isolated from the town and from physicians. During the six years of her stay, she underwent full medical treatment, including gold therapy, and in the meantime received training and worked as a clerk. Her state of health improved to such an extent that four years ago she got married, but she still visits the Homes regularly during the holidays with her husband and two fine children.

Maria became ill with rheumatoid arthritis when she was only ten years old. At the Institute for Rheumatic Diseases she received surgery on her hands and feet and had numerous blood transfusions; so far no great success has been achieved, still she loves living at Konstancin. She retains her keen sense of humour and works for three hours a day. For Maria, Konstancin is home indeed, as both her parents are now dead, and she has nowhere else to go.

Bolesia became ill when she was six and had been in fourteen different hospitals by the time she was admitted to Konstancin six years later. Owing to a very serious degree of decalcification, her bones were too brittle to bear her weight and she had to be supported by specially made straps. Before coming to the Homes Bolesia had been a lonely reticent and slightly retarded child with whom it was difficult to establish contact. In the friendliness and security of Konstancin, however, she blossomed out, she began to trust people, and developed immensely, both psychologically and mentally, becoming the soul of the Home. We nicknamed her *Sunshine*. She died at the age of sixteen, but during those last years of her life she reached a maturity which was very largely due to the conditions created for her and the other young disabled at the Foundation's Homes.

Up to the present there have been very few Homes which have not only looked after the physical well-being of their Residents, but have also tried to create for each individual the conditions in which they may learn to the best of their ability to live with their handicap. The possibility of reconstructing his or her personal life is most important to the patient and often more so than a physical cure. For many people who have been cured physically have found it impossible to adjust again to the realities of everyday life, and have suffered greatly from maladjustment and depression.

The average person who goes to Konstancin is struck by the normality and independence which is shown by the girls. For everyone is determined to lead as normal a life as possible and to do as much as they can for themselves, though several have had major surgery six or seven times and received implants. It is exceptional for anyone not to study and work, however disabled, or to be thought of as different in any way from an average person. In addition to their studies they also learn to carry out extremely delicate work, including the finest embroidery. Despite their disabilities and suffering the girls are usually cheerful.

While at the Home they also complete their studies, and many have gone on to qualify as dressmakers, teachers and accountants or to full courses at University; they read mathematics, economics, etc. Thus many of the girls are able to earn a small salary according to the number of hours which each is able to work in the Homes, while others leave after making a complete recovery. The minority who are chronically disabled may look forward intensely to the privacy of small flatlets nearby or within the Home. Every individual girl, according to her interests, capabilities and disabilities can continue her general education up to O or A level (Matura). Many are proficient in English and French, particularly in English. They are virtually given every opportunity to do their own housework, including laying the table, tidying up their rooms and dressing themselves, and many enjoy cooking and indeed prepare their own breakfasts and suppers. A weekly rota is drawn up. The main meal of the day, lunch, is however cooked for them.

At Konstancin there is, too, a workshop which resembles a small bright, busy factory, where the girls work in shifts making various articles which are subsequently sold by the Co-ops, who pay them a wage on the 8th day of each month. The girls are also responsible for the designing of the tea-towels, platters, tea-cosies etc., which are sold in the Foundation's shops; the most colourful and fascinating activity in the workshop itself is the making and dressing of dolls in Polish regional costumes. The whole process is completed by the girls themselves, the starting material being merely a piece of wire. Hours are spent in creating and discussing their art and designs, the mixing and blending of colours. Both girls and staff join in and these talks are stimulated by all sorts of ideas. It can be truly said that they have created the design centre for many of the things in the Foundation.

They take great pride in their appearance and are frequently at night or early in the morning before work to be found washing and setting one another's hair. They have a pure unspoiled beauty, a love of life and a great sense of gaiety and jokes. The kitchen is a gathering place—one day, when funds can be raised, we hope to renovate and enlarge it. We hope too to include more bathrooms and loos, also to build an attractive linkway between the two Homes which would make such a difference to everybody, especially in winter.

At Christmas and Easter the Foundation's tradesmen are invited to spend these feasts in the Home, and on Easter Monday the old folk tradition of throwing cold water (dyngus) on each other from 5 a.m. onwards is carried out with great glee. New tradesmen are often caught out! When many of the girls and staff came to stay at Stagenhoe for a holiday, they received a bouquet of flowers with the message: "For all the girls from all the boys."

All the girls at Konstancin agree that the most important thing about the Homes is that while receiving long-term medical treatment they can also study and work and they very much appreciate the opportunity to make friends, to belong to a big family and to lead a full social life, which is naturally most important in helping them to overcome their disability. Outings provide great enjoyment, going to the Opera is one of their favourite pleasures and Warsaw is famous for its opera and operetta (these two theatres have been rebuilt.) Although Kraków is 200 miles away they love going there too, for it has the oldest Polish University (600 years) and the whole city, the former capital of Poland, is full of beautiful buildings including the Royal Castle of Wawel with its historical associations with the monarchy.

When driving in Poland often over distances of hundreds of miles, I am welcomed and stay in many places—mainly in the Homes and hospitals, but also countless individuals everywhere offer me wonderful hospitality, yet I always eventually come back to the Homes at Konstancin as my base and headquarters they are to me the Polish Cavendish. In the little town itself one of the churches has an illuminated clock and cross which is a welcome sign after hours of driving. I always feel completely at ease with the girls and am assured of a cordial reception whatever hour of the day or night I arrive. Even though I insist that they should not wait up for me, they invariably do so, and when they hear the Land Rover approaching they come out to greet me and help me carry in my things. If messages need taking, one of the girls, a student named Leokadia, always offers to drive her car whenever she is available. It is a very joyful place full of gaiety and vitality, and often in the evenings the sound of records and singing fills the Homes. Television is also popular, especially such serials as *The Forsyte Saga*. A great favourite is football, for which incidentally the entire country comes more or less to a standstill.

The late Professor Eleanora Reicher, Head of the Institute of Rheumatic Diseases in Warsaw, was one of the people instrumental in starting the Homes at Konstancin. In the course of my work in Poland I had often visited the Department and the Hospital and later the large newly built institute, and Professor Reicher frequently invited me to make use of her own small flat in Polna Street as a base. She was a wise and witty person and reminded me greatly of Mama because of the similarity of their outlook on life. Indeed, when they met they had a lot in common. Professor Reicher had been hidden in a convent during the occupation, but she continued working as a doctor. She was outspoken and very shrewd. In her company after surgery hours the Professor often had ministers, artists—she herself was no mean painter and writer—specialists and people from all walks of life and there were great discussions and talks on many subjects which I was privileged to hear. One of her friends, the late Professor Lenoch of Prague, an outstanding rheumatologist, was sometimes present. He too was a man of many talents. She always insisted on my having a warm meal; and her lifelong companion would, however inconvenient the time, produce stewed apples.

She had a quality of greatness and leadership which enabled her to handpick a staff who were to work so lovingly and faithfully at the Homes, many of them women doctors, physiotherapists, a psychologist and teachers. They are always there but in the background, not consciously exercising their authority. The Institute of Rheumatic Diseases together with the Home staff decide upon admissions, maintenance, cost of food, new appointments, drugs and treatment for Konstancin. This is all done in close co-operation with the Ministry of Health and Social Welfare and the Foundation.

As mentioned in an earlier chapter, the Foundation's first Home was in a converted prison near Bad Nauheim in Germany, but the first which we actually built ourselves was this one in Poland; and it seems particularly fitting that the foundation stone of the Living Memorial should have been laid in this way in a country which was so despoiled by the war.

The Poles faced huge problems in clearing the rubble and rebuilding from scratch. A love of building had always been with me since early childhood, and I am only sorry that I have never had the opportunity of studying the subject. I was inspired by the enthusiasm of everyone concerned, including Local Authorities, architects, builders, craftsmen and women too who worked in the archives and on the building sites.

Traditional family ties are still strong, and most of the women, whether married or single, find it possible to follow a profession right through to retirement at the age of 60 thanks to the willingness of grandparents and other relatives who help in sharing to look after their families and children. In Poland, as at Benenden, "The great variety of their jobs bears witness to this." However hard they work, and it is customary never to get up later than 5 to 6 a.m. every morning, they never lose their femininity and have the gift of looking attractive. They have proved to me how important it is to attempt to keep tidy. Also, in the conditions and circumstances in which we have had to work to stick to a routine and be disciplined.

In this ruined country as described the few buildings that were left relatively undamaged had already been converted into schools or hospitals, so as far as our own work was concerned it was obvious that the Foundation would need to provide simply designed buildings for use as Homes or hospitals. Naturally building regulations vary according to the part of the country. The hard winter brings frost penetration when the ground becomes solid, sometimes to an average depth of over two feet, so obviously great care must be given to the fill and foundations. Soil tests are essential. Clearly too we must always adhere to the fire regulations and in the Foundation's standard Homes at strategic points 9-inch fire-check walls in brick are built with 2-hour fire-check doors. From the beginning sets of drawings had to be prepared by the Foundation and translated in every detail after which the Ministers and Local Authorities would take these to the planning stage incorporating their own contributions—services: roads, electricity, sewerage, central heating and water. To eliminate more lengthy and voluble site meetings it was necessary for me to ask the Minister of Building and Works as well as the Minister of Health and Social Welfare to pass the Foundation's set of fourteen drawings to be used officially in all parts of Poland. Since 1969 a standard Home/hospital has had a surgery, functional accommodation for the staff and 47 beds—24 singles, 7 trebles and 1 double.

Once a site has been selected, the building materials are ordered in Britain, apart from local supplies of sand, cement and gravel. The reason why the Foundation has to ship out its own materials is that, as virtually the whole country has had to be restored, there is no local material available or else it is in such short supply as to be rationed. Furthermore most of the soil is sandy, which adds to our problems. There is a lack of aggregate. At the beginning it was rare to get a concrete mixer so we mixed by hand, and during the long cold winters when temperatures dropped to between 10 to 15 degrees centigrade celsius we used to warm ourselves around braziers when we could get them. But because of the severity of the climate it also meant that the actual erection, once the foundation was in, could only go on between April and the end of October, when the carcass of the building had to be bricked and we could then work on the interior. The summer months are warm and the temperature is usually well over 25 degrees centigrade even climbing occasionally to 35 degrees centigrade. When we have been on building sites in hot weather the delight of washing under a pump or in a bucket is inexpressible.

During the first years I was on my own, and so I

inevitably had to face up to the problems of erection and renovation, shipping and the complications of dealing with bills of lading, ship's manifest, etc., myself. I was allowed to search the docks when necessary with the forwarding agent for materials dispatched, and despite the clearest of shipping instructions to the companies in Britain the materials were not always properly labelled. Incidentally, twice the dockers at one of the ports in England on hearing what the facing *bricks were to be used for waived their loading charges.

During the past eight years, however, I have been fortunate in receiving assistance from builders and tradesmen of different nationalities who have joined the Foundation to help me as well as from Local Authorities. I have been particularly helped for short periods by Graham Hughes, Peter Denton, John Hughes, Brian Jones and Engineer Karzel. The bringing in of teams of builders from abroad—by agreement with the Polish Ministries— has been made necessary by the fact that there is no un- employment in Poland, where masons and labourers are at a premium. These teams reinforce the local people in their work on the Foundation's Homes. The Foundation teams are invaluable to us in our work, share the life of the Community during the time they spend on the Continent, and over twenty of the visiting tradesmen have married Polish girls, the wedding celebrations lasting several days and nights in the fashion typical of the country. This was a situation one could never foresee and the ramifications were numerous and highly disconcerting as once a programme has been drawn up every pair of hands is needed to keep it on schedule. To be taken aside in the middle of hard work on a building site or during the course of renovation (Remont) to be asked for advice or told by the tradesman that he wished to marry, added unexpected complications. I remember on one occasion a young British bricklayer had to get special permission from his Anglican Bishop before he could marry a local Polish Catholic girl. In the midst of all the difficulties I found myself an unofficial adviser on marriage problems to

* McCarthy's Salmon Pink Calcium Silicate.

worried mums and dads in both countries. Unfortunately, there is always a shortage of suitable qualified tradesmen— and if we had more, many more new Homes and/or Hospitals could be built, and much additional renovation done. Of course, some of the sites are isolated, conditions difficult and the food unfamiliar to foreign helpers.

In addition to the hundreds of Poles who make small homemade gifts for the Foundation, the British Embassy has a tradition of inviting the Diplomatic Corps and the Poles to attend a Pantomime, Plays or a Fair during December. The Directors of the Theatres and their staff in Warsaw eagerly lend costumes free of charge and great efforts are made and there is much excitement. The proceeds are spent on the Foundation's work of relieving suffering.

A pause and a walk in the peace of the woods en route is always welcome. I love listening to the cuckoo, wood pigeons and grasshoppers and smelling the soil. Some- times too, I have a good sleep. After sweeping the dust or snow out of the driving cabin, I climb back again refreshed. Usually, the country roads in Poland are long and straight with an even surface (except in winter). Moreover, a large percentage of the population walk or use public transport —buses and trains—while children are accustomed to walk to school, even over a long distance.

Life has a far gentler pace and I like the earthy feeling. In villages or on farms, if time permits, I stop to refill my thermos and I am often offered food. There are thousands of small farms, and once a week the farmers take their produce by horse and cart to market, which is a great gathering place. Regrettably a number of carts carry no lantern or light, so at night, or in fog or snow, particular care has to be taken. In recent years, the police have rightly become very strict on drivers. Radar has been introduced in many areas to enforce a lower speed limit. Fines and spot-checks which include breathalyser tests and inspection of the vehicle's electrical system and tyres etc. are common. This also acts as a brake on those who drink and I personally approve of the strict enforcement of rules for safety on the roads, both in Poland and elsewhere. When stopped by a policeman one is usually saluted and asked to produce one's licence as well.

Humour and jokes are part and parcel of the average Pole's life, without which the people would probably not have survived as they have throughout the centuries, and particularly in desperate situations. However tense and difficult site meetings prove, when I have resorted to butterscotch and smoking *Sport* (the equivalent of *Woodbines*), their resilience and ability to make jokes have usually prevailed. One afternoon after receiving kind hospitality from a Building Engineer, whose daughter played Chopin through part of the lunch, we reluctantly took our leave to find a site situated right out in the country along partially cobbled roads. The site was further away than was anticipated. On arrival, at an office, we were greeted by a person who said he knew everything about the construction of the Foundation's proposed Home. John Mill, who was accompanying me as the Foundation's Surveyor, and I had to try to prevail upon him and to explain that although the building to be erected was of one storey, nevertheless there was a great deal which needed to be understood. We did this against the background of the Nuns singing Compline in their Chapel, the service being relayed on a Tannoy system. The cook at the local Home appeared and insisted that we should partake of homemade sausage with bread and butter, and in the midst of the excitement and enthusiasm of the locals I repeatedly asked to be shown the site in order to pace it out. We were led through woods, under a moonless sky, and by the light of their hurricane lamp and my torch we subsequently paced out on a field, thick with cauliflowers and rhubarb, the dimensions for our proposed 10,000 sq. ft. building. I asked one of those present pertinent questions as to the availability of services and how close we were to them. Whereupon he replied that the water was the best in the district and leading me to a well he lifted off the cover under which . . . . we saw a dead rat floating. Mr. Siemiradzki, from the Ministry of Health and Social Welfare, a colleague with whom I had worked for years, and the other Poles present gave, in no uncertain manner, their opinion of this rash remark, but there was laughter too. Subsequently, to give them their full credit they cleared the entire site and put the foundations in almost record time, but here as on some other sites we continue to have our difficulties, especially with the plumbers.

On another occasion, many years ago, I had a meeting in an Orthopaedic Hospital, and as is the custom in Central Europe and in other countries on the Continent, if the rooms are heated, it is very impolite not to remove one's overcoat. Mine, an inexpensive nylon (which was given to me by my husband for Christmas and called an *Eskimo*) was taken by a consultant and hung in a corridor just outside the room in which the meeting was held. It was a very cold night (some 10 degrees centigrade celsius) and snowing, and everyone knew that I had to move on to my next appointment in Warsaw by the following morning. When the meeting was over the others put on their coats but mine was not to be found, which was unusual. They were exceedingly embarrassed and insisted upon rousing the local professor and the Director from their beds and alerting many of their colleagues about the situation—much to my dismay. The police were also informed too, and a detective appeared wearing dark glasses and looking the part. He proceeded to take down a long statement asking me the name of my father and whether I had attended a High, Lower or Middle School. He also requested detailed description of the coat with its braid—calling it *Eskimoskie Futro*.

I think they all had visions of the van *Joshua* being driven off because my coat had in its pocket all the keys of the van and my rosary. At that time padlocks were in short supply, and the doctors contacted a rather voluble mechanic who had his own workshop on the outskirts of the city. He came in record time to assist me in removing the front panel of the van in order to install an ignition because that key too had been on the ring which had disappeared. This was done very quickly despite the snow-storm, and the various doctors set off in all directions looking for padlocks from their friends because we had to saw off 5 padlocks on the van including the one on the petrol tank. Meanwhile, I had driven to the workshop where the owner wanted to keep us warmed up with the help of Bigos (a Polish speciality which consists mainly of stewed cabbage and sausage), and sips of Vodka while work was in progress. He was exceedingly cheerful but his young apprentice kept his full concentration. On completion of the work, and bedecked in a borrowed coat which did not fit me, and large gloves also lent by friends, I left for Warsaw. On arrival, I found that the grapevine had informed the Ministry and other people, so a stream of Poles greeted me, each carrying one or more carnations: their tradition requires an uneven number of flowers. They had come to tell me that the loss of my coat was a dishonour to their country and themselves. The following day the Prime Minister sent me a special handmade coat, lined with sheep-skin and with matching hat and gloves, and which has been called after him ever since.

Since the establishment of the Homes at Konstancin, many others have been built by the Foundation in different parts of Poland. As everywhere, the needs are numerous and great, but special priority is given to patients suffering from cancer. The Poles had already rebuilt their Cancer Institute and were trying to establish centres with X-ray, radium and eventually (but only in certain places) cobalt equipment, so the Foundation has played only a very small part. I was deeply moved by the many people with cancer whom I met during the course of the work while on the rounds with the doctors and social workers. I remember, for example, the bedridden woman of seventy, a terminal case, who shared a room with her daughter and two small grandchildren: doctors and neighbours had tried to get her admitted to six different hospitals, but none had a free bed. Then there was a former milliner, aged sixty, who, as well as suffering from cancer, had had a nervous breakdown: she was homeless and sleeping rough in a park in a temperature of 8 degrees centigrade celsius.

A housewife suffering from cancer died alone because her husband, on whom she depended, had to work in another part of the town. The country has a tradition of voluntary workers who also participate in these visits and play a valuable part. The problems and frustrations of individuals were exacerbated by the political difficulties and strained relations of the post-war era. I would like to express recognition and appreciation to all the Staff in each of the Homes and hospitals—especially to those who are married and therefore have two jobs in life and yet try to give their loyalty and time to both a family and the patients. The domestic staff (Salowees) play a more than valuable and vital role both on day and night duty in supporting their seniors including the Nuns.

Feasibility surveys are carried out continuously by the authorities and I participate in these. I felt from the beginning that something should be done to help the very hard-pressed authorities and people who were battling so heroically to alleviate this terrible misery. In the 1950's it was estimated that about 30,000 people died of cancer in a year without hospital treatment because of the shortage of beds. The Foundation's first very simple Home for cancer patients was built at Zyrardow, thirty miles from Warsaw, but subsequently others were built within the complex of General Hospitals, so that they might benefit from the facilities which include chemo-therapy, radio-therapy and radium-therapy treatment and surgery.

I myself frequently had the privilege of comforting dying patients in the Homes for terminal cases, some of them only in their teens or early twenties, and I recall many of them vividly. Even though we could provide no cure for them, we had the consolation of knowing that they were being looked after by people who cared about them, and that they were conscious of this.

It is my custom on arrival in the van or Land Rover to greet the staff and patients: those who are ambulant stand in or near the doorway and passage with flowers—usually carnations or handmade gifts. Their welcome is made all the more moving by one or two of them saying or reading a message thanking me for coming and including in their

thanks those I represent. Once a Bod recalled and recited
these lines to me from Kipling:

I have eaten your bread and salt

I have drunk your water and wine

The deaths ye died I have watched beside

And the lives that ye led were mine.

After being briefed on the diagnosis by the consultants
I then go on the rounds with the sister in charge and
consultant talking to each individual, making notes, sitting
with them and listening to their stories and their experiences. When consultants used Latin extensively it
called for even greater concentration on my part. At the
beginning certain drug products were difficult to obtain
and we seemed to spend hours going through Mims (a
pharmaceutical magazine). A considerable number of
doctors in Britain were collecting drug samples while
other drugs had to be ordered especially.

It is a very humbling experience, going around, sharing
their thoughts, cares and joys of patients and staff. Often
their endurance is heroic, while others cry as they realise
they are departing from life so soon or will have to leave
behind their young children. Sometimes we have a husband
and wife as patients at the same time. I remember particularly a young boy with an inoperable tumour who
became blind, and couldn't accept the fact that he
had no future. He needed a lot of companionship,
and became steadily more demanding as his disease
advanced.

There was, too, an engineer with cancer of the lungs who
kept his empty tin of New Zealand peaches as he whispered
"Just imagine who the donor is and what that country
looks like". Then there was another woman whose jaw
was ulcerating; although by profession she was a teacher
and had a remarkably brave war record in the Resistance,
she could only write the word "Drink". There are hundreds of others, and almost each room holds memories
of individuals who have been treated, discharged and
readmitted. The average mortality rate is between 40%–

50%. It would be much higher but for our endeavours to prevent the number of terminal and malignant cases from becoming an unduly high proportion. This is a cruel and factual dilemma which lives with me all the time. Trying to comfort and support the bereaved relatives and friends can be very exacting too, and there are always poignant moments, relieved, however, by the stoic courage and humour of the patients themselves; and when I am with them I feel it almost impossible to tear myself away.

During the years of working, I found that these were the top priorities: patients with rheumatoid arthritis (mainly young girls and women), cancer and cardiac cases, physically disabled young married couples, victims of severe accidents, hemiplegics and retarded children. Even if we limit ourselves to working in these fields, the demands on the Foundation and all concerned are great, however, and we cannot do as much as we would like to. In the circumstances the best course is to rely as before on the Ministers, the Local Authorities and local practitioners to tell us what they intend doing, and then to co-operate with them as best we can. They themselves have built a re-markable number of Homes, and each of the twenty-two districts (Wojewodztwos) has a well-qualified staff in its Medical and Social Welfare Departments.

There are, of course, other Homes caring for short-term patients, who are discharged after treatment; and wider social problems, including rehabilitation, are also studied. The vastness of the need may seem depressing, yet, as one of our colleagues, Professor Koszarowski, head of the Polish Cancer Institute, has said: "If we speak only of problems, it sounds hopeless; but it isn't. Our lives are made up of problems, troubles, expectations, successes and failures. We must persevere and go forward." This is my own view. We always have to bear in mind the wide prevalence of cancer, the needs in hospitals, the availability of beds for both acute and malignant patients, discharge facilities and domiciliary care.

The timing and pressures upon the Local Authorities and the Foundation to get the materials on to the site in time, plus the saga of the documentation (preparation of the site drawings and services) added to the frustrations of ensuring that materials are not held up by lack of co-ordination between the supplier and the shipping company in Britain . . . well, these alone would fill a book. Our unbounded appreciation goes to the companies who keep their prices down and stick to their word about delivery and "D-Days", also to the Poles and Yugoslavs for giving free freight to the Foundation's supplies.

The first company with whom I placed an order were most co-operative—they also waited until funds could be raised and provided materials at almost cost price. Their drawings were headed: *When in doubt, ask.* As I was usually at least a thousand miles or more away and could not resort to a telephone because of cost and the lack of clarity on the line, the local engineer and myself were faced with a number of practical problems, and drew up a Snag List which was composed either into a long ELT (European Letter Telegram) or into an airmail letter which could take days to arrive.

Finally, when the Home or Hospital is erected and completed, the lights are lit, the water flows through the taps, and the staff welcome the children or patients enabling them to relax and relieving them of their pain, then all of us who have been engaged in the work as a team know that our efforts have not been in vain. Each time a renovation is carried out or a new Home is built, it feels like giving birth to a child.

Regrettably, I have not mentioned the many other places, hospitals and Homes, each of which, as always in life, has its own characters, personalities, humour, squabbles and differences. Every visit has given pleasure but was also a challenge and a headache. I have found a dignity and thoughtfulness which reminds me of so many gracious people—young, middle-aged and old. Director Raczynski (he himself had to undergo a serious operation, performed skilfully by a woman surgeon), works with the Order of Nursing Sisters of St. Vincent de Paul. They are in charge of the local authority Home at Góra Kalwaria (Hill of Calvary) which is linked with the Foundation's

Homes. Director Raczynski is a tall reserved man who has had to shoulder a lot of responsibility. Like his colleague, Mr. Mikolajczyk, at Radzymin, and others in their position they share the deep concern for trying to improve the quality of life with the appropriate local authorities. This is even harder as they grapple with the pressures and persistence of hundreds who want to be admitted. The would-be patients who apply are usually people who have lost everybody in their family, and are often very heavy nursing cases. Some of them are quite indomitable. I remember how one Bod insisted upon singing *Rule Britannia* with the final line running *Poland and Britain never will be slaves.*

After going the rounds at the Homes at Góra Kalwaria among the 127 patients, the sisters would say: "Do come and have some coffee"—regardless of the time of day or night. This means a four course meal (mainly vegetables) beautifully prepared and presented in a simple room which was also their head sister's bedroom; canaries flitting freely about the room added an unusual touch. Our conversation would turn to the Bods and the children's needs in other countries. On one occasion when we were talking about the frolics and the fun of the girls of Konstancin, Director Raczynski said: "I think their lives *here* at Góra Kalwaria have a different sort of expression but it is very moving, and when you hear the patients and they talk to you, there is still much life in them". As Rupert Brooke once wrote: 'Old age is only a different kind of merriment from youth, and a wiser one'.

I have always felt a special affection for Poland and the Poles, and visits to that country are a source of joy, no matter how many problems face us there in our work. The Poles are renowned for their hospitality, and I have many happy memories of warm welcomes. Their courtesy, too, is remarkable—though unfortunately this doesn't extend to queuing for public transport!—and it is pleasant for example to see the male engineer on a building site kissing the hand of a female plasterer, while she is still holding a trowel with the other. The greetings, cordiality and good humour of the Poles with their many jokes ensure that the atmosphere usually remains pleasant during discussions, however marked differences of opinion among such strong individualists may be.

Leaving the sites and Homes in Poland after my regular visits is always a wrench, especially when I am saying goodbye to the mentally handicapped children. On my departure, as on my arrival, all the patients and staff gather to greet me or see me off with flowers and handmade gifts, and the sincerity of their affection makes these occasions particularly poignant. I always hate leaving, and wish that I could spend more time with them.

There is much to be done in Poland, as elsewhere, as I have already emphasised, but when I feel discouraged, I remember the words of a physician I met during the early days of our work there. She was lying in her small room in the last stages of tuberculosis. She suffered terribly, yet she discussed constructively and at great length the gaps and priorities in the treatment of diseases. She told me: "There are thousands of sick people and the world will always have them, but it is important that you concentrate on and cope with a few priorities. Everyone is going to ask you to provide a Home or hospital for their category of patient. In developing countries where problems of poverty, sickness and disease seem overwhelming, and in our country which has suffered such devastation, you must not be side-tracked but must concentrate on giving assistance to those whom the physicians and specialists can help by offering medical and nursing care on a short or long term basis. Even with limited funds you are the person to relieve the pressure on their overloaded waiting lists and to save them from having to turn away many who need to be admitted to hospital. By founding Homes and small hospitals for both the acute sick and the disabled you are providing and releasing beds in hospitals which would be otherwise blocked. It is you we are looking to because you have dedicated your life to try and do this".

These words from the mouth of a dying person made me feel very humble and brought to my mind words scribbled on

the wall of an underground cell in the infamous Gestapo
Interrogation Headquarters in Aleja Szucha in Warsaw:

> *It's easy to talk about Poland*
> *It's harder to work for her*
> *Still harder to die*
> *And the hardest is to suffer.*

———

	%
Dwelling houses destroyed	72
Industrial buildings	90
Health Service buildings	90
Historic buildings and monuments	90
Schools and institutions of higher education ..	70
Theatres and cinemas	95
City and State Archives	90
Road and railway bridges	100
Tramway tracks and rolling stock	85
Waterworks and sewage systems	30
Railway junctions within the city	95
Railway stations	100
Electricity works	50
Telephone exchanges	100
Street surfaces	30
Trees	60

CHAPTER 16

Yugoslavia

Early one evening while I was waiting for a meeting with the Yugoslavs in the van overlooking the Plitvica lakes, a group of tourists from Britain came strolling by and, noticing the name on the van, stopped to tell me they were supporters of the Foundation. Rather than spoil their holiday, I refrained from telling them what had happened in that neighbourhood during the two World Wars and the centuries of foreign occupation preceding them, and I felt too that it would be hard for them to imagine the tragedies which had occurred in many districts of the country. Yugoslavia attracts a large number of tourists, but few realise the sufferings the Yugoslav people have undergone, or the gaps still existing in society and the efforts of the people themselves to meet the many existing needs.

It is a country of thickly-wooded mountain ranges where the snow remains on some of the highest peaks all year long, a country of lakes, waterfalls and rivers, of winding roads offering breathtaking views, a country of great plains where farmers reap their barley, of white beaches, of castles built by the Crusaders, and of stone villages gathered round the domes of their churches or the slender minarets of their mosques.

Here the Nazi invasion of 1941 caused four years of terror and suffering. Twenty-five divisions were stationed in Yugoslavia by the Axis powers, apart from the quisling units, and thirty-four major concentration camps were established, as well as many smaller camps. The invader attempted by all means to break the resistance of the people. He did not succeed, however, for under the leadership of the resistance forces Yugoslavs retreated to the forests and mountains and began to wage partisan warfare with great courage, determined to achieve the liberation of their country. It was a time of dramatic change and of

197

many difficulties caused by the differences between various sections of the resistance, traces of which have not entirely disappeared.

A very notable aspect of the resistance in Yugoslavia, and one which does not normally receive much recognition, is the Partisans' medical service. Encircled by the enemy and very short of supplies, the Partisans performed miracles of courage and devotion in looking after the wounded. Many of their hospitals were situated in underground shelters or caves to which a vertical shaft gave access. Down this shaft the patient was lowered, and immediately afterwards the entrance was camouflaged with tree trunks, moss, bracken, or whatever was available. In other places the wounded were taken into the houses of patriotic local families, where they were looked after by a semi-trained nurse. Only when a fairly large area had been liberated was it possible to run open hospitals. All Partisan hospitals, when located, were ruthlessly bombed by the Germans, and to seek out those that were hidden, task forces of between fifty and two hundred men dressed in Partisan uniforms and accompanied by tracker dogs were sent out.

The dangers encountered in transporting medical supplies from occupied territory to the Partisan units are graphically illustrated by the following passages taken from the diary of a young Partisan girl:*

"The fascist terror is rampant. The citizens of Zagreb hurry along the streets. Many faces already reflect hunger, poverty and fear. A young girl, head bowed, walks quickly down the street, her eyes always on the lookout for plainclothes policemen or fascist patrols. She has a large parcel tied with string under her arm. At last she reaches her destination. It is a shabby workers' lodging house. She enters cautiously and only when the tired face of the housewife is lit up by a smile does she relax a little and hand over the parcel. 'Take good care of this,' she whispers, 'it contains medical materials and it should be sent as fast as possible to our men in the forest—to the Partisan wounded. You see we have managed to collect a

* From the book *Partisan Hospitals in Yugoslavia*—reproduced by kind permission of the author Dr. Djerdje Dragic.

lot. Ruzica took something from the dispensary where she works; Zdenja raided her father's surgery; the hospital orderly got us a few things; I managed to buy a little in various pharmacies; and there we are.'

"The same night the parcel travels further, now carried by a brawny young worker. He has left the suburbs, and the city is behind him. Here in the forest one can breathe more freely—one can escape. Suddenly, the young man stops dead in his tracks, whistles softly, and hears an answering call from a nearby copse. This is the place of rendezvous. 'The contact is waiting,' mutters the young man, and hurries towards the copse. 'Halt!' echoes softly but firmly behind a tree.

"The password is whispered and the young man's heart is thumping as the thought that perhaps this is not the partisan contact but an ambush organised by the fascists or the police. If it is, his fate is sealed; there await him torture, prison, death. . . . But, in reply, he hears the password, 'Freedom to the people'. A cordial greeting is exchanged, the parcel handed over. The worker whispers to the courier 'Take good care of this; it contains medicines and dressings for the patients in the Central Hospital in Petrova Gora.'

"The courier now proceeds rapidly, and is already on his way through the dense forest and undergrowth. There is a point where the route passes near a German blockhouse, but there is no moonlight, and this makes matters easier. This is the thirty-seventh time that the young courier has made his way by secret paths and roads between the enemy garrisons and strongpoints. Every day he risks discovery by the fascists. But he is cautious, particularly this night when he is carrying a precious parcel of medicines for the wounded."

After the defeat of the Axis powers, when a national government was established under Marshal Tito, Yugoslavia was a ravaged country. 1,700,000 people—almost a fifth of the population—had died during the War, and there was an immense task ahead.

I had already been working with the authorities in Yugoslavia for some time when, during the late 1950s, Professor M. Andrejevic, an authority on geriatrics, drew my attention to the need of establishing a geriatric unit in the city hospital in Belgrade. I warmly welcomed his suggestion, feeling that this was an occasion for the Foundation to carry out one of its primary aims—to operate in complete liaison with the local authorities and to support them in their efforts. The Homes which were subsequently established in Belgrade comprise two medical units and one surgical unit, together with a centre for physiotherapy and occupational therapy for patients who otherwise would be blocking hospital beds

While these Homes were being built, however, others were already being started in different parts of the country. There was much to be done, but equally there were many problems with which to contend. Yugoslavia is a country covering more than 200,000 square miles, and although it is politically a single state, it consists of six autonomous republics. There are four official languages and two alphabets, and the people differ greatly in their ideas, traditions and religions, etc. Nonetheless, some of my most vivid memories are of the enthusiastic co-operation I received from the Yugoslav people—central and local authorities, doctors, social workers and engineers, and the inhabitants of the countless towns and villages where my travels brought me—and of the energy with which they have helped in the finding of suitable sites and the establishment of the Homes.

In most cases the local authorities propose the site for the Home, and also introduce me to the various categories for whom they want to cater. It is always difficult to make the final decision, bearing in mind the priorities and conducting lengthy discussions and surveys, and whatever group ultimately benefits from the facilities we provide, I feel terrible about the others, particularly when I see from the tours of villages and towns and of the existing hospitals the number of people who could be helped if Homes were to be erected and established for them.

I remember one blind woman who said "Can you imagine what it is like to be left alone, to have nothing and no sight. If only the world could show some heart."

Many of the younger generation were killed and consequently there is a grave need amongst the frail and elderly who cannot care for themselves. In addition, the local people, who are fully aware of their own responsibilities, use every effort to persuade us to build a Home in their area.

Invariably I am asked to join colleagues and the local dignitaries at their meal: depending on the part of the country, the main dish may often be mutton, accompanied by plum brandy and Turkish coffee, none of which I could digest. Perseverance, enthusiasm and courtesy are general and in the earlier days time appeared to be of little account. I recall one official meal at which the excellent local fish was announced as the main course, though in fact it had not yet been caught—much less cooked! I remember too with affection the nuns ready to prepare a feast at any hour of the day or night, and who always woke me at 4.30 a.m. when I was staying with them, to attend the first Office of the day.

Distances were so great that occasionally I would not reach the potential site until night had fallen, and thus was able to inspect it only by the beam of the car headlights. One night as we were searching for a particular site, we came up against a bridge in the process of being constructed by the Army, and the Yugoslavs insisted on climbing up on the very high concrete slab, standing on each other's shoulders to do so. We were challenged by a sentry, who allowed us to proceed when the nature of the Foundation's work was explained to him, and proceeded to the edge of the slab in the fading light, hearing the fast, rushing river below us in the dusk. After some minutes the Yugoslavs were persuaded to return to the Land Rover, however, and we continued the journey, finally locating the site, after a further search, on the other side of the river.

Itineraries were often very arduous, and eventually various officials, among them Doctor Olga Milosevic (Marshal Tito's personal doctor, who had fought with the Partisans and had lost her husband and daughter in the War), insisted that stops for food and rest be included when planning the site-prospecting expeditions.

In the early days many of the roads were merely dirt tracks, and some sites could not be reached except on foot in summer or by sleigh in winter. Once or twice I travelled by a small twin-engined aircraft. I remember that air turbulence made the flight far from smooth, but the pilot was so eager that it seemed no risk was too great for him to take in spite of the turbulence and very bad visibility.

The Yugoslav physique is strong and at times it was an effort to keep up with what my companions proposed. We were concentrating our activities mainly in Serbia, Montenegro, Croatia and Macedonia, making use of every means of transport, sometimes scrambling by torchlight over overgrown boulders, and, when the occasion called for it, rising at 6 a.m. for breakfast with the local mayor and being shown around a factory and a new housing area before setting out on a day's drive.

It is now some sixteen years or more since the establishment of the first Home, and these years have seen a blossoming in the work done in Yugoslavia, where thousands of individuals have been treated and cared for in twenty-two Homes, including two for physically handicapped children at Strumica and near Belgrade. There have been great changes too in Yugoslavia itself, for the country has largely recovered from the effects of the War and the foreign occupations of the past centuries, with signs of a new prosperity everywhere. There has been a spectacular increase in the number of medical students, but, as in so many countries, relatively few after qualifying like working in isolated areas. This in itself presents a problem.

I try to visit all the Yugoslav Homes once every eighteen months, driving some six to seven thousand miles in three or four weeks. Usually I enter Yugoslavia from Austria, and after a long drive through the night have the wonderful experience of seeing the dawn over the mountains; but there are other occasions when I travel down the Hungarian road, which in winter is covered with snow and ice. Generally my rendezvous with the Yugoslavs is at Zagreb at 6.30 a.m., preceded by Mass at 6 a.m. in the Cathedral.

From Zagreb, after meetings and visits to local Homes and individuals, I start my itinerary. One night we came upon an accident: a bus carrying a football team had overturned, having swerved right across the road before plunging into a wood, and the passengers were trapped underneath. We helped to extricate some of them, who were in great pain and suffering from shock, and I gave water from my thermoses to those lying by the roadside, working by torchlight in the dark.

At Gospic, an hour's drive from the underground Partisan hospital at Petrova Gora mentioned earlier, which is being preserved, the Foundation, together with the local authorities, has built in a very simple way two Homes for the disabled of different ages, both men and women. This area was ruthlessly destroyed by the Occupation forces, and I am always deeply impressed by the people's lack of bitterness and by their acceptance of suffering. There are other areas where memories of the suffering in the First World War are very vivid, and the efforts made by the Scottish nurses among the Serbs are often mentioned: there were thousands of casualties as a result of typhus, hunger and the bitter cold.

After a couple of days at Gospic I usually drive on to Risan on the coast, a distance of several hundred kilometres, by what is now a new road. Originally the patients in the Homes here were accommodated in two old houses in a small village very close to the sea. These houses had very steep stairs, no heating, and many flies in the hot summer, in addition to which there were no flush loos and water had to be drawn from a well. Many of the patients were incontinent, yet somehow, despite these appalling conditions, the nuns who cared for them managed to keep them clean. I cannot remember ever hearing the nuns or the Warden or his staff grumble.

The Authorities and I searched for a level site in the neighbourhood—a difficult proposition, for there are many mountains and hills—and finally a site was found; beautiful, with a fine view of the sea, although not level. When cleared it provided room for three Homes and a laundry, and, in addition, for accommodation for the nuns (of whom there are now nineteen), enabling them to have their own little chapel. For these Homes a central heating system was designed by the Foundation's honorary heating consultant and the parts were sent out together with nearly all the other materials for the buildings.

Discussions on building problems, water pressures, plumbing, etc., continue endlessly and on almost every site everyone—whether qualified or not—joins in enthusiastically.

From Risan I continue on to Pristina and Kragujevac. The old road used to take me over one of the highest mountains, Čakor, and for miles around there was beautiful scenery. The terrain is very rocky and the road full of twists and bends, with many tunnels blasted through the solid rock. Often it is quite deserted apart from the sheep grazing on the mountainside. In the autumn the flocks are driven down to the local villages because of the severity of the winter, when there is heavy snow, while in summer it is extremely hot. It is on these drives and others like them that I enjoy listening to taped music, especially *Kumbaya My Lord*, which is a favourite with the Yugoslavs accompanying me. These cassette tapes were a gift to us from a film company, and my husband records on them music from *Your Hundred Best Tunes*, a Sunday evening BBC radio programme, also the Proms.

On the way to Pristina, besides making calls at different hospitals and having meetings and discussions with social workers, I also sometimes find myself persuaded by the Yugoslavs accompanying me to divert from my route in order to see the frescoes in a mountain monastery.

At Pristina the Foundation has built two Homes with the help of the local authorities, which are wholly responsible for running them. The nuns who staff these Homes occupy one end of one of the buildings and have their own chapel, where they start the day with a Service at 5 a.m. An occupational therapy room is included in this Home, and colourful local people come in with handwork and encourage the patients to do more in the way of handicrafts. They have a warm humour and great generosity. I sleep in the nuns' sitting/dining room next door to the chapel, and the Sister in Charge insists upon my having her bed, while she herself moves out into rather a crowded room with three or four other nuns. They make great preparations for me to have a bath, almost hovering over me to see that I get undressed properly! One night the

Warden insisted on giving me a present by booking a telephone call home to my children, and there was tremendous excitement when the call came through: now he repeats this kind gesture on each visit.

The disabilities of the patients vary here as some are psychiatrically disturbed, whilst others are fully ambulant or in wheelchairs. They are classified in rooms, and anyone who has the opportunity of having a single room enjoys it tremendously.

At one of the other Homes the nuns observe silence during meals, while one of them reads aloud. One day when I was with them and solemn reading was in progress two of us suddenly remembered a joke we'd been told by the patients and had such difficulty in restraining ourselves that the reading had to be abandoned.

At Travnik in Bosnia, while walking with one of the Sisters at 6 o'clock one morning I remarked upon the weather—the temperature was 6° centigrade celsius and she replied "Yes, it is rather chilly!"

On another occasion when there were threats during a very serious international crisis, a few of the Yugoslavs asked whether, in the event of another invasion, I would go with them to the mountains as they intended to join the Partisans again. After being cut off from any news for weeks an aerial was found which enabled us to use their radio and tune into the B.B.C. in London. Instead of alarming news we heard a very English voice describing the stabling of horses at Newmarket, a Victorian play, and a calm, objective news bulletin and commentary. The Sisters had decided earlier it was better to pray for peace and kept leading me to the Chapel.

From Pristina I drive down to Bitoli. Now there are new roads, but in the old days one had to take a winding road and it was a journey of several hours. Bitoli is almost on the Greek frontier, and it is from Bitoli that I used to go to Greece while working there. The town is very old, and it has now been greatly developed with industry. In the First World War part of a French Division fought there, and there is a large French cemetery; in very rough hill country some of the trenches remain. In Bitoli the Foundation has built two Homes on the site of a demolished house dating from the Turkish occupation, which lasted for nearly four hundred years.

The Nursing Sisters here work in the local hospital as well as in our Homes. They and the staff, like many of their compatriots, have a warmth and love of the Bods, with goodness and gaiety. One of the Sisters in fun occasionally tells our fortunes by tipping the remains of a cup of Turkish coffee upside down and then reading the lines on the saucer.

At Kragujevac, one of the principal towns in Serbia, the authorities asked the Foundation to erect two Homes for the disabled of different ages. These Homes are on the outskirts of the town where in 1942, 7,000 of the inhabitants were massacred in one day, including children from Form 5 of the local school.

There is a healthy competition between different Homes. The Wardens and their staff (despite the distances) like to make up a convoy and join me when possible on these journeys. We have had to take care in the last few years as many of the Yugoslavs are regrettably fast drivers with a bad accident rate.

In this way my journeys through Yugoslavia continue, meeting everywhere kindness, flowers and hospitality. My memories of these difficult journeys are innumerable: the lakes and waterfalls on the drive to Gospic; a lamb strapped to the back of a donkey; buses careering around corners on mountain passes; a brass band blaring at the opening of a new Home; nuns saying their Office in the chapel; and an old man of 108 in one of the Homes performing a folk-dance, whilst in the next room a girl of 23, deprived of a normal life by polio, is weeping in her wheelchair.

As in all countries where folk-lore survives strongly, the wanderer in Yugoslavia may hear a variety of adages whose origins or first causes are long forgotten. One that has followed me around and remains in my mind for no reason that I can think of is: "Don't boast in Sarajevo, don't ride a horse in Travnik, don't lie in Mostar, don't sing in Banja Luka". I wouldn't dream of shocking Banja Luka!

In collaboration with local authorities the Foundation has now created a Council in Yugoslavia on which Miss N. Novakovic represents the appropriate Federal Ministry and the Wardens of our Homes sit *ex officio* at regular meetings. There is need for more Homes, and the Yugoslavs wish for them as much as I do. The authorities and the people themselves have done and are doing much, but we share their painful awareness that many thousands remain in need of the succour with which we cannot yet reach them. We know, too, that even among those admitted to our Homes there are many with problems still to be tackled adequately—by medical and nursing care, or by rehabilitation, or by helping the lonely and rejected to come to terms with incurable disease or irremediable disabilities.

In July 1972, a group of twenty-four visitors from Yugoslavia came to Stagenhoe. Besides Miss Novakovic and Dr. Olga Milosevic the group included Wardens and nuns from our Homes. They visited our own and other Homes in England and several hospitals. They followed their itinerary with great enthusiasm and were tirelessly eager for first hand acquaintance with British methods of coping with social and medical problems. From one of this party I received the following letter:

Upon my return home to my dear city of Zagreb I would like to thank you and your colleagues for the kind welcome that I was greeted with during my stay in your really great country. My impressions were deep, but in my heart I shall always remember this journey, your great concern, and not only yours but that of your collaborators, your children, the elderly and the disabled. I keep hearing the words of the gentleman who said when we visted Papworth Industries near Cambridge on 3rd August that the word 'unable' was never mentioned.

Thanking you, your dear children and all your friends, I now look forward to your coming visit and remain for ever grateful.

D.S.

207

CHAPTER 17

Greetings on Frontiers

"Gee, that must be exciting," someone once exclaimed when he heard that my work involves travelling. "Do you fly everywhere?" The answer is generally no, except in certain large countries where distances are very great, or in cases when the only quick way of reaching my destination is to travel by air. Nowadays, despite the many improvements, flying is still very tiring, especially through the night, with long waits, overcrowding, stop-overs, and rapid changes of time and climate. In the course of my travels I have experienced tropical storms and emergency landings.

In an average year I drive approximately 40,000 to 50,000 miles to the Homes, new properties and official engagements in Britain, as well as driving to and in the other countries where the Foundation works. I make regular visits to various countries on different continents, chiefly in Europe, the Middle and Far East—including India. My husband and I visit Australia and New Zealand every five years. Distances there are vast, itineraries complex and always crowded, giving little time for privacy or rest. To go straight into a meeting and give a talk after having travelled by air for 24 hours calls for considerable stamina! For its work in both countries the Foundation has a co-ordinating Council, whose Chairman since 1972 has been The Honourable Mr. Justice John Nagle. Active Committees—called Councils or Support Groups—are, besides continuing their contributions for the overseas work, now founding Homes and more Shops in several places in Australia and New Zealand.

The warmth of the welcome awaiting us wherever we go, especially in the schools and among young people, compensates for fatigue. We are always heartened by the generosity and goodwill we encounter, and on each visit are struck anew by the beauty, the size and the potential of these two countries. The Maoris' traditional welcome and in particular their singing is deeply moving.

Visits abroad include not only countries in the which the Foundation already works, however, but also those in which the authorities and people have learnt of the work we do and invite me, or other representatives of the Foundation, to discuss with them ways in which we can co-operate in caring for the sick and disabled.

The major part of a tour of Central Europe, on the other hand, will be spent visiting all the Foundation's Homes in Poland and Yugoslavia, and attending meetings to discuss the existing Homes and hospitals and to plan the founding of new ones and the renovation of others. Several suggested sites for new Homes will be visited, and, where possible, a few will be chosen.

The work is planned at least two to five years ahead, according to priorities in the area, the funds that are available locally and the plans of the people themselves. Wherever I work (with a few exceptions) the Local Authorities are responsible for providing staff, giving grants for the day to day running, and the provision of food and medical supplies, the Foundation being responsible for maintenance, renovation and the building of extensions. Autonomy is aimed for, as the Homes clearly have to be administered locally.

Another important aspect of the Foundation's work is assistance given in the homes of individuals who are sick or disabled or in any kind of need, by providing drugs or treatment, wheelchairs, walking aids, hoists or any other special equipment which enables such people to be looked after at home rather than in hospital and to live a more normal life, retaining or achieving a large measure of independence. For those recommended by our case-workers as being in financial need because of sickness or other misfortune, the Foundation provides small grants in some countries, and clothing is also distributed. I spend as much time as possible with the social workers and going on the rounds with them.

In Germany the Foundation's principal work remains prison visiting and aftercare, which has already been described in the chapter on The Boys, and I visit those who have been discharged, either to their own countries or to the Foundation's Home, which accommodates a few of the Boys who have found jobs locally. Their adjustment to life in the world outside prison is often slow and difficult.

Inevitably there is much work to be done and always will be, and these long journeys are accordingly a vital necessity, enabling me to keep in contact with all aspects of the Foundation's work, to help extend it, and to bring it to the attention of those who are not aware of what we do. Outsiders sometimes envy me for being able to do so much travelling, imagining my travels to be some extended form of holiday, but they would soon realise their mistake if they could see what is really involved. Not only is my schedule everywhere taken up almost entirely by very vital meetings and discussions concerning the Foundation, but often—as on visits to the Continent—I drive myself, and great distances have to be covered: driving between one Home and another in Poland or in Yugoslavia can mean some 300 to 700 miles. In addition the weather can often be very bad: in winter there are blinding blizzards, with snow and ice on the road and sleeting rain; the side and near windows of the Land Rover fog up, and it is difficult even to see the wipers on the windscreen. In the cold, one's hands very soon become chapped and the cream specially prepared and made by a very disabled artist friend in Pilsen has a most soothing affect. In summer again the heat can be intense and the dust very troublesome, and one sticks to the seat as one drives.

Depending on the places concerned, my visits abroad mean that I will be away for about six weeks to two months each time. Every eighteen months two to three months are spent in the various countries of Central Europe, where I visit the Foundation's Homes, sometimes breaking my journey in Belgium. There the Foundation is a registered charity and has as its distinguished Chairman Professor H. Brugmans (former Rector of the College of Europe). In Belgium, as in other countries, we have very hard working Support Groups who include psychiatrists and other members of the medical profession as well as lay people. At the moment they are preparing to open four Homes. As already mentioned, the Belgians have for years played an active part in raising their own funds and give personal service in helping with the organisation of the Holiday Scheme.

I have to plan every day and night of the itinerary with great precision with all who are involved, paying meticulous attention to details, for unless I do this I am unable to fit into the time available the large volume of work awaiting me in these countries. Furthermore the itinerary has to syncronise with the availability of Ministers, Local Authorities, social workers and others with whom we work so closely. It is probably true to say that the weeks involving these journeys are the most strenuous and intensive part of the year.

As the start of the journey draws near, the sense of urgency in planning the itinerary, arranging appointments and getting everything together increases. The last week before I leave is one of great pressure and activity. We are always grateful when we do not have too many interruptions, as there are crucial meetings with builders, engineers and contractors about the non-delivery of building materials which are urgently required on site to enable the erection and building work to proceed during the good weather between April and the end of September, before the severe winter starts. It is always vital to get the carcase up and clad with brick so as to enable us to proceed with the internal work during the winter months.

In past years we would be busy also packing *Joshua*, the two-ton van which was given us anonymously, but nowadays it is the Land Rover. The gathering together of equipment, material, wheelchairs and gifts is a major task, for the loading has to be done in such a way that things needed first on the journey are packed last into the van or Land Rover, so that at each place we are able to find the relevant goods immediately and not waste time unloading and reloading. I have little space for my clothes—usually one suitcase marked "Personal" plus an overnight bag—

but I take certain supplies of food and fuel so that I can be independent and make hot drinks during the long night drives.

Apart from this there is also the correspondence with the Embassies of the countries concerned about passports and visas for the builders' tradesmen—plumbers, bricklayers, decorators, carpenters, electricians and floor-layers —who make up the teams going out to renovate existing Homes abroad or to erect new ones. While some of the tradesmen work only on the renovation and restoration of the Foundation's properties in Britain, others come to one of the British Homes first for us to get to know each other, and after assisting us for two to three months they proceed overseas. They have read the advertisements placed by the Foundation in trade journals, and most of them join because they feel this is a practical way of doing something worthwhile and assisting others by using their own trade and experience.

Before I leave, pictures form in my mind of what lies ahead—the long drives; talks with Bods and doctors, specialists, social workers, consultants, engineers and others; their cultures and traditions. When I leave Jeromy and Elizabeth's rooms and our own I feel very sad, and the first miles of the way pass in silence, but then there is the warm welcome at Dover aboard the Townsend Car Ferry and the sight once more of familiar faces.

During all these years I have driven many different vehicles on my journeys. After the international organisations withdrew from their work on the Continent and I continued alone, I drove a second-hand car. Later, because I had to convey people and goods, vans were necessary: sometimes these have been called after the prophets, including *Job*, *Daniel*, *Ezekiel* and *Elijah*, and there was also an Austin 30 named *Alice* by a German Minister, after *Alice in Wonderland*. The vehicles are thus named because it makes them more personal, and they seem to become part of one's life. Once I get into the cab the vehicle becomes something very personal to me: driving reminds me of riding, of getting into the saddle and staying there.

When I used the van *Joshua* there were two side lockers which were locked but not sealed, so that access to the tool and food boxes proved easy. Inside the cab, opposite the driving seat, I keep the jack and wheel-brace, and in a net above my head an extra pair of driving gloves, scarf, dark glasses and a second-hand fur cap. Behind the gear lever on the left is an extra container which holds a bottle of fruit juice, cups, tissues and thermoses. Other supplies include things such as powdered coffee, butterscotch, butter and cheese and a sponge bag. When I stop for refreshment I use either the top of the engine or the adjoining seat as a table.

On these journeys I have on occasions had to try and cope with various mechanical problems, and I am grateful for what I was taught in the FANY. In 1952 I also worked briefly at Rootes' well-known service centre in London, to gain more knowledge and to refresh my memory on the maintenance of vehicles. I firmly believe that before drivers receive their licences, they should be instructed on the necessity of maintaining and servicing the vehicle regularly, and told more graphically of the dangers to themselves and others of driving aggressively, and also the results, with possible multiple injury and disablement for the rest of their lives.

Quite a number of women were still employed at Rootes, and had been considered as assets and equals, and indeed their language and humour equalled the men's. We were attired in boiler suits and carried a tool box. On admittance each vehicle received a job card which had to be followed strictly. Time was allocated for every part of the work. In those days the charge-hand was very strict, and if we omitted to use wing covers or were seen dawdling he used strong language. Once the work was finished the vehicle was driven to the inspection area, and if the Inspectors were displeased it came back until the job was done to their complete satisfaction. As in the FANY the engines were cleaned down and painted over with paraffin so that literally no dirt or dust could be found. Journeys are planned so that most of the driving is done at night. I are prefer this because hours can be saved avoiding the

213

appalling volume of daytime traffic, particularly on the Autobahn and motorways of Western Europe, and the huge juggernaut lorries, the roar and speed of which are horrible; also in summer it is cooler. I have seen so many terrible and macabre accidents that I prefer to drive steadily. The curves of many hills, roads and motorways stretching ahead are familiar to me, often remembered in connection with some particular journey—usually one made in bad weather. When I get tired I always stop and pull in for a rest, keeping the engine running in very cold weather, and when I want to sleep I lock both doors and stretch out across the engine or the seat with my old pram pillow behind my head.

At the end of each night's journey I note the distance, the route, the time it takes during the winter and the time the same journey takes during the summer, knowledge which has been acquired during previous journeys, for I have always noted and filed the distances, routes, weather conditions and travelling times. Necessity has obliged me to drive at all times of the year and in all weathers, and this information has proved most useful, as I know whether I am behind or ahead of schedule.

Living out of a suitcase and always carrying about files, boxes and drawings with me has been a part of my life for so long that it's a wonderful feeling to reach a place where I know I have more than two nights to spend. Being able to stretch out, to wash and get the dirt off and then luxuriate in a hot bath, not having to get up early or answer the telephone—these are very rare treats. Letters, however, are with me all the time, awaiting me at every stop, and have to be answered whenever possible.

It is by choice that I generally travel alone on these European journeys, for I prefer not taking the responsibility for a companion. Moreover, these drives provide some of the rare occasions when I can find quietness and solitude away from the telephone and other distractions. There is time for meditation, which I find absolutely necessary. On the quieter roads it is like a spiritual retreat: one can admire the flowers, trees and birds, and I

214

like especially watching the sky, the starlit nights, the sunrises and sunsets.

During these long journeys, one is aware all the time of the number of people who are waiting for assistance, and of the great gaps in the existing services and the many we never reach. The volume of requests for help is very great, and one can become exhausted. After a day filled with discussions, meetings, difficulties, frustrations, greetings and farewells, it is essential to find solitude for a while.

Whenever I stop for brief breaks—preferably in a wood to listen to the birds and to enjoy nature—I brew up coffee and write up my notes, but all too soon it is necessary to continue my journey, for the itineraries, as has already been mentioned, are tight and have to be kept to punctually.

My constant criss-crossing of frontiers on my journeys has taught many of the Customs Authorities to recognise the Foundation's familiar blue vehicles. Usually I have no trouble with the frontier authorities—indeed, I am generally greeted with kindness and good humour—but one finds that in practice it depends upon the officials who happen to be on duty on a particular night. If the man in charge knows one, then there is no need to produce the *laissez passer* document (which is in five languages) —one is waved through.

Occasionally, though, a bored or difficult official examines the *laissez passer* and goes round the sealed van with his torch.

One year, because of thick fog, I was late for a rendezvous at 2 a.m. at the frontier post at Aachen. The son of Doctor Wagner, an old friend and senior official of the German Red Cross, had waited with a letter for me from his father, but then, believing that I had been detained or had decided to return to Belgium until the fog had cleared, he left the letter with the Customs Authorities and went

home. On arrival at the frontier post, I presented a letter
from the German Ambassador to Britain, but the officials
refused to accept it. Confronted by five men, I tried to
strengthen my position by saying: "Well, to prove to you
who I represent, here is a letter from the Red Cross, this
one which you have just handed to me, in addition to the
letter I have just shown you from your Ambassador." They
denied, however, all knowledge of the fact that Doctor
Wagner's son had been waiting for me, and demanded
DM20 for the transit of *Liebesgaben* (gift parcels or
comforts). An unnecessary and time-wasting argument
followed, which lasted for nearly two hours, but finally the
point was won by my bluffing and saying: "Look it up in
your *Gesetzbuch*, and under such-and-such a paragraph
you will find that *Liebesgaben* may be taken through free of
charge." On another occasion, an official complained:
"This is an ambulance, yet there are no patients in it—we
don't understand." To which I replied: "How could
there be patients in it when it is full of walking aids,
wheelchairs, etc?" On another occasion the authorities
wanted me to count the number of clout and twist
nails.

At Waidhaus on the German-Czech frontier, near
Flossenburg (where Bonhoeffer was hanged on 9th
April 1945), I invariably meet with courtesy from the
Germans before I go through a stretch of no man's land
and on to meet the friendly Czechs, waiting at the frontier
post on a steep hill. They offer the use of their loo and give
me boiling water for the thermos. One night, however,
when I was accompanied by Ann Batt of the *Daily
Express*, we found Czech officials on duty whom I did not
know. They told me that a new regulation had been made,
and that for any vehicle of two tons and over in weight tax
had to be paid. I asked them for their co-operation, but
they explained that the authorities to whom they had to
refer had gone home; they gave up their office to us and we
stretched out on chairs with the border officials' thick
coats over us, for it was very cold despite the stove in the
room. We dozed until Prague could be consulted at 6 a.m.
and officials there confirmed that we might proceed. On

arrival in Prague, however, thanks to the Legal Adviser at the British Embassy, who had contacts in the right quarter, a special certificate was issued, as has been done every year since, which enables me to travel into Czechoslovakia freely and without paying tax.

On the many journeys through Czechoslovakia, the women who often serve on the petrol pumps have got to know me, and spontaneously offer me the use of their loo. Members of the Czech Army too have helped me to find street numbers, or to empty petrol from the jerry-can into the petrol tank.

Often I spend a night in Prague, an historical city of great beauty, known as "the city of a hundred spires" and "the golden city". Of Prague the poet Frantisek Kosic wrote: "She has always been a symbol of dignity, tenderness and mystery, a real mother to her sons, whose hearts are deeply imprinted with her suffering. She has also been a witness to their greatest glory and joy."

A member of the Czech Government used to ask me to a working breakfast at which he discussed the problems of the disabled. He himself had been a prisoner in the Terezin (Theresienstadt) concentration camp and would say to me: "I agree that Terezin must remain in the past. We forgive, although we do not forget. I always remember that the Germans gave birth to Beethoven and Goethe."

These journeys through Europe are memorable not only because of the friendliness and hospitality of the majority of the people I meet, but also because of the intense interest shown by the people of Central Europe in English literature and history. It is not at all unusual to be asked at two in the morning in any town, city or village there to expound upon the *Canterbury Tales*, to describe Oxford or to explain the meaning of expressions such as "the back of beyond", "being at a loose end" or "somewhat the worse for wear". It is sometimes far from easy to get over to the enquirer in simple terms the significance of such expressions—particularly at that hour of the morning.

In winter the avenues of dark, snowladen fir trees are particularly lovely. The tapes on the cassette give me great pleasure and companionship as I drive on my way, and

I think about my husband and the children and look forward to hearing from them. I am reminded of notes and letters which were often given me or left for me by Mama before such journeys in the past, and the following I have always carried with me :-

Child of my love, fear not the unknown morrow,
Dread not the new demand life makes of thee.
Thy ignorance doth hold no cause for sorrow,

For what thou knowest not is known to me.
Thou canst not see today the hidden meaning
Of my command, but there no light shalt gain.
Walk on in faith, upon my promise leaning,
And as thou goest, all shall be made plain.
One step thou seest, then go forward boldly,
One step is far enough for faith to see.
Take that, and thy next duty shall be told thee,
For step by step thy Lord is leading thee.

One of the most wonderful things about these journeys is the kindness of other people, both known and unknown. Total strangers have often invited me into their room and given me a warm and wonderful welcome, and many times after Mass a priest has invited me to breakfast with him and has given me the opportunity of having a good wash. I really cannot describe the hospitality and kindness of friends along the way, and the meals which they prepare at all hours, including chicken soup, noodles and cream cakes. One kind host woke up the local grocer at 4 a.m. to provide extra ingredients for a meal in spite of my pleas. In the days when there was hardly anything to eat, they would offer me their only piece of bread or their last drop of coffee, and in the presence of such incredibly warm and generous hospitality one felt very humble. Nothing was too much trouble. When there were not enough beds, they would be shared, and on many occasions people have offered me the use of their own bed. I can still hear the familiar voices of women friends on the routes awakening me in English with the words, "Darling, it's time now."

I can always rest assured that people, particularly in Central and Southern Europe will go to great lengths to give personal assistance regardless of the weather conditions. One night during one of the longest and worst winters in Poland, when the snow was unusually heavy and drifts several feet high, a tractor was sent out to tow the van because the last two miles of the road leading to the Home I was making for was blocked and ridged with frozen snow: I remember particularly the glow of the rear lights on the tractor and the chugging of the engine in the dark. The driver was young and perhaps not fully convinced that I was really trying to keep the van upright, and at one point he called out me: "Come on, you can only die once!" On the return journey, after two days at the Home, the tractor was replaced by two horses.

At Kudowa, the Polish-Czechoslovak frontier crossing, I am offered hot coffee. On another occasion, at the border post at Cieszyn, when the frontier formalities were over and before I climbed back into *Joshua*, the Polish customs and passport officials (a woman and several men), came to kiss me goodbye and hand me some tulips. At this, the Czech Customs and passport officials added: "Although we haven't any flowers for you, you know that you have our hearts." They waved me farewell as I drove off on another stage of the long journey over the bridge linking the two countries, with the gushing river below and the water gleaming in the moonlight.

After miles and miles of travel, it is a real pleasure to enjoy at last a bag of hot chips in Belgium on my way back to England, to see the lights in the docks at Zeebrugge, to be given a bed on board the car ferry and to reach Cavendish again, sometimes in the still of night as the church clock strikes three, or at other times driving through the early hours of the morning, hearing the dawn chorus through green lanes and quiet villages, reflecting on the past weeks, and the hospitality, the kindness and the courage of the children and adults who in spite of so many difficulties and disappointments have expressed such great warmth, affection and fortitude.

CHAPTER 18

A Time to Build Up

At Cavendish as I write, old dreams are becoming new realities.

To the front of the Home we have just completed a new building to house, among other things, a museum explaining the history and work of the Foundation to visitors. There have been great moments in this development. The frames and trusses were acquired from Timber Frames (U.K.) Limited at Honiton in Devon, and one weekend directors of the firm themselves came all the way from there to fix the trusses. Redland Tiles Limited of Reigate, Surrey gave us the roof tiles and free service to lay them. Langley London Limited presented the ceramic floor-tiles and the Blue Circle Group the Sandtex for the exterior walls. At a time when inflation was badly hitting the building trades, these were generous gestures indeed. There are many others to whom we are profoundly grateful—many wish to remain anonymous.

Our next expansion, from the east side of the present building, will give us the new kitchen and dining room which we have long needed and additional bedrooms for patients and staff. Initially it was estimated that these extensions would cost about £100,000, but with sudden and dramatic rises in the price of materials the probable cost has increased greatly and goes on increasing.

In 1974 the Foundation was fortunate enough to find a lovely family home in the village of Oxenhope, near Keighley in Yorkshire. This beautiful house, with its well-kept garden and large windows looking out to the moors, is now used as a home for those with cancers—short-term and long-term patients—including others following treatment.

It is a regrettable fact that due to ignorance and lack of education, cancer is still thought about as an horrific disease, but it should be known that, in Britain at least, from 40 to 50 per cent of cases are cured, and proceed to lead a fully active and normal life, provided the diagnosis is made early enough. In fact, it is important to realise that 80 per cent of patients die of other diseases than cancer.

Even for those who suffer from cancer, treatment can, in many cases, keep the disease under control for many years. A typical example is Mrs. P. S. who discovered a lump in her right breast in 1958 at the age of 35 years. She was advised to have the breast removed and X-ray treatment was given following this, to make sure that no residual local disease was left to grow.

Mrs. P.S. remained well and attended hospital for a check-up at regular intervals. Unfortunately, further trouble occurred in 1962 and this time she was advised to have the function of the ovaries stopped by X-rays. After thinking about this, she agreed and as a result remained well until 1973. On this occasion further problems appeared and she was advised to have drug therapy. Mrs. P.S. has responded well to this treatment.

At all times she has been fully active in her work and as a housewife. She knows her diagnosis and prefers it this way. She also feels that it is important that others should know how well she has fared, if only to reassure them of the outcome. As a result of these views Mrs. P.S. has willingly taken part in interviews for radio programmes.

This story illustrates hope, produced by reassurance, which might easily have been replaced by despair.

For those whose disease is more advanced without response to treatment, possibly alone, or who feel a burden, it is vital that they should be strengthened by specialised attention and devotion, which cannot always be given in hospital or in the family environment. Available statistics show that many large areas of Britain have no Homes such as we are founding for cancer patients who are in dire need of them.

It is the policy of the Foundation that no Home should be parochial in outlook and therefore does not collect funds for its own exclusive use in its own area only, but rather for the international work and well-being of the Foundation as a whole.

So we go on searching for further suitable properties. . . .

We are ever hopeful of becoming more effective by con-
solidating our efforts and opening new Homes, in Britain
for patients with cancer and for physically handicapped
children, and overseas, mainly for sufferers from leprosy,
etc. Lack of sufficient funds and leadership is often the
main obstacle, but apart from this there are, as every social
worker knows, regrettably large numbers of people whose
problems are of such a nature that no solution of them seems
possible however hard one tries. Who did, I wonder, write:
    "I expect to pass through this world but once:
    any good thing therefore that I can do, or any
    kindness that I can show to any fellow-creature, let me
    do it now; let me not defer or neglect it, for I shall not
    pass this way again nor can I take anything with me"?
I am writing these words in my office, which leads out
of our bedroom on the first floor of the Home in Cavendish. This small room, with its latticed window, was built
on to the back of the house fifteen years ago; before that we
all shared two offices, and I never hoped or expected it
would be possible to have one of my own. The Polish
Minister of Health gave me a sheepskin rug, which he
insisted that I have in the office, much to my embarrassment. It was received with delight by Jeromy and
Elizabeth, and now when their friends come to stay, their
sleeping bags are put on top of the rug and they hold
midnight feasts by torchlight.
    The furniture in the office was also bought with money
given by the Bods, and collected gradually by a friend, who
let us have it in a dilapidated state, after which it was
renovated, with the exception of a small rosewood table
given to me by my mother.
    On the desk among the letters, files and ring books
stand three coloured miniatures—of my husband and our
two children. Nearby are trays marked 'Pending',
'Action', 'Urgent', 'Building'. 'Caseworkers' and 'Personal Secretaries'. Along the pine windowsills and on
the walls there are gifts and mementoes that I have
received during the past thirty years. Pictures of Our Lady
and of St. Francis made out of corn were given to me by the
Minister of Culture in Poland; a wooden model of the

222

Kragujevac Memorial was made by an English girl who was an air-ferry pilot during the War; a vivid and beautiful tapestry was woven lovingly from threads retrieved by Russians in Leningrad during its appalling siege; the statue of St. Christopher was sculptured in wood by an Italian; the crystal vase was a gift from cancer patients in one of the Foundation's Homes; a meticulously carved model of a fifteenth century galleon was made by a young disabled man and presented by the Mayor of Kotar in Yugoslavia when I received the freedom of that city; and there are pictures which were painted by well-known artists in the countries where I have worked. Indeed this room holds many treasured gifts, some of them the donors' only possessions. I always find it exceedingly difficult to accept such presents, but each gift reminds me of the giver and of all that he or she did and meant, and moreover refusal would have upset them greatly.

From my desk I can hear the gentle, continuous splashing of the fountain outside, and look out over the garden—the lawns and flower beds, the old well covered with honeysuckle, the many lovely trees, the pond, the tennis court and the extension called the Old Forge beyond.

On one side of the garden is *Mulberries*, the bungalow where my mother came to live in 1967 with Miss Bainbridge, who had been with her over forty years and cared for her until she died here on February 14th, 1974.

All through her long life, spent mostly in Yorkshire and Suffolk, with many visits abroad, countless people looked upon Mama as their friend. Her interests were wide and various, and her impulse was always to give. She took part wholeheartedly in the life of the local community, and gave freely of her time to help people. For many years she was a magistrate, besides which she served on over thirty committees, and had the ability to make each member feel that he or she was wanted, so that all worked together as a team. Her sense of humour was infectious. She was gay, cheerful and charming, often told jokes against herself, and was never pompous or touchy. Inwardly serene and happy, her smile won people's hearts. Few have left so beloved a memory.

223

Without Mama's wisdom, constant encouragement and active participation it is difficult to imagine the Foundation ever having consolidated or expanded. I could consult her at any time, and, in spite of all her other activities, she was always available to guide me and to help me cope with the correspondence, the meetings and the various problems. She would often pass on to me quotations applicable to the moment or remind me of prayers, such as the following, which I find among my papers:—

What can I wish on this your birthday morning
Save that the Friend, the faithful and the true
In his great Love all earthly love transcending,
Be near today to bless and comfort you
And with his smile make glad the day now dawning.
Chasing the shadows from life's darkest place
God's perfect Peace your heart and mind enfolding
Till in his Joy you see Him face to face.

For as long as I can remember her, Mama seemed to have an instinct for instant recognition of the moment when somebody was most in want of companionship or of solitude. This gift, and her uses of it, naturally endeared her to people and the Bods at the Home. She would perceive and respond equally to their need of someone to rejoice with them in their joys, or to share quietly in their sorrows, or simply to give them by her company the reassurance and encouragement that their perplexities craved for. Mama would herself prepare special dishes for them, pick strawberries, invite them for meals, or accompany them to flower festivals and concerts. They loved her for her gaiety and the interest they shared in so many subjects, but above all for her compassion and affection for them and her respect for them as human beings.

It would be impossible to quote from the hundreds of letters and cables received before and after her death, but the following extracts may sum up their feelings:

I shall always picture her as a luminous and lovely person full of fun and energy. She was the leader and guide of our group, and however late or early, your mother found out what we liked most, and those who were unwell she would care for and look after. When

224

she was driving or accompanying us, she would often sing. We loved too to hear her playing the piano.

Please feel we will stand by you, realising that it was she who laid the foundation-stone of your work. Her activity will always remain a clear signpost, not only to you, but to countless others who enjoyed her friendship and love.

When I am at home in Cavendish the day begins early; I prefer to rise early and have always enjoyed getting up when I feel fresh to start the work of the day. My husband and I prepare our own breakfast in the kitchenette in the passage by our room. We eat very simply, especially as my husband has to keep a gluten-free diet.

The pressure of correspondence is unrelenting, and a morning mail of between thirty and forty letters is a light one. The post covers a variety of subjects, so that many hours of each day are devoted to the dictation of correspondence and other matters. These are dealt with by very willing secretaries and assistants, who are literally my left and right hands. We work as a team. Every letter received is acknowledged personally when I am at Headquarters, or by the secretaries/assistants when I am absent, so those who say "Please treat this clothing or this postal order as an anonymous gift" earn our particular gratitude.

Much time is also occupied by discussions with colleagues and particularly with members of the Foundation's Council, on whom I depend for advice, guidance and decisions. I also like, however, to relax when I can with members of the staff and to discuss personal problems, and I try always to be accessible to every one of them. There are all kinds of official visitors to be received, and a great part of each day is devoted to talks with medical and social workers. Local Authorities, builders and architects, members of the Foundation's Support Groups, and others.

In addition, there are meetings to be attended and talks to be given on the work of the Foundation, all of which entails long hours of driving, I like doing fieldwork, being among people on the rounds of the sick and on building sites, rather than occupying myself with administration, fund-raising and talks, but of course this is necessary, and it takes a great deal of time.

As mentioned, a part of each year is spent abroad. I keep in close touch with the various Homes, Groups and Shops in Britain, though it is unfortunately never possible for me to spend as much time with them as I should like; it is always a joy to visit them, and I only wish that I could do so more often.

In relationships with other people, consideration and warmth have both meant a great deal to me at all times. Coming from Yorkshire, I believe in being frank but without hurting a person's feelings, if this is possible; I try to remember that there are always two or more sides to a problem. Having lived and worked with people from all walks of life—and Central Europeans in particular—one has noticed and appreciated their etiquette and pleasant manners; they would think it over-familiar to use a person's first name until requested or permitted to do so, and then only when they have got to know that person extremely well, and they act with a courtesy which has never failed to make a deep impression on me.

At 10 p.m. the telephone, which is manned continuously, is at last switched through to our room, but even this does not mean the end of the working day. Tradesmen on one of the sites once rang up at 11.30 p.m. to say that the window frames had not arrived, and I remember another occasion, having been several weeks on the road and trying to get an early night, when I was awoken at 10.40 p.m. by the Chairman of one of my husband's Homes with the news that the Home had been burnt down—patients and staff were fortunately safe. On occasion an enthusiastic supporter in Canada has also phoned to Cavendish, not realising that it was 2 a.m. in Britain.

To the young I enjoy talking about our work with special pleasure and with the most intense hope. It is a paradox of our time that we have a "generation of concern" growing up in a world dominated at almost every level of society by the disease of materialism and greed. Hence, I am convinced we have a right and obligation to make sure that the concerned, including the youngest of them, know exactly what our problems are among the neglected, impoverished, sick and handicapped, and how concern for them can be expressed in positive action. Too often hospitals, for instance, are unfamiliar areas and the people living there unreal, so that the artificial divisions between the sick and those leading "normal lives" persist in quite an unnecessary way.

"Your summons," writes a friend in Australia and former Bod in S.O.E., "is a summons to seek and face the facts, to deny ourselves, to dedicate ourselves, to be there with those who are suffering. It is a challenge to all the young who find life insipid."

I do not believe the young want to be ostriches shielded by sterile sand from uncomfortable perception of other people's sufferings. On the contrary, I find that when I can tell them plainly where and why there is urgent need for, say, more nurses or social workers or physiotherapists or occupational therapists, I can count on an eager and practical response. Often, alas, the eager are thwarted because they lack the required education, or fail their examinations on the very path they are keen to climb. Young people with a really genuine vocation should not be denied a chance to fulfil it simply because they cannot attain the required academic standards. There seems great need for more regular and recognised schemes to harness this urge into useful, satisfying channels with the participants following practical courses of instruction. Perhaps this scheme could become international? Practical jobs are of vital importance in any community. Routine work, like making beds, washing up and peeling potatoes, and including "tender loving care," are of just as great value as the more high-powered duties.

The media concentrate so much on cruelty, horror and ill-will. They pay all too little attention to the constructive work of goodwill being done by so many people.

Once a prisoner whom I was trying to help flung at me the reproach: "I think you could have done more—that is what you are here for." I believe that these words apply to my entire life and to all that I have tried to do. As I look at my life and examine my conscience, remembering my failings and conscious of my failures, I can only hope that

227

the sincerity of my endeavours will to some extent help to compensate for both. And, as always, I remember the kindness, goodness and generosity of countless others and the active support which it has been my privilege to receive in all my efforts.

It has been hard to describe the events I have set down here, partly because it meant reliving some dreadful experiences. In writing I have been confronted once more by the suffering and despair I have witnessed, and have remembered again the faces and voices of so many people I have met. There was a boy who asked for a taste of butter again before he died—"Oh, the cross I have borne has been so heavy"; and the woman, also dying, who asked to feel a pair of shoes—"Thank you for finding them," she said; "I hope those who walk in them will find happiness and peace". There was the child of seven in Auschwitz—"Can I taste a piece of bread before I die?"; there was a man with leprosy dying in the streets, homeless, amid the scurrying leaves.

I see before me once again crowds queuing outside hospitals where beds line the corridors and patients are sleeping on the floors under the beds; hospitals where the pressure is so heavy that patients have to share the beds if they are to receive care and treatment and not be turned away.

I remember terminal patients with T.B. meningitis, and the cry typical of this disease. I remember too the penetrating and overpowering smell of ulcerating cancer, and how I would pull up by the side of the road after visits to cancer hospitals, and get out of the van to breathe the fresh air.

There has been suffering, some of it so terrible that I cannot bear to describe it even today; but there is also courage and selflessness, hope and generosity, humour and warmth, and these things I remember too as I write: the woman who walked two miles to hand me a donation of 2/6d for example; and the Borstal boys working at Hickleton who gave up their pocket money when 30/- disappeared from the collecting bowl in the front hall.

Some words come to my mind again. An eight year old child, brought to England to be educated, asking on a visit to Windsor: "Does the Queen wear her crown all the time?" A Bod, on the completion of a new Home: "I never dreamt I would have a room to myself, isn't it marvellous? Please try to thank those who have given me this privacy." Mr. Z, whose wife had lost her first husband, two children and her brothers during the War and was then killed herself in a road accident while visiting England under the Holiday Scheme—his lack of bitterness and solace he derived from hearing and reading how happy she had been in her last few weeks. "You have made up for something of what she lost, and she lived in a fairy land with flowers whilst with you." I am often asked how many one has worked with and for—the answer can only be approximate, probably about 250,000 children and adults of over fifty nationalities.

There have been horrors, there has been suffering, unhappiness, frustration and disappointment—but in looking back on my life I realise that the beautiful and the good outweigh everything else, and it is these things of which I prefer to think. The smile of an Indian child who was eating his share of ice cream and sweets for some celebration. The Bod who said that the golden dream had begun. The smell of incense and hay: laughter and mellow cornfields in autumn, and how beautiful the mountains look in the fading light and at sunrise during my long drives. Returning to Britain after the War, and the pealing of church bells which I had never thought to hear again. The Big Wheel at Walton-on-the-Naze illuminated at night during the week before the War, and the nostalgic songs we used to sing: *Red sails in the sunset;* and later, with the Bods, *We'll meet again, Wish me luck as you wave me goodbye,* and the old Polish Folk Melody, *Time for us is quickly passing.* The sunrise in Trunley Wood, carpeted with anemones and cowslips; and the orchard at Thurlow, the trees heavy with apple blossom; and the rooks wheeling and cawing through the air at Scarcroft.

But this is a time to look forward, for: "in today, already walks tomorrow".* In this book I have attempted to give a brief outline of what the Foundation has so far done. It is the past that has taught us how much the future holds in promise and opportunity and how great the demands will always be.

* Samuel Taylor Coleridge

CHAPTER 19

And the Morrow is Theirs

For the cause that lacks assistance,
For the wrong that needs resistance,
For the future in the distance,
And the good that I can do.

George Linnaeus Banks.

If I have learned anything in a life that has seen its share of tumult, suffering and complications, I have learned to believe that we are made to live in harmony, and to be compassionate, and disciplined and between the one and the other there is a link.

The scope and future of compassion is immense, because through compassion the human family, as time goes on, is bound closer together. Suffering, pain and distress bring a sense of isolation and a need for companionship and support. Compassion unites us and makes us discover one another and ourselves. It does not cancel out the suffering or the evil, but it offers us a way of living with it. And this way of living enriches each of us, quietly, as a gentle shower before dawn gives life to the tired soil and the thirsty bush.

Wherever we look, in whatever part of the world, we find human and social problems in countless different forms. At times there are sudden world disasters which call us forth from our ordinary routine and commitments and which for a passing moment draw us together in a common desire to help. We sense the urgency and the challenge, and so we rise to the occasion.

But there is also the long-term, the continuing daily need of innumerable fellow human beings—a cry that is far less spectacular and seemingly less urgent, and, for the very reason that it is always with us, all too easily accepted as an inevitable part of life. This calls for a different kind of response for the bit-by-bit cracking of the surface and the

230

piece-by-piece filling of the holes—a task where there will often be no results to see and to which there will probably never be an end. That every human being has the right to a reasonable standard of living, to education and medical and nursing care when ill, few would deny. But the sad truth is that many do not enjoy these rights, millions do not have food for more than the barest subsistence, nor is there any foreseeable likelihood that they will. That this gap should be closed, indeed that its very existence constitutes a violation of justice, if not a threat to the future peace and security of mankind, most would agree. But how to close the gap and how to face up to the sacrifice which is required—so small a sacrifice by comparison with that demanded by war—still eludes the mind and the will of governments. Yet it is people themselves who make communities and nations, and who have it within their power to create better or worse ones, even to imbue governments with a will and a purpose that otherwise they would not have.

I am conscious of our own immortality, and that whatever we do, wherever it might be, does count, not only here and now but in that great future for which we have all been created. It may sometimes be that we are given a certain opportunity only once and that if we fail to respond it will not be given to us again. But if we seize the opportunity, even if we should not succeed in achieving our goal, the effort involved can be offered up to God who is our Judge and who is able to turn every defeat into victory.

Experience as a field worker has taught me that it is the effort made by one individual that makes all the difference to another individual's life. It has shown me that no matter who we are or what our position in life, there is always something that we can contribute if we have the desire and the will. It may be by personal service in one's spare time, by arousing the interest of other people, by organising a function, by building, by nursing, by collecting clothes or bric-a-brac for a jumble sale or a gift shop, or by going without something in order to make a small gift; or, on a different level, it could be by prayer or by indentifying oneself in whatever way one can with another person's

231

predicament and need. The very fact of knowing that someone else, perhaps at the other side of the world, is interested and concerned, is enough in itself to give encouragement and new strength, and to lighten the burden of the sufferer.

When compared with what needs to be achieved, all this may seem hopelessly small and inadequate, but it serves little to look at the whole sum of the problem, better that we focus our attention on what we ourselves can do or be harnessed to do.

If one has ever had the privilege of working with those who have the will and the single-mindedness to succeed, and who believe in the light at the end of the tunnel no matter how dark and how interminable the tunnel may be, one knows that almost anything can be achieved.

"A little more and how much it is, a little less and what worlds away."

The War and its aftermath followed by the struggle to maintain peace have all been our teachers. They have taught us more clearly than ever before the one-ness of the human family, the basic truth that we are all children of one Father. John Donne captured this spirit in his immortal words:

> "No man is an island, entire of itself; every man is part of the continent, a part of the main. Any man's death diminishes me, because I am involved in mankind."

Surely, though we are scattered about, we are all meant to be parts of a single Continent? Yet, if we are to be whole, it will not come about easily or without sacrifice; we will have to suffer together, often be called upon to pay a heavy price. It will not be enough for the rich and the powerful to condescend to give the needy a few scraps that are left over. It is more important than ever that all of us share what we can reasonably afford, that we understand the necessity of our own personal involvement, however modest this may be.

To strive for unity in a world that, sadly, is still divided is a debt we owe to all those throughout the ages who in different ways have dedicated themselves to this cause, above all to those who have laid down their lives in its pursuit. If we are to succeed, the goal must ever be kept in mind. We cannot afford to yield to weariness or despair. No matter what the situation in which we find ourselves, or how dark the horizon, we must not lose faith—faith in our fellow men and in ourselves as well as in the all-seeing Providence of God. Faith that even though evil will always be present, within ourselves as well as in the world at large, good will finally triumph. Faith, as we used so often to sing, that all their and our tomorrows will be happy ones.

> *Who would once more relight Creation's flame,*
> *Turn back to sanity a world that goes insane,*
> *To bridge this awful chasm of despair?*
> *The faint, small voice of Hope calls out,*
> *Do you answer? Will you dare?*

—Qedrwl.

ROSEMARY FOR REMEMBRANCE

Enquiries in writing only please to:

SUE RYDER FOUNDATION,

Cavendish,

Nr. Sudbury,

Suffolk.

Index